THE PUBLIC INTERNATIONAL LAW OF TRADE IN LEGAL SERVICES

This book examines the international legal regime covering trade in legal services. While legal services are a vital component of the economies of many developed and emerging countries, they remain poorly liberalized with numerous restrictions undermining market access for foreign suppliers. Although some modern bilateral and regional trade agreements have begun to address barriers to trade in legal services, few go beyond the basic commitments of non-discrimination and transparency contained in the WTO GATS. This book approaches the pressing need to open the global market for trade in legal services across the four modes of supply: cross border, consumption abroad, commercial presence, and temporary movement of natural persons. It considers changes under way within the legal profession brought about by alternative business structures and technology. Both underscore the importance of reconceptualizing trade in legal services as one that should be as open as possible with a view to maximizing competition while safeguarding the needs of clients.

David Collins is Professor of International Economic Law at City, University of London.

CAMBRIDGE INTERNATIONAL TRADE AND ECONOMIC LAW

Series editors

As the processes of regionalization and globalization have intensified, there have been accompanying increases in the regulations of international trade and economic law at the levels of international, regional, and national laws.

The subject matter of this series is international economic law. Its core is the regulation of international trade, investment, and cognate areas such as intellectual property and competition policy. The series publishes books on related regulatory areas, in particular human rights, labour, environment and culture as well as sustainable development. These areas are vertically linked at the international, regional, and national levels, and the series extends to the implementation of these rules at these different levels. The series also includes works on governance, dealing with the structure and operation of related international organizations in the field of international economic law and the ways in which they interact with other subjects of international and national law.

Books in the series

The Public International Law of Trade in Legal Services
David Collins

Industrial Policy and the World Trade Organization: Between Legal Constraints and Flexibilities
Sherzod Shadikhodjaev

The Prudential Carve-Out for Financial Services: Rationale and Practice in the GATS and Preferential Trade Agreements
Carlo Maria Cantore

Judicial Acts and Investment Treaty Arbitration
Berk Demirkol

Distributive Justice and World Trade Law: A Political Theory of International Trade Regulation
Oisin Suttle

Freedom of Transit and Access to Gas Pipeline Networks under WTO Law
Vitalily Pogoretskyy

Reclaiming Development in the World Trading System, 2nd edition
Yong-Shik Lee

Developing Countries and Preferential Services Trade
Charlotte Sieber-Gasser

WTO Dispute Settlement and the TRIPS Agreement: Applying Intellectual Property Standards in a Trade Law Framework
Matthew Kennedy

Establishing Judicial Authority in International Economic Law
Edited by Joanna Jemielniak, Laura Nielsen and Henrik Palmer Olsen

Trade, Investment, Innovation and their Impact on Access to Medicines: An Asian Perspective
Locknie Hsu

The Law, Economics and Politics of International Standardisation
Panagiotis Delimatsis

The WTO and International Investment Law: Converging Systems
Jürgen Kurtz

Export Restrictions on Critical Minerals and Metals: Testing the Adequacy of WTO Disciplines
Ilaria Espa

Optimal Regulation and the Law of International Trade: The Interface between the Right to Regulate and WTO Law
Boris Rigod

The Social Foundations of World Trade: Norms, Community and Constitution
Sungjoon Cho

Public Participation and Legitimacy in the WTO
Yves Bonzon

The Challenge of Safeguards in the WTO
Fernando Piérola

General Interests of Host States in International Investment Law
Edited by Giorgio Sacerdoti, with Pia Acconci, Mara Valenti and Anna De Luca

The Law of Development Cooperation: A Comparative Analysis of the World Bank, the EU and Germany
Philipp Dann

WTO Disciplines on Subsidies and Countervailing Measures: Balancing Policy Space and Legal Constraints
Dominic Coppens

Domestic Judicial Review of Trade Remedies: Experiences of the Most Active WTO Members
Edited by Müslüm Yilmaz

The Relevant Market in International Economic Law: A Comparative Antitrust and GATT Analysis
Christian A. Melischek

International Organizations in WTO Dispute Settlement: How Much Institutional Sensitivity?
Marina Foltea

Public Services and International Trade Liberalization: Human Rights and Gender Implications
Barnali Choudhury

The Law and Politics of WTO Waivers: Stability and Flexibility in Public International Law
Isabel Feichtner

African Regional Trade Agreements as Legal Regimes
James Thuo Gathii

Liberalizing International Trade after Doha: Multilateral, Plurilateral, Regional, and Unilateral Initiatives
David A. Gantz

Processes and Production Methods (PPMs) in WTO Law: Interfacing Trade and Social Goals
Christiane R. Conrad

Non-Discrimination in International Trade in Services: 'Likeness' in WTO/GATS
Nicolas F. Diebold

The Law, Economics and Politics of Retaliation in WTO Dispute Settlement
Edited by Chad P. Bown and Joost Pauwelyn

The Multilateralization of International Investment Law
Stephan W. Schill

Trade Policy Flexibility and Enforcement in the WTO: A Law and Economics Analysis
Simon A.B. Schropp

THE PUBLIC INTERNATIONAL LAW OF TRADE IN LEGAL SERVICES

DAVID COLLINS
City, University of London

CAMBRIDGE
UNIVERSITY PRESS

CAMBRIDGE
UNIVERSITY PRESS

University Printing House, Cambridge CB2 8BS, United Kingdom

One Liberty Plaza, 20th Floor, New York, NY 10006, USA

477 Williamstown Road, Port Melbourne, VIC 3207, Australia

314–321, 3rd Floor, Plot 3, Splendor Forum, Jasola District Centre, New Delhi – 110025, India

79 Anson Road, #06-04/06, Singapore 079906

Cambridge University Press is part of the University of Cambridge.

It furthers the University's mission by disseminating knowledge in the pursuit of education, learning, and research at the highest international levels of excellence.

www.cambridge.org
Information on this title: www.cambridge.org/9781108423526
DOI: 10.1017/9781108526265

First published 2019

Printed and bound in Great Britain by Clays Ltd, Elcograf S.p.A.

A catalogue record for this publication is available from the British Library.

ISBN 978-1-108-42352-6 Hardback

CONTENTS

ACKNOWLEDGEMENTS

I would like to thank the British Academy for its generous support of the research and writing of this book. I would also like to thank the faculty, fellows, and staff of the Center for the Study of Law and Society at the University of California Berkeley School of Law, where a significant portion of this manuscript was written during my sabbatical there in the autumn of 2017. Thanks also to my former student Ben Robinson for assistance with preparing the index. Finally, I wish to express my gratitude to the International Committee of the Law Society of England and Wales, on which I have had the pleasure to serve as a member for almost ten years, during which time I gained valuable insight into trade in legal services and met many warm and inspirational legal professionals. Finally, I would like to thank Ben Robinson for help with indexing and proof-reading of the manuscript.

ABBREVIATIONS

AARPI	L'Association d'Avocats à Responsabilité Professionnelle Individuelle
ABA	American Bar Association
ABS	Alternative Business Structure
AFAS	ASEAN Framework Agreement on Services
APEC	Asian Pacific Economic Cooperation
ASCM	Agreement on Subsidies and Countervailing Measures
ASEAN	Association of South East Asian Nations
BIT	Bilateral Investment Treaty
BPRL	United Nations Basic Principles on the Role of Lawyers
CAFTA	Central American Free Trade Agreement
CARIFORUM	The Caribbean Forum
CCBE	Council of Bars and Law Societies of Europe
CEPA	Hong Kong–China Closer Economic Partnership Agreement
CETA	Comprehensive Economic and Trade Agreement
CFIUS	Committee on Foreign Investment in the United States
CIS	Commonwealth of Independent States
CJEU	Court of Justice of the European Union
CLA	Commonwealth Lawyers Association
CPC	Central Product Classification
CPTPP	Comprehensive Progressive Trans Pacific Partnership
DETA	Digital Economy Trade Agreement
DIFC	Dubai International Financial Centre
ECHR	European Convention on Human Rights
EEA	European Economic Area
EFTA	European Free Trade Association
FIFO	Fly in Fly Out
FIRB	Foreign Investment Review Board
FLC	Foreign Legal Consultant
FTA	Free Trade Agreement
FTZ	Free Trade Zone
GATS	General Agreement on Trade in Services

GATT	General Agreement on Tariffs and Trade
GCC	Gulf Cooperation Council
GDP	Gross Domestic Product
GDPR	General Data Protection Regulation
GJB	Gaikoku-Ho-Jimu-Bengoshi
IBA	International Bar Association
ICC	International Chamber of Commerce
IIA	International Investment Agreement
ISO	International Standards Organization
ITA	Information Technology Agreement
JD	Juris Doctor
JLV	Joint Law Venture
LCIA	London Court of International Arbitration
LLB	Bachelor of Laws
LLM	Master of Laws
MERCOSUR	Southern Common Market
MFN	Most Favoured Nation
MIGA	Multilateral Investment Guarantee Agency
MOOC	Massive Open Online Course
MRA	Mutual Recognition Agreement
NAFTA	North American Free Trade Agreement
NCA	National Committee on Accreditation
NDIAC	New Delhi International Arbitration Centre
NYIAC	New York International Arbitration Center
OAB	Brazilian Bar Association
OECD	Organisation for Economic Co-operation and Development
QLTS	Qualified Lawyers Transfer Scheme
RCEP	Regional Comprehensive Economic Partnership
RTA	Regional Trade Agreement
SAAS	Software as Service
SCC	Supreme Court of Canada
SIAC	Singapore Arbitration Centre
SPS	Sanitary and Phytosanitary Agreement
SRA	Solicitors Regulatory Authority
STRI	Services Trade Restrictiveness Indices
TBT	Technical Barriers to Trade Agreement
TFA	Trade Facilitation Agreement
TFEU	Treaty on the Functioning of the European Union
TISA	Trade in Services Agreement
TPRM	Trade Policy Review Mechanism
TRIPS	Trade Related Aspects of Intellectual Property Rights
TTIP	Transatlantic Trade and Investment Partnership

UNCITRAL	United Nations Commission on International Trade Law
UNCTAD	United Nations Committee on Trade and Development
USSC	United States Supreme Court
WPDR	Working Party on Domestic Regulation
WTO	World Trade Organization

TABLE OF CASES

World Trade Organization

Panel Reports

China – Measures Affecting Trading Rights and Distribution Services for Certain Publications and Audiovisual Entertainment Products, WT/DS363/R, (12 August 2009)
China – Certain Measures Affecting Electronic Payment Systems, Panel Report, WT/DS413/R (adopted 31 August 2012)
European Communities – Conditions on the Granting of Tariff Preferences to Developing Countries, WT/DS246 (1 December 2003)
United States – Measures Affecting the Cross-Border Supply of Gambling and Betting Services, WT/DS285/R, (10 November 2004)

Appellate Body Reports

Argentina – Measures Relating to Trade in Goods and Services WT/DS453/AB/R (9 May 2016)
Brazil – Measures Affecting the Import of Retreaded Tires, WT/DS332/AB/R (3 December 2007)
European Communities – Regime for the Importation, Sale and Distribution of Bananas, WT/DS27/AB/R (26 September 1997)
Turkey – Restrictions on Imports of Textiles and Clothing, WT/DS34/AB/R (21 October 1999)
United States – Measures Affecting the Cross-Border Supply of Gambling and Betting Services, WT/DS285/AB/R (20 April 2005)

International Investment Arbitration

CMS *v.* Argentina, ICSID Case No. ARB/01/8 Award (12 May 2005)
Pope & Talbot *v.* Canada, UNCITRAL (10 April 2002) [NAFTA]
Salini *v.* Morocco, ICSID No ARB/00/4, Decision on Jurisdiction, (23 July 2001) [Italy-Morocco BIT]

European Court of Human Rights

Golder *v.* United Kingdom, 4451/70, ECHR (21 February 1975)

Court of Justice of the European Union

Case C-550/07, P Akzo Nobel Chemicals Ltd and Akcros Chemicals Ltd *v.* Commission [2010] ECR I-08301
Case C-225/98, Commission *v.* France, Nord Pas de Calais [2000] ECR I-7445
C-55/94, Reinhard Gebhard *v.* Consiglio dell'Ordine degli Avvocati e Procuratori di Milano, ECR-I-4165
Case C-324/98, Telaustria Verlags GmbH and Telefonadress GmbH *v.* Telekom Austria AG [2000] ECR I-9315
Case C-340/89, Irène Vlassopoulou *v.* Ministerium für Justiz, Bundes- und Europaangelegenheiten Baden-Württemberg [1991] ECR I-2357

United States

Application of Griffiths, 413 U.S. 717 (1973) (USSC)
United States *v.* Microsoft, Ct of Appeals Second Circuit, Docket No. 14-2985 (14 July 2016) [currently on appeal to the USSC]

United Kingdom

Prudential PLC and Prudential (Gibraltar) Ltd *v.* Special Commissioner of Income Tax and Philip Pandolfo (HM Inspector of Taxes), [2013] UKSC 1 (23 January 2013)

Canada

Andrews *v.* Law Society of British Columbia [1989] 1 SCR 143, 56 DLR (4th)

India

Bar Council of India *v.* AK Balaji & Ors (W.P. 5614/2010) (High Court of Madras) (21 February 2012)

Bar Council of India *v.* AK Balaji & Ors [Civil Appeal Nos.7875-7879 of 2015] (Supreme Court of India) (13 March 2018)

Canada

India

1

Introduction

The Globalization and Regulation of Legal Services

1.1 Legal Services and the Modern Economy

The explosion of the Internet since the beginning of the twenty-first century has facilitated a new generation of legal services being provided across international borders. At the same time, the increasing globalization of the economy means that legal issues are taking on an international dimension, necessitating professional advice across multiple jurisdictions and in international law. New business models, such as virtual law firms, conflict with traditional regulatory structures at the national and subnational levels. These forms of service delivery, including the controversial outsourcing of legal tasks to professionals in other countries, raise an urgent demand for an investigation into how laws on data protection and privacy, as well as ethical obligations of legal practitioners, fit into international frameworks governing trade in services. At the same time, there has been an expansion of other kinds of professional services to cover areas traditionally performed by lawyers, such as accountants, surveyors, and new varieties of legal professionals. These alternative business structures (ABSs) offer other services, which are bundled with legal advice, raising problems of categorization under public international law. Changes that are underway in the legal profession itself and the process of obtaining qualifications in countries such as the United Kingdom, generally in the direction of liberalization, underscore the need to reconsider barriers to international practice as well as often outdated or inadequate rules on mutual recognition.

Trade in legal services has grown in the manner alluded to above, in step with globalization itself. Globalization has influenced the legal sector by expanding the need for legal services that cover multiple jurisdictions and may be flexibly applied by the same provider or firm. Simultaneously, it would seem that there has been a growth in international law, specifically the range of commercial and noncommercial issues that are dealt with at the international rather than the domestic level. These include high-profile commercial fields such as foreign investment and international trade as well as e-commerce, tax, and arbitration. International commerce has led to an increase in the number and size of economic actors engaging in transactions, often ending up in disputes that require resolution in international tribunals. Just as companies operate across many countries, so highly mobile consumers and workers find themselves interacting with legal regimes beyond that of their home country. This so-called legal pluralism means that a single individual may potentially be subjected to multiple legal or even quasi-legal regimes imposed variously by the state, substate, transnational, and international communities.[1] Tied to this, the emergence of transnational business governance regimes is shaping the expectations of transparency and predictability on the part of parties engaged in international business transactions.[2] The demand for multijurisdictional advice has capitalized on the expansion of telecommunications as well as worldwide alliances of law firms with offices in many jurisdictions, which are better able to embed themselves in the legal cultures of a diverse range of legal systems.[3] The rise of the Foreign Legal Consultant as a category of legal professional is perhaps emblematic of this development. While such professionals have the competence to advise on criminal or family matters, their role would seem to have been designed to serve the commercial interests of multinational actors, including those of a contentious nature that end up in arbitration.[4]

Economic development through globalization has led to the emergence of what commentators have described as a new model of legal services oriented towards providing legal advice to businesses rather than the traditional one in which lawyers, often sole practitioners, represent clients at local courts. There is now a pressing need for legal services in jurisdictions that lack expertise in business law, notably the emerging markets of Asia. This has generated considerable export activities for US and European law firms.[5] Legal professionals serving these international business clients across a range of jurisdictions have a vital role in constructing governance regimes with a view towards facilitating greater movement

[1] P. Schiff Berman, *Global Legal Pluralism* (Cambridge University Press, 2012).

[2] M. C. Regan Jr, "Lawyers, Globalization and Transnational Governance Regimes", 12 *Annual Review of Law and Social Science* 133 (2012).

[3] G. Muller, *Liberalization of Trade in Legal Services* (Wolters Kluwer, 2013) at 6.

[4] S. Moritsch, "Research Paper: International Trade in Legal Services – FTAs and Beyond GATS Commitments", International Bar Association Trade in Legal Services Committee at 1.

[5] Muller, *Liberalization of Trade* at 5.

of goods, services, and capital across international borders. Their work has in turn instigated a greater need for law firms in an ever-intensifying process. In that sense, lawyers are both the agents and the beneficiaries of globalization.[6]

International legal services make up a sizable sector of the economy in many advanced countries. The United States was the largest legal services market in 2016, accounting for about US $290 billion, or 45 per cent of the global market. The United Kingdom was the second largest, accounting for about $45 billion, or 7 per cent of the global total and approximately 20 per cent of the European market. Germany was in third place, accounting for about $25 billion, or 4 per cent of the global market. These countries are followed by France, which represented about 3.5 per cent of the global market, or $20 billion, and Japan, which accounted for 0.5 per cent.[7] Data from emerging markets such as China and India are harder to verify, but the growth rates of these countries coupled with their increasing integration into the global economy and global legal architecture suggest that the legal services markets in these countries will expand considerably in the coming years. The legal services market could grow faster than the global economy itself. This is because of the explosion of the international risk culture, that is, the increasing legalization of society, in which more and more regulations cover more aspects of life, particularly in a commercial context, as well as the expansion of judicial extraterritoriality, seen, for example, in the number of transnational courts.[8]

Consumers using legal services are changing their patterns of consumption, with a clear trend towards the purchase of legal services from nontraditional suppliers. This applies to clients who are individuals as well as firms. A study conducted in 2017 revealed that approximately 52 per cent of in-house legal departments are considering acquiring legal services from nontraditional law firms. Clients are increasingly seeking firms that offer a range of professional services, such as accounting, finance, and even marketing. Expertise in digital commerce, data protection, privacy, and internet security are also frequently sought from legal services providers.[9] Many commercial clients, particularly newer firms, now have the

[6] Regan Jr, "Lawyers, Globalization and Transnational" and Y. Dezalay and B. G. Garth, eds. *Lawyers and the Rule of Law in an Era of Globalization* (Routledge, 2011).

[7] "The EU and the Legal Sector Report", The Law Society of England and Wales, 2015.

[8] A. Hook, "Sectoral Study on the Impact of Domestic Regulation on Trade in Legal Services", OECD and World Bank (undated) at 11.

[9] Legal Services Market Global Report 2017 (12 Jan 2017) www.prnewswire.com/news-releases/legal-services-market-global-market-report-2017-300390461.html.

expectation that their lawyers will be able to offer business-oriented advice in addition to conventional legal advice.[10]

Commentators have begun to draw attention to how the legal profession is changing through the application of technology and how law firms have often been slow to accommodate these changes, insisting on delivering their services in an obsolete manner that is not cost effective and will ultimately lead to their own demise.[11] Rapidly changing product, market, and network configurations reduce the period in which static legal solutions are effective. Legal services are thus required that can be developed and deployed quickly and in a global manner.[12] Although global supply chains and online delivery of services have led to an economy that has become increasingly complex, some observers believe that the legal infrastructure has lagged behind.[13] Globalization appears to have driven much change in the sector; as open markets have created greater demand for legal services, technology and liberalization have unlocked the capacity of a range of legal professionals to serve foreign clients.[14] The resistance to the changing nature of the legal services market from within the highly conservative legal profession, particularly among its older members, including senior partners, judges, and law professors, has been criticized by some commentators.[15]

1.2 Definition of Legal Services

At a fundamental level, legal services suppliers provide advice to clients, who may be individuals or corporations, about their legal rights and obligations. Legal services suppliers also represent clients in civil or criminal cases as defendants or claimants, in commercial transactions, and in various other noncommercial matters such as family law and estates. These issues are not always easy to categorize formally for the purposes of integrating global markets.

[10] A. Weinberg and J. Heine, "Counseling the Startup: How Attorneys Can Add Value to Startup Clients' Businesses," 15 *Journal of Business and Securities Law* 39 (2014).

[11] R. Susskind, *Tomorrow's Lawyers* (Oxford University Press, 2017) at 3–6 and M. Kowalski, *Avoiding Extinction: Reimagining Legal Services for the 21st Century* (American Bar Association, 2012). Kowalski's book is curiously framed as a novel.

[12] G. Hadfield, *Rules for a Flat World* (Oxford University Press, 2017) at 151.

[13] Ibid. at 130.

[14] Susskind, *Tomorrow's Lawyers* at 3–6.

[15] B. Barton, *Glass Half Full: The Decline and Rebirth of the Legal Profession* (Oxford University Press, 2015) at 174.

The World Trade Organization (WTO) specified the classifications for legal services used in the original General Agreement on Trade in Services (GATS) negotiations, which we will discuss in more detail later. These specifications were based on the UN Central Product Classification (CPC) Group 181 for legal services, which is divided into four classes:

8611 – Legal advisory and representation services in the different fields of law
8612 – Legal advisory and representation services in statutory procedures of quasi-judicial tribunals, boards, etc.
8613 – Legal documentation and certification services
8619 – Other legal advisory and information services.[16]

The CPC definition is problematic because it is geared toward domestic law and consequently does not capture the reality of trade in legal services. This is one reason why it has not been possible for states negotiating for liberalization of legal services even to agree on a common format and terminology. Indeed, WTO members scheduling commitments for legal services have done so in a range of ways. This incoherence weakens the value of international treaty commitments on legal services and may offer at least one explanation of why progress in this area has been unsatisfactory. Several WTO members have submitted proposals to the Council for Trade in Services for alternative definitions. It has further been questioned whether the language of barriers to trade is appropriate in the context of legal services regulation, in which, at least in the United States, discussions about the validity of regulation of lawyers have not used this vocabulary,[17] possibly because it is a sector that has traditionally been highly circumscribed. The language of barriers appears – perhaps unsurprisingly for the WTO – to be imbued with reflexive liberalism.

Furthermore, the fragmented nature of the legal services industry in countries such as the United Kingdom, where there are multiple licensing regimes for solicitors, barristers, conveyancers, and others (in contrast to the United States, where there is one regime for lawyers), poses additional problems in terms of GATS classification in that different degrees of liberalization may be permitted within "legal services", which tend to be viewed more holistically elsewhere. The United States proposed a definition for

[16] World Trade Organization, Document W/120, Services Sectoral Classification List (July 1991).

[17] L. Terry, "From GATS to APEC: The Impact of Trade Agreements on Legal Services", 43 *Akron Law Review* 875 at 974–976 (2010).

legal services that included the provision of legal advice or legal representation in areas such as counsel on business transactions, participation in the governance of businesses, mediation, arbitration, and other nonjudicial dispute resolution services as well as, very expansively, public advocacy and lobbying.[18] Canada recommended that there should be common definitions for foreign legal consultancy services and for the practice of international law.[19] Australia made similar suggestions.[20] Interestingly, India put forth the idea of dividing legal services into subsectors that concentrate on individual professions, such as lawyers and judges.[21] A group of WTO member states issued a joint statement on services to the Council for Trade in Services that was based on the International Bar Association (IBA)'s resolution for a more appropriate definitional framework. This statement was based on the idea that there should be common definitions for all forms of legal services, taking into consideration the varied approach adopted by WTO members in submitting their GATS schedules and capturing the fundamental distinction between advisory and representation services.[22]

The term "service supplier" is defined in GATS, rather unhelpfully, to mean any person that supplies a service.[23] Article XXVIII (b) goes on to state that "supply of a service" includes the production, distribution, marketing, sale, and delivery of a service. A "person" means either a natural person or a juridical person. Footnote 12 to Article XVIII (g) explains that service suppliers also include forms of commercial presence without the legal status of a juridical person, such as branches or representative offices that are not organized as legal entities, an elaboration that is particularly relevant for law offices. This latter provision clarifies that members do not have the power to exclude certain entities from the scope of GATS by virtue of their national laws, which may not grant legal personality to certain businesses or may not recognize certain foreign juridical persons, such as associations.

[18] Legal Services, Communication from the United States, Council for Trade in Services Special Session, S/CSS/W28 (18 December 2000).

[19] Initial Negotiating Proposal on Professional Services, Communication from Canada, Council for Trade in Services Special Session, S/CSS/W/52 (14 March 2001).

[20] Negotiating Proposal for Legal Services, Revision, Communication from Australia, Council for Trade in Services Special Session, S/CSS/W/67/Supp.1/Rev (10 July 2001).

[21] Proposed Liberalization of Movement of Professionals under the GATS, Communication from India, Council for Trade in Services Special Session, S/CSS/W/12 (24 November 2000).

[22] IBA Resolution in Support of a System of Terminology for Legal Services for the Purpose of International Trade Negotiations, IBA Council Meeting, San Francisco, September 2003.

[23] Article XXVIII (g).

With attention drawn to the above definitional issues, some preliminary comments need to be made about the terminology used in this book. The term "legal services provider" is the dominant phrase that will be used to describe any individual or firm that is providing legal services, which itself can encompass legal advice and representation in court as well as assistance in matters that have a legal dimension, such as document review and other routine tasks. In the past, some lawyers associations, notably the American Bar Association (ABA), has resisted the use of the phrase "legal services" because of the concern that it somehow diminished the legal profession, which comprises lawyers and only lawyers. The extraordinary position of lawyers as distinct from other kinds of legal services providers is grounded in legal professional privilege, which prevents communications between lawyer and client on legal matters from being disclosed without the client's permission. The UK Supreme Court recently established that this privilege may be exercised only by qualified lawyers (solicitors and barristers), not by other kinds of legal professionals, such as paralegals.[24] The unique character of lawyers is also seen in the prohibition, in some US states, against the unauthorized practice of law. For most people outside of the legal profession around the world, however, lawyers tend to be seen as simply another kind of service provider.[25] This perception may take hold as other types of legal professionals begin to undertake work that was traditionally the exclusive domain of the classic lawyer.

The term "legal services" should also be contrasted with "the practice of law" or the "profession of law" because these terms unfairly underpin questionable claims of distinctiveness on the part of legal services. In the domain of international trade, which is the focus of this book, legal services tend to be thought of as merely another category of services, such as health care or engineering, both of which could equally lay claim to a special status as professions. This view is rooted in the theory that the concept of profession is a fluid one that is premised fundamentally on the notion of asymmetrical knowledge between the provider and the consumer as well as, somewhat more ambiguously, the fulfilling of a social role beyond simply that of self-interest or personal profit.[26] In this book, the term "lawyer" is used for convenience to refer to someone possessing a legal qualification authorized by a regulating body in the individual's home state or

[24] *Prudential PLC and Prudential (Gibraltar) Ltd* v. *Special Commissioner of Income Tax and Philip Pandolfo (HM Inspector of Taxes)*, [2013] UKSC 1 (23 January 2013).

[25] Terry, "From GATS to APEC" at 970.

[26] R. Susskind, *The Future of the Professions* (Oxford University Press, 2015) at 24–25.

host state. Thus, the term "lawyer" includes both barristers and solicitors as well as attorneys and practitioners with similar titles as used in other jurisdictions.

1.3 The Regulation of Trade in Legal Services

It is important to draw attention in this introductory chapter to the main kinds of regulatory barriers that are imposed on the supply of legal services because these are the focus of many of the liberalizing efforts with respect to trade in legal services. Equally important is a consideration of the justification behind these measures, which often impede the modernization and globalization of the legal profession in terms of who is entitled to provide legal services and, by extension, what qualifications such individuals must possess and, in some cases, where they originate.

1.3.1 The Nature of the Regulatory Barriers to Trade Legal Services

The legal services industry is among the most restricted of all sectors of the economy. The Organisation for Economic Co-operation and Development's Services Trade Restrictiveness Indices (STRIs) for legal services range from 0.11 to 0.73 on a scale from 0 to 1, with an average of 0.31.[27] The regulation of the legal profession, as with most industries, has historically been the purview of national and in many cases subnational governments. The provision of an enabling legal framework is the responsibility of the state, just as it is implemented and enforced through legal institutions, including properly functioning courts, effective legal counsel (prosecution and defence), an independent and competent judiciary, and diligent investigating authorities.[28] Such laws traditionally create a monopoly for individuals who are qualified under the jurisdiction's rules,

[27] M. G. Grosso, H. Nordås, F. Gonzales, I. Lejárraga, S. Miroudot, "Services Trade Restrictiveness Index (STRI): Legal and Accounting Services", *OECD Trade Policy Papers* 171 (4 November 2014). The STRIs are composite indices that take values between 0 and 1, where 0 represents an open market and 1 represents a market that is completely closed to foreign services providers. The indices are calculated for forty countries – the thirty-four OECD members and Brazil, China, India, Indonesia, Russia, and South Africa – and are based on regulations that are mentioned explicitly in the GATS, regulations that are mentioned explicitly in regional trade agreements, and other regulations that the OECD has identified as relevant.

[28] N. Katangaza and C. Thurston Smith, "Lawyers without Borders: The Case for Legal Services Liberalisation", 20:3 *International Trade Law and Regulation* 45 at 46 (2014).

prohibiting unqualified suppliers from offering legal services and controlling the extent to which individuals from outside the jurisdiction can enter the domestic market. Domestic competition authorities focus on regulating legal services markets, whereas professional regulatory bodies such as bar associations and law societies devote their attention to regulating the individual services suppliers themselves.

Entry rules to the legal profession may be subdivided into three categories, the least onerous of which is registration, in which individuals who provide a certain service must identify themselves to a regulator. This is followed by certification, which is similar to registration except that it also permits the use of certain titles or designations, such as Queen's Counsel (QC) for experienced barristers. The most stringent entry rule (and the most market-distorting one) is full licensing, which prohibits anyone from providing legal services unless the individual is specifically granted the permission to do so, typically after demonstrating skill by passing examinations or undergoing training.

Conduct rules seek to prevent poor-quality service and often involve insurance to mitigate harm that may be done as a consequence. Conduct rules also involve ethical rules and guidelines. Many jurisdictions maintain laws designed to protect the public from unqualified foreign lawyers. These consist of rules that essentially compensate for differences in training and qualification procedures across various jurisdictions. They include educational and experience requirements as well as restrictions on the types of legal advice that a foreign lawyer may provide.

Business structure rules limit the nature of the business entity through which the individual may deliver legal services, such as partnerships with non-lawyers and corporations, often described as ABSs. These regimes are relatively liberal in the United Kingdom and Australia but remain tightly controlled in the United States and various Asian countries, including Japan.[29] Corporate law provisions regarding company structure that restrict the type of business form that law firms can adopt, for example, are another example of this kind of law. There are, of course, sector-specific measures, typically captured in primary legislation governing the legal profession, that may be imposed through codes of conduct, as well as measures concerning education and training. All of these can affect the extent to which foreign practitioners may access the market.[30] There are laws aimed at constraining the ability of otherwise qualified foreign

[29] N. Semple, *Legal Services Regulation at the Crossroads* (Edward Elgar, 2015) at 33–44.
[30] Hook, "Sectoral Study on the Impact of Domestic Regulation" at 3.

lawyers from providing services in the domestic market. These measures include hiring restrictions, partnership and association restrictions, data protection and privacy rules, restrictions on naming of firms, residency requirements, and, in some cases, discriminatory taxes. There are regulations that effectively prohibit legal practice by foreign lawyers solely on the basis of their nationality. These measures include citizenship requirements for local bar membership, prohibitions on foreign ownership, and visa requirements.[31]

The closed community of legal specialists who are permitted to provide these services in most countries is regularly criticized for offering insufficient choice to consumers. Many believe that the legal profession is an unjustified monopoly and that its rules, in many countries, are restrictive and anticompetitive.[32] There are parallels between the liberalization of markets domestically (ABSs and delivery by non-lawyers) and the liberalization of markets internationally (enlarging spheres of legal services delivery for foreign providers). Reform initiatives for the former are often linked to the latter, and just as the areas of practice available to non-lawyers are expanded, so also are foreign providers' opportunities. Some jurisdictions regulate foreign lawyers in the same manner as they regulate local non-lawyers. Commentators have spoken of the global "ripple effect": When liberalization of the kinds of services that can be supplied by non-lawyers takes hold and better serves the needs of clients, global businesses that benefit from new forms of service delivery will expect similar services in their own countries.[33] Foreign lawyers may be the first to answer this call.

Most jurisdictions around the world allow legal services providers to offer services regarding the laws of the jurisdiction or jurisdictions in which they are qualified as well as in international laws. Such individuals are usually permitted to form partnerships with local legal practitioners and other foreign lawyers and to use their firm's name. Restrictions based on the nationality or residency of the service supplier are uncommon. In many jurisdictions, legal services suppliers are subject to local legal professional ethical and disciplinary rules.[34]

Domestic legislation on the provision of legal services tends to set out the objectives of the regulation, the scope of the market that is subject

[31] These categories were initially described by D. N. Menegas, "GATT as a Framework for Multilateral Negotiations on Trade in Legal Services", 7 *Michigan Yearbook of International Legal Studies* 277 at 280–282 (1985).

[32] Susskind, *Tomorrow's Lawyers* at 6.

[33] Ibid. at 9.

[34] Katangaza and Thurston Smith, "Lawyers without Borders" at 48.

to the laws contained in the legislation, and an outline of the rights and obligations of legal professionals in that jurisdiction, including the manner in which legal professionals are to be supervised by the state. As we noted above, the regulation of legal services is primarily aimed at establishing the qualification of individual practitioners as well as the delineation of the types of services that they are entitled to provide and from which nonqualified individuals are excluded. In developed countries with advanced economies, there may be additional information on transactional or nonadversarial work, whereas less advanced countries tend to focus on the practice of law in the courts. In developed countries, there are often distinct regulators for the legal profession, whereas in less developed countries, this role is undertaken by local courts. There, the courts will be charged with monitoring practitioners and disciplining those who have failed to uphold the standards of the profession. Engaging in the delivery of legal services in these countries can be problematic for foreign practitioners because of the lack of regulatory sophistication on the part of the courts, which may not be accustomed to supervising lawyers from outside their own jurisdiction. The practice of law by foreigners can be fraught with uncertainty and can lead to resentment by local lawyers who feel that their own control over the profession is at risk.

Many jurisdictions, especially in the developed world, will have not only a regulator but also a local bar association that represents legal practitioners as a group and promotes their interests, often engaging in training and outreach initiatives, including client development and, in some cases, law reform proposals. These tend to be voluntary associations, which in some cases have been delegated the power to regulate the legal profession by governments. This lends a degree of independence from state interference with the profession, which may be useful when there are international obligations covering the practice of law. The trend in many developed countries has been to shift from self-regulation by professional bodies toward autonomous regulators that are focused on the market rather than on the individual service providers. The Solicitor's Regulatory Authority (SRA) in the United Kingdom is a good example of this approach.

1.3.2 *Justifications for Regulating Trade in Legal Services*

There are a number of justifications for controlling foreign access to the domestic market of legal services, some of which have been alluded to already. First, there is the somewhat abstract notion that foreign lawyers lack the shared cultural values of the host state, particularly if they are involved in local court proceedings that affect citizens' personal or property rights. Flowing from this view, some regulatory barriers imposed on foreign suppliers of legal services may be justified on the basis of safeguarding the interests of citizens against lawyers who do not understand the nature of the society in which their clients live and work.

Relatedly, there is the concern that foreign qualified lawyers lack the necessary competence. National regulators may assert that, as they have no control over the foreign educational standards, the lawyers whom this foreign system produces may be substandard and thus may pose a danger to their clients and society at large. Clients are now readily identified as consumers, which invokes considerations of consumer welfare as a justification for the regulation of lawyers.[35] These concerns are exacerbated when there are fundamental differences between legal systems, as is the case between civil and common law countries.

Problems of market failure in the legal services sector, such as information asymmetry (the clients cannot accurately price the value of the services because they do not appreciate the level of complexity of their own needs) and adverse selection (clients cannot tell the difference between good and bad legal services, so they choose the cheaper one, which creates a perverse incentive for good lawyers not to improve their own services),[36] may be felt equally, if not more so, across international boundaries. These situations result in inefficiencies or social costs. Professional services such as legal services are correctly described as credence goods, meaning that their quality is very rarely adequately evaluated by the consumer because it is highly technical, requiring external quality assurances, such as bar association membership, licensing, or high standards of education, such as law degrees from accredited institutions.

Third, there is some apprehension among national regulators that foreign lawyers may be more susceptible to committing malpractice, possibly because of lack of familiarity with the domestic legal system but also because their ethical profiles cannot be verified. Foreign legal practitioners who do not obtain domestic qualifications may escape supervision by domestic regulators for money laundering. Local citizens using these lawyers may suffer from the inability to bring or enforce claims for compensation when the service suppliers do not hold assets in the domestic jurisdiction. This issue is more acute given that modern lawyers tend to

[35] M. Trebilcock and L. Csorgo, "Multi-disciplinary Professional Practices: A Consumer Welfare Perspective", 24 *Dalhousie Law Journal* 1 (2001).

[36] Semple, *Legal Services Regulation* at 24–26.

handle sensitive data belonging to their clients. These problems are likely also to generate negative externalities, that is, harmful effects to third parties. A client may choose to hire an incompetent lawyer, perhaps from another jurisdiction, if the outcome may harm others but not himself, as in the case of a poorly drafted will.[37] Concerns about competence because the localized character of the law arguably justify screening processes, such as examining the extent and relevance of foreign training and experience as well as supplementary education or examinations. Clients will seek competent providers of legal services and will identify whether a foreign supplier fits this category; otherwise, they will use other suppliers.[38]

Fourth, it is sometimes thought that the presence of foreign lawyers may inhibit the establishment of a domestic legal profession. This "infant industry" style argument is particularly relevant for developing and emerging market countries that are seeking to move beyond agrarian or basic industrial economies toward service industries. In some countries with poorly developed legal markets, regulatory barriers to entry of the legal profession may be erected on the basis that these preserve the standing of the local legal profession and, in so doing, contribute to the independence of the legal profession more generally.

Finally, there is the strategic or diplomatic justification that foreign lawyers should not be able to offer their legal services if their home state does not grant reciprocal access. Asymmetrical access to legal markets combined with difficulties in negotiating services (unlike tariffs on goods) often means that markets remain less open than they could be.[39]

1.3.3 Benefits of Liberalizing Trade in Legal Services

Having set out some of the reasons why trade in legal services are so highly constrained, it is crucial to consider the benefits of liberalizing trade in legal services. A starting point in this discussion is the recognition that a growing trend has been observed in which governments are subjecting many more occupations, especially professional ones, to extensive

[37] B. H. Barton, "Why Do We Regulate Lawyers: An Economic Analysis of the Justifications for Entry and Conduct Regulation", 33 *Arizona State Law Journal* 430 (2001) at 470.

[38] A. Amos-Stewarta, K. Broughton, and B. Schwartz, "All Talk and No Action: Access to Canadian Markets under the General Agreement on Trade in Services", 11 *Asper Review of International Business & Trade Law* 91 at 119 (2011).

[39] M. J. Chapman and P. J. Tauber, "Liberalizing International Trade in Legal Services: A Proposal for an Annex on Legal Services under the General Agreement on Trade in Services", 16 *Michigan Journal of International Law* 941 at 953 (1995).

licensing requirements. While professionals such as legal practitioners may possess specialized knowledge that is not readily verifiable by members of the public, placing clients or potential clients in a position of vulnerability, the regulation of professionals imposes a cost on society. Whether done consciously or not, establishing monopolies over the provision of certain services raises costs to consumers. Clients of limited means are driven to unlicensed poor-quality providers, and occupational licensing drives up costs to a level that many people are unable to afford, further restricting supply and creating professions that are socially exclusive. Such monopolies are harder to justify given technological advances that have rendered many of the tasks performed by legal professionals highly routine and capable of automation. The creation of very specific job requirements discourages innovation and competition within a sector. It can also frustrate individuals' efforts to change professions in mid-career, which may be attractive to individuals who are seeking entry into the legal profession.[40]

The exacting regulatory regime for lawyers (and other legal services providers) is the most significant barrier to the liberalization of trade in legal services on either a multilateral or a preferential basis. This regime is derided by many as self-serving and anticompetitive, designed to limit new market entrants rather than to benefit consumers.[41] Some legal professional associations that provide registration and certification of lawyers have been accused of adopting ideological standpoints on matters that exceed their mandate, including judicial appointments from a particular political party and their support of what might be termed extraneous causes such as diversity and inclusiveness. The ABA and the Law Society of Upper Canada (Ontario) have recently drawn criticism in this regard.[42]

Many of the justifications for control over the delivery of legal services from foreign suppliers are questionable. While consumer (or client) protection is unquestionably an important policy objective, market access for foreign legal professionals is not likely to present much of a threat. This is because the type of services provided by foreign law firms tends not to

[40] J. R. Shakleton, "Conspiracy against the Public: Occupational Regulation in the UK Economy", Current Controversies No. 56. Institute of Economic Affairs (December 2017) at 25.

[41] "Competitive Restrictions in Legal Professions", Policy Roundtables, Competition Committee, OECD, 2007, Paris at 9.

[42] For example, Senator Tom Cotton spoke at the 2017 National Lawyer's Convention (16 November 2017) about the ABA's support of certain judges. See also J. Kay, "Law Society's Inflated View of Lawyer's Importance Leads It to Compelled Speech", *The National Post* (Canada) (26 October 2017), regarding the Law Society of Upper Canada's requirement of its members to uphold progressive policies.

be consumer focused. The end user of these services is more likely to be a sophisticated multinational enterprise with extensive sectoral knowledge, deep resources, and the capacity to verify the authenticity and expertise of the supplier. Furthermore, benefits may accrue to ordinary consumers because improvements in the legal services sector can underpin a more stable business environment generally, fostering increases in foreign direct investment.[43]

In terms of safeguarding the development of a local legal profession, local legal services providers who view foreign entrants as a threat to their monopoly may be misguided. The kinds of law firms that enter a foreign market tend not to provide the kinds of legal services in which local firms specialize, such as private client, criminal, or family law work. Foreign entrants probably lack not only the qualifications but also, perhaps more important, the local knowledge to offer an effective challenge to the dominance of local providers. Internationally mobile legal services providers are more likely to establish and practice with a view toward serving international businesses, either on a temporary basis or in conjunction with local lawyers. Because foreign legal services providers tend to offer a service that is tailored to offer assistance on an aspect of an international transaction, it tends to follow that liberalization of legal services should yield a rise in the level of domestic productivity.[44] Moreover, the idea that there is an infant industry of legal services in some jurisdictions that deserves protection from the stresses of international competition has not always been supported by dedicated action on the part of states to promote the local industry, such as the removal of regulatory barriers preventing access to the profession among a broader segment of domestic society. Again, it is not evident that protection in the sense of the creation of legal obstacles to the entry of foreign legal services providers actually assists the local profession to develop to the point at which it can function competitively in the international legal market, since success in this environment is predicated on satisfying the demands of sophisticated international clients. It is widely recognized that lawyers have for some time been performing routine work for which they are overqualified and for which they are overcharging their clients. Regulations that ensure a monopoly on legal services supply among a small group of elites in most countries has perpetuated this malfunctioning market.[45]

[43] Katangaza and Thurston Smith, "Lawyers without Borders" at 48.

[44] Ibid. at 47.

[45] Susskind, *Tomorrow's Lawyers* at 59.

The decline of the legal profession in a general sense is now a common theme in many works, raising doubts about the genuine purpose of market access restrictions. There has been a pronounced downturn in employment numbers for law graduates as well a drop in revenue per lawyer, particularly at large US firms.[46] The reasons for the struggles of large law firms are numerous but seem to focus on outsourcing and computerization, with the classic highly paid lawyer taking on a limited supervisory role as part of a larger supply chain.[47] There now appears to be a vast oversupply of lawyers and law graduates in many developed countries, particularly the United States.[48] Enrolment in law schools has fallen in the United States, yet law schools around the developed world produce more graduates each year than can be sustained by the demand for new lawyers.[49] Rather than training lawyers to serve the needs of their clients, law schools are viewed as agents of social policy that are far removed from reality and tend to fit within a narrow range of political ideology.[50] The opening up of legal markets overseas could create opportunities for these individuals for whom those at home have been exhausted.

Liberalization of trade in legal services may benefit the consumers of legal services. Creating a monopoly for the provision of legal services through tight regulation can raise prices for the users of that system. This problem is exacerbated by the high barriers to entry on the part of lawyers themselves. Of course, while there are many thousands – in some countries, hundreds of thousands – of qualified legal practitioners, very few of these will be able to provide adequate legal services to their clients. In other words, tight control of the profession in many countries reduces the number of suppliers, raising the cost of services. When national authorities restrict access to the domestic legal market by foreign providers, they further constrain the supply of this service, raising the prices even more. Many consumers end up being unserved or overpaying for the service. This problem is exacerbated further when there is a lack of legal aid available to impecunious consumers. Furthermore, without sufficient competition from abroad, domestic lawyers are not compelled to increase the quality of their services because they do not need to do so to remain attractive to their clients. They do not invest in technology or the acquisition of

[46] Barton, *Glass Half Full* at 45–52.

[47] Ibid. at 73.

[48] Ibid. at 122.

[49] B. Tamanaha, *Failing Law Schools* (University of Chicago Press, 2012).

[50] W. Olson, *Schools for Misrule: Legal Academia and an Overlawyered America* (Encounter Books, 2011).

knowledge, and the profession in turn stagnates. The presence of foreign lawyers within a domestic market should increase the quality of the service while lowering the price. Restricting the entry of foreign firms will not insulate domestic providers entirely anyway, because savvy consumers will seek these services offshore, either by travelling or by using telecommunications unless, of course, these forms of legal services delivery are restricted as well.[51]

With regard to suspicions about the competence of foreign lawyers and the need to safeguard consumers, evidence suggests that this may be a false fear. Commentators have urged that, contrary to the objections raised by lawyers, the removal of discriminatory qualification requirements (such as nationality, residence, or even education at a domestic university) has not led to a weakening of the regulatory framework for legal services.[52] There are indications that the liberalization of legal services across international borders may necessitate stronger regulatory control. Cross-country studies on the impact of institutions on the performance of services generally illustrate that countries with robust regulations coupled with enforcement have larger and more dynamic services sectors.[53]

For example, the unwillingness of US regulators to recognize foreign competence is puzzling, given that the discipline of attorneys in the United States has been a notoriously neglected area. It is believed that up to 90 per cent of complaints against US lawyers have been summarily dismissed.[54] This suggests that maintaining quality or ethical standards within the profession is not as significant a priority as one might think. In the words of one prominent commentator, "there is good reason to doubt the sincerity of bar association warnings about the potential harms to clients by non-lawyers".[55] The same may be said of potential harm inflicted by foreign lawyers.

The pursuit of competition in the delivery of legal services sector with a view to serving consumer interests characterizes reforms to the regulation of the legal profession in jurisdictions such as England, Wales, and Australia. These systems feature independent regulators acting as mediators between the state and the profession, and they tend to focus regulatory efforts on the services themselves rather than on the individual who provides the services. This consumerist motivation for the liberalization

[51] Katangaza and Thurston Smith, "Lawyers without Borders" at 48.

[52] Ibid. at 47.

[53] M. Amin and A. Mattoo, "Do Institutions Matter More for Services?", World Bank Policy Research Working Paper 4032, 2006, The World Bank, Washington DC.

[54] Barton, *Glass Half Full* at 211.

[55] Ibid. at 212.

of international trade stands in sharp contrast to the professionalist-independent tradition of regulating legal services. This model, which is found in the United States, is constituted by a unified, isolated profession that is largely self-governing and focused on the individual practitioner rather than on the service itself.[56]

It has been suggested that segmented markets for legal services increase the costs of commercial matters that have a transnational element. This is because they require the involvement of separate lawyers in each jurisdiction covered by the transaction or dispute when having fewer lawyers but with multijurisdictional expertise would suffice. This can lead to duplicate billing as well as transaction costs resulting from excess communication and transportation. Clearly, liberalizing trade in legal services will help to facilitate international transactions, securing efficiency gains from this type of commerce.[57]

It is often asserted that the principle beneficiaries of the opening of world markets are the providers of services based in industrialized countries rather than the consumers. In the case of legal services, these providers are the large US and, to a lesser extent, UK law firms. This is precisely why it is superficially tempting to consider legal services emblematic of industrialized countries' attempt to control the markets of less industrialized countries that lack such firms.[58] The exclusion of foreign law firms may be self-defeating because the professional skills that many clients seek, especially in relation to cross-border transactions, may shift toward centres of international legal expertise in other jurisdictions. The home jurisdiction will thus lose out on this potentially lucrative legal work, representing not just lost income through services outflow but also the suppression of the development of the local legal profession, which would have thrived under the competition generated by foreign firms.[59]

It is crucial to keep in mind the important role of lawyers as agents of the court and further as enablers of access to justice. Access to justice is in turn an essential component of a functioning democratic society.[60] In this sense, liberalizing trade in legal services to allow the participation of lawyers from abroad in the justice system can be an important means of

[56] Semple, *Legal Services Regulation* Chapter 4.

[57] R. J. Goebel, "Lawyers in the European Community: Progress towards Community-Wide Rights of Practice", 15 *Fordham International Law Journal* 556 at 556–57 (1991–92).

[58] S. Cone, "Legal Services in the Doha Round", 37(1) *Journal of World Trade* 29 at 38 (2003).

[59] Cone, ibid., at 40.

[60] A. Wooley, "Why Do We Regulate Lawyers?" in D. L. Blaikie, T. Cromwell, and D. Pink eds. *Why Good Lawyers Matter* (Irwin Law, 2012).

strengthening domestic institutions such as courts but also regulators, governments, and private commercial parties. It is no coincidence that the countries with the highest scores in the Rule of Law Index tend to be those that are most open in the sense of being economically globalized. It has been widely recognized for some time that stronger legal systems are closely tied to a more open legal profession.[61]

Open trade in legal services may be a valuable purpose of international rule making in part because it is an inevitable aspect of globalization, as we suggested at the beginning of this chapter. Commentators have lamented the failure of legal markets to provide coherent solutions to problems that have become increasingly cross-border, as evinced by global supply chains and digital commerce.[62] Some commentators hold that there is a system of decentralized or networked governance within the global business community that has been generated in part by the legal professionals who serve it. This is manifested in multiple transnational legal orders that aim to direct the behaviour of global firms. Such orders consist of a collection of formalized legal norms, often associated with non-state actors, meaning organizations that exert authority over the understanding and practice of law across international boundaries. These organizations or actors endeavour to legitimize the norms they create through processes of persuasion and negotiation.[63] A transnational legal order purports to order social relationships that transcend national boundaries but seeks to influence and is ultimately reflected in national law-creating legal bodies. As they are imprinted on local legal norms, creating a degree of harmonization globally, these systems exclude what is normally viewed as "soft law" because they are binding. Legal services providers are regarded as important participants in the construction of these transnational governance regimes, particularly in fields of international law, where they exert key influence. One of these is international trade, in which governmental negotiators tend to be qualified legal practitioners. Legal practitioners working in-house for extractive sector companies are thought to have played a key role in the development of ethical standards for multinational enterprises.[64] Legal practitioners working for transnational clients may have further contributed to globalization through their role in formulating

[61] J. H. Barton, "Negotiation Patterns for Liberalizing International Trade in Professional Services", University of Chicago Legal Forum 103–104 (1986).

[62] Hadfield, *Rules for a Flat World* at 193.

[63] See T. Halliday and G. Shaffer, *Transnational Legal Orders* (Cambridge University Press, 2015).

[64] Regan Jr, "Lawyers, Globalization and Transnational".

transnational governance regimes that harmonize commercial and human rights.[65]

Critics of open trade in legal services may warn against granting access to the delivery of legal services to individuals who do not have a sense of national loyalty to the host jurisdiction, possibly because these legal services professions do not share the values of local members of the legal profession. This view ignores the reality that members of the legal profession worldwide do, generally speaking, adhere to common overarching principles based on trust and client confidentiality. It also overlooks the need for diversity of opinion, which is needed in any professional regime.[66] Legal services providers underpin transnational law making and, in so doing, enable globalization through contractual innovation, in which they act as advisors as well as drafters producing tailored contracts that serve their clients global business needs; through standardization, in which they function as intermediaries promoting the dissemination of these strategic contracts, possibly resulting in the emergence of model contracts (sometimes seen as "soft law"); and finally by acting as public experts in hearings or negotiations, advocating for a norm to become legally binding. This last role requires recognition by a national or ultimately transnational authority.[67]

Legal services providers are viewed as the natural drivers in the construction of fields of transnational governance that reduce barriers to cross-border activities through the establishment of legal systems that are independent of local interests. This is done in part through the invocation of traditional liberal legal principles such as predictability, equality, and protection of private property.[68] Legal services providers are further likely to play a key role in transnational governance regimes because the service of a multinational enterprise may involve the exploitation of differences between national regulations, requiring legal advisors to acquire knowledge of the national laws of various jurisdictions. A vital component of this expertise is an understanding of how local custom and practices affect the way in which the law is actually applied, particularly where it diverges from how the law appears in statutes. This kind of expertise, which may be available only to the international service provider, is regarded as an

[65] Ibid.

[66] Stewarta et al., "All Talk and No Action" at 119.

[67] S. Quack, "Legal Professionals and Transnational Law-making: A Case of Distributed Agency", *Organization* 14(5) at 643–66 (2007).

[68] This can be seen quite readily in the sphere of international investment law, in which such principles are enshrined in both investment contracts and investment treaties. See, e.g., J. Salacuse, *The Three Laws of International Investment* (Oxford University Press, 2013).

important source of professional capital that can enable the professional to define the problem that diverse national regulations create in a given field and to prescribe solutions to it.[69]

Trends in the regulation of the legal professions toward a more co-regulatory model and away from a self-regulatory one, along with pressures to segregate regulatory and representational services suppliers, have had the result that legal services are increasingly being treated as simply one of many types of services. This may ultimately mean that legal services providers, including fully qualified lawyers, may in the future be brought under the umbrella of generally applicable legislation of the governing jurisdiction, such as consumer protection laws. This could mean that governmental authorities will become increasingly less tolerant of what some lawyers have traditionally regarded as lawyer exceptionalism. A number of domestic competition authorities have contemplating their own systems of lawyer regulation.[70]

1.4 Instruments of Liberalization

From the point of view of international trade, it is important to establish that assurances that are intended to combat harmful market failures such as those noted above are legitimate, meaning transparent, nonarbitrary, and in the public interest. Because qualifications for legal services providers (as with many other professions) tend to be variable across jurisdictions, the major problem is that local regulators are required to assess foreign qualifications, training, and experience. This can be a difficult process, often requiring letters of recommendation from senior members of the profession, such as law firm partners or judges. Foreign legal professionals may be required to demonstrate their skill and familiarity with the local legal system through additional education, training, and examinations. Verification procedures must not be so onerous that they operate as a disguised restriction on international trade, or else they risk falling foul of international treaties, as will be explored further in this book. Qualification requirements for legal services providers are particularly harsh because the profession is divided across national and sometimes subnational lines, reflecting the highly localized character of the law.[71]

[69] Regan Jr, "Lawyers, Globalization and Transnational".

[70] L. Terry, "Trends in Global and Canadian Lawyer Regulation", 76 *Saskatchewan Law Review* 145 (2013).

[71] Grosso et al., "Services Trade Restrictiveness Index".

Several countries with a federal structure of government have undertaken initiatives to open up legal services internally, across subcentral jurisdictions, recognizing that such barriers have acted as a drag on economic development. While Canada and Australia have enjoyed considerable success in this regard, there appears to be little interest in pursuing this aim in the United States. The removal of subcentral restrictions on the supply of legal services from these medium-sized economies may create a larger domestic presence from which national firms can internationalize. As in the international context, the primary concern in the regulatory reform of the practice of law in federal states tends to be differences (perceived or real) in education or qualification requirements in different subcentral jurisdictions. While it is not the case in the provinces of Canada or states of Australia, the highly unequal level of difficulty among state bar exams in the United States would surely act as a disincentive for many law graduates to take the bar exam in California, for example. The "easiest" jurisdiction in which to qualify could then become a passport to qualification in the more difficult or more prestigious states, lowering the overall quality of legal practitioners to that of the weakest jurisdiction. Exchange of information about disciplinary processes between subfederal regulators may be a further problem. Individuals who have committed a disciplinary offence might simply move to another jurisdiction in the country if they are disqualified in their home state.[72]

The liberalization of legal services has been taken up in some countries by competition authorities who focus on the effective functioning of markets from the perspective of consumer interests, as suggested earlier. This may be problematic because competition regulators are designed to address the behaviour of firms, whereas most legal regulators devote their efforts to the supervision of individuals – the practicing lawyer or paralegal. As was alluded to above, the nature of legal services also arguably calls for distinct regulatory approaches. The policy justification as well as the manner of regulation of a lawyer who represents an individual client in court defending the client's rights against the state can be quite different from the regulation of a lawyer who undertakes transactional work for a commercial purpose.

Of vital importance to this book is the international dimension of legal services regulation, meaning essentially that which affects international trade. The regulation of the legal professional is increasingly affected by the actions of international bodies as if it were any other service rather than

[72] Hook, "Sectoral Study on the Impact of Domestic Regulation" at 32.

one deserving of special status. For example, the European Commission, along with the European Central Bank and the International Monetary Fund, has insisted on the regulatory reform of legal services as one of the conditions of bailouts of financially troubled EU member states such as Greece. Similarly, the WTO and the Asian Pacific Economic Cooperation (APEC) treat lawyers much the same as they do other services providers. The Organisation for Economic Co-operation and Development (OECD) developed policies on competition that have had an impact on lawyer regulation.[73] The Financial Action Task Force issued recommendations that some countries have implemented that regard lawyers as being the same as other gatekeepers of financial services in relation to money laundering and terrorism, despite the fact that these rules may conflict with lawyer confidentiality rules in many jurisdictions.[74] These approaches must be viewed in light of the resistance from within the legal services profession in many countries against the treatment of the legal profession like any other industry because this ignores the crucial role of the lawyer as an agent of the justice system and as a servant of society.[75]

Multilateral controls over the actions of national regulators have been viewed as the chief means to enable the further expansion of the legal services industry. Calls for an international regime governing transnational legal practice have been made for decades, even before the onset of the transformative era of global telecommunications through the Internet.[76] Some countries that have been relatively closed to trade in legal services have addressed the issue of liberalization alongside that of regulatory reform generally. Opening the market for legal services to foreign suppliers has been done in tandem with policies aimed at increasing the number of domestic legal professionals.[77] This is the case in Japan, Korea, and India, to mention some prominent examples.[78]

[73] Organization for Economic Cooperation and Development, Competitive Restrictions in Legal Professions (2007), online: www.oecd.org/dataoecd/12/38/40080343.pdf. This report built on the work of a prior report that addressed professional services generally rather than legal services specifically.

[74] L. S. Terry, "An Introduction to the Financial Action Task Force and Its 2008 Lawyer Guidance", *Journal of Professional Law* 3 at 10 and 24–27 (2010).

[75] Hook, "Sectoral Study on the Impact of Domestic Regulation" at 34.

[76] Chapman and Tauber, "Liberalizing International Trade in Legal Services".

[77] Ibid.

[78] The notion that domestic reform is an essential precondition for international liberalization is captured, to an extent, in Article XVI of the General Agreement on Trade in Services of the WTO, which precludes numeric restrictions on services suppliers, whether domestic or international.

At the bilateral or regional level, free-trade agreements (FTAs) covering services may offer additional liberalization beyond which is attainable globally, although only a small number of regional or bilateral agreements have done so. Under WTO law, there are few limitations on these preferential arrangements, chief of which is that they must have "substantial sectoral coverage".[79] This condition is understood in terms of number of sectors, the volume of trade affected, and modes of supply. Accordingly, FTAs should not provide for the a priori exclusion of any mode of supply. In other words, there cannot be sector-specific services FTAs, such as one for legal services. Whether or not this restriction makes sense economically, it unquestionably represents a barrier to the liberalization of legal services. Presumably it would be easier for two or more states to find agreement in relation to the regulation of a particular industry – the legal profession, for example – than it would be to do so across all services, including potentially even more contentious ones such as financial services or telecommunications. In services negotiations, most states have one or more "sacred cows", meaning sectors that they refuse to open to international suppliers, a problem that is exacerbated by "turf-conscious ministries" that cannot recognize the value of concessions to other sectors beyond those covered by their own departments.[80]

1.5 Aims and Structure of this Book

This book will explore the ways in which international law addresses the important and expanding trade in legal services, covering essentially the capacity for lawyers to work in other countries (either in person or virtually) and for law firms to establish offices overseas. This book will consider the role of modern forms of delivery of legal services such as virtual law firms, ABSs, and associated challenges such as data protection and automation. It will examine how the various multilateral and regional, trade agreements control domestic laws that affect trade in legal services. Although no specific domestic regimes will be considered in depth, several examples of national laws will be mentioned to give an overview of the types of restrictions that are imposed by some of the leading jurisdictions in the world, including both developed and emerging economies. This

[79] Article V 1 (a).

[80] R. Adlung, "Trade in Services in the WTO: From Marrakesh (1994) to Doha (2001), to ..." in A. Narlikar, M. Daunton, and R. Stern eds. *The Oxford Handbook on the World Trade Organization* (Oxford University Press, 2012) at 374.

approach should help to illustrate how public international law facilitates trade in legal services with a view to uncovering how it may be modified to improve the international flow of legal services both as a tool of economic progress and development and as an agent of democracy and rule of law.

One of the themes of this book is that open trade in legal services is central to international trade itself because of the need for security and predictability of lawyers' intervention in many forms of commercial activity. Allowing the legal advisor to travel along with the traded goods fosters a trusted adviser relationship between lawyers and clients. Legal professionals are also able to develop local knowledge. Law firms working together across international borders can develop their expertise to provide multi-jurisdictional advice that will empower the activities of firms that operate globally. Lawyers from the same organization can collaborate more effectively on the same transaction than can lawyers who are not part of the same office.[81] From the perspective of the economy generally, restricted trade in legal services has undermined the ability of many states to capitalize on these types of efficiencies to enhance their own economic development. There are a number of countries around the world that should be importers of legal services but, as a consequence of market access barriers, have not attained this status.[82] Commitment to the rule of law as fostered by open markets for legal services brings benefits beyond those enjoyed by commercial parties; it serves a vital role in the proper functioning of all democracies.

It is surprising that those who argue in favour of deregulation of legal services to reduce the burden on society because of excessive rules very rarely recommend opening up trade in legal services from other countries as a solution.[83] Commentators have argued that domestic regulation of legal services, particularly in countries where the legal profession is self-regulating, should foster innovation and accessibility.[84] Yet the benefits of liberal trading rules are strangely ignored. One way to address the ever-increasing demand for globally-oriented legal services is to increase the numbers of those who have the knowledge, training and qualifications to

[81] Katangaza and Thurston Smith, "Lawyers without Borders" at 47.

[82] Hook, "Sectoral Study on the Impact of Domestic Regulation" at 3.

[83] See, e.g., G. Hadfield and J. Heine, "Life in a Law-Thick World: The Legal Resource Landscape for Ordinary Americans", USC Law Legal Studies Paper No. 15-2 (9 January 2015), and E. Iacobucci and M. Trebilcock, "An Economic Analysis of Alternative Business Structures for the Practice of Law", Law Society of Upper Canada Symposium on Alternative Business Structures (4 October 2013).

[84] Semple, *Legal Services Regulation* at 8.

supply it. ABSs in which non-lawyers with expertise in matters such as international tax is one answer. Foreign legal services suppliers with familiarity with other jurisdictions is another.

Clearly liberalization in legal services (as in other spheres) cannot be presumed to be advantageous in all circumstances. While legal services is unquestionably a "market" in the sense that services are offered in a competitive manner for financial gain, law must still be viewed, to a degree, as a special kind of profession in that the users of the service are both customers and clients, the latter grouping requiring from law service providers an additional duty based upon trust, integrity, and ethics. Unlike other professionals, lawyers also owe a duty to the court itself that stands apart from, and may often be in tension with, the duty owed to the client and to potential future customers. The extent to which this should affect the service's openness is a matter of much debate and constant re-evaluation, particularly in terms of whether lawyers deserve their exemption from many rules covering trade and competition.[85] Critics have argued that claims that lawyers constitute a profession whose motivation is primarily an altruistic one in the service of society and therefore is deserving of special status and self-regulation are not easy to justify.[86] Commentators have described the view that all legal work is highly specialized and requires a sacrosanct relationship between consumer and supplier as an unhelpful romantic fiction. Much less legal work requires customized delivery than lawyers would like the public to believe. Legal services are in fact highly adaptable to methods of mass production and routinization that could lead to better and less costly results.[87] The OECD authored a report on precisely this issue, assessing whether the manner in which the legal profession has been regulated in many developed countries is still appropriate, given changes in the legal profession as well as the globalized nature of legal practice.[88]

The structure of this book is as follows. Following on from this introduction, Chapter 2 will take a closer look at the chief international legal instruments that affect trade in legal services, notably the WTO's GATS. Chapters 3–6 will build upon the GATS' approach to services liberalization, each focusing on a separate mode of services delivery: cross-border, consumption abroad, commercial presence, and temporary movement of natural persons. In examining cross-border legal services, Chapter 3 will

[85] J. Goldsmith, "The Core Values of the Legal Profession for Lawyers: Today and Tomorrow", 28 *Northwestern Journal of International Law and Business* 441 (2008).
[86] Semple, *Legal Services Regulation* Chapter 7.
[87] Susskind, *Tomorrow's Lawyers* at 26.
[88] Competitive Restrictions in Legal Professions, Policy Round Table, OECD, 2009.

consider the application of technology to create new varieties of legal services. The exploration in Chapter 4 of consumption abroad will look at the creation of centres of legal excellence to attract foreign clients and the related issue of restrictions placed by states on the export of legal services. The discussion of commercial presence in Chapter 5 will concentrate on the regulatory approach of states toward the law firm and its status as a kind of foreign direct investment. Chapter 6 will investigate obstacles facing the individual practitioner serving foreign clients on a fly-in-fly-out basis. Chapter 7 will examine the important principles of domestic regulation and mutual recognition as tools of integrating the regulatory outlook of disparate jurisdictions. Conclusions and recommendations will be presented in Chapter 8.

With these debates in mind, the focus of this book is public international law, that is, the law governing interactions between states rather than between private parties. Clearly, there are international rules governing the transaction for legal services itself (i.e., the purchase and sale of professional advice for money). These include laws such as those related to breach of contract by the legal professional and laws that would facilitate a claim of professional negligence, for example. These laws are within the sphere of private law and are therefore outside the scope of this book. Moreover, as commentators have noted, the elimination of trade barriers to legal services is valueless if domestic regulations impose barriers that prevent competition between domestic and foreign lawyers. This is why effective liberalization must include the removal of anticompetitive measures between domestic as well as foreign providers.[89] While these matters are important, this book will not consider reforms to the regulation of the legal profession at a comprehensive level, focusing instead on trade in legal services as controlled by public international law.

The book's concluding recommendations include both increased liberalization commitments under multilateral and bilateral regimes and the consideration of a more informal role for international organizations that embraces cooperation among stakeholders such as national regulators and professional bodies. There will also be emphasis on diplomatic or soft law solutions, such as bilateral negotiations for mutual recognition and market access through professional associations.

[89] Muller, *Liberalization of Trade in Legal Services* at 16.

2

The International Legal Framework Governing Trade in Legal Services

2.1 Introduction

Lawyers and legal practitioners are regulated primarily by laws that are created and enforced at the domestic level. There is no such thing as an international qualification in law; nor is there an international bar. This is because law, perhaps uniquely among professional disciplines, is jurisdiction specific. In theory, every sovereign state (including subregional ones such as the Australian states and Chinese provinces) has a distinct legal regime governing criminal law, commercial law, family law, and so on. Laws do not exist in nature; they are created by legislatures and shaped by judges. In practice, there is broad overlap among the various legal systems, with a high degree of uniformity in the substantive content of the law. There are principles of fundamental justice, and there are universal ethical and moral obligations associated with holding the designation lawyer, barrister, advocate or attorney.

Given the decentralized or nation-state nature of most laws' origins, it would be tempting to conclude that international law, meaning binding laws that govern the relations between states, has limited relevance to regulating the practice of law, even when the practice crosses borders in one or more ways. This is far from true. Indeed, international law plays an increasing role in dictating the way in which legal services are governed. With trends such as globalization and advances in communication technology, as discussed in Chapter 1, the role of international law will certainly expand in the coming years. Domestic laws appear to be an increasingly inadequate system through which legal services are administered and coordinated.

This chapter will introduce the framework of international law by which international legal services are regulated. Because the practice of law is a service, the relevant international legal regimes are those governing services, or, more specifically, trade in services. Services, comprising such industries as finance, transportation, and professional services such as those of lawyers and accountants, represent a vital sector of the world's economy and one that grows every year. The World Bank reports that as of 2016, services comprised close to 70 per cent of the world's GDP.[1] Yet trade in services makes up only 13 per cent of the world's GDP.[2] This disjunction suggests that, in contrast to goods, which are highly mobile across the world, services tend to be locally supplied and consumed. This makes sense when one thinks of certain types of services such as dentistry, which must be supplied at the point where they are consumed. It makes less sense for a service that may be offered over the Internet, as is certainly feasible with legal advice. But a dentist may travel overseas to attend to patients who live in other countries, or patients may wish to travel from their own country to see a specialist dentist who works elsewhere, both of which are scenarios that are readily transferable to legal advice. Thus international trade in services becomes more practical and commonplace. Why, then, are such activities evidently not commonplace, as shown by the minor role they play in the world's economic output? Clearly, logistical barriers are one answer; it is not always easy to travel abroad to see a dentist or a lawyer. But a significant element of the disparity between the fiscal importance of services and their role in trade is the consequence of regulatory barriers erected by governments, typically in the form of domestic laws.

The capability of foreign entities to access services markets is dictated by institutional barriers that are found in domestic legislation. This is precisely why the liberalization of any service requires extensive political and diplomatic engagement between or among states over a prolonged period. The more countries become involved, the more difficult this process becomes. In an era in which there is significant antiglobalization animus, this is even more the case.

International economic law, which aims at liberalizing the laws affecting trade and investment for the purposes of economic advancement, seeks to address the institutional barriers through the establishment of disciplines that minimize the trade impact of domestic laws while ensuring that this does not interfere with legitimate policy goals. In the context of services, perhaps the most important of these is consumer welfare. The chief instrument for the liberalization of trade in services is treaties, which are formal agreements between sovereign states that contain binding commitments to engage (or refrain from engaging) in certain courses of action. This chapter will consider some of the major treaties governing trade in services. It

[1] https://data.worldbank.org/indicator/NV.SRV.TETC.ZS (accessed March 2018).
[2] https://data.worldbank.org/indicator/BG.GSR.NFSV.GD.ZS (accessed March 2018).

will begin by examining multilateral treaties, the most important of which is the General Agreement on Trade in Services (GATS) of the World Trade Organization (WTO), followed by the new – but currently moribund – Trade in Services Agreement (TiSA). It will then turn to regional and bilateral treaties. Only a sample of treaties will be considered, given that there are many hundreds of such instruments governing trade as well as investment in services. Finally, this chapter will set forth some of the key non-treaty-based materials that affect the international trade in legal services, which, although not binding in the sense of treaties, nevertheless carry significant weight as sources of international rule making. This discussion will introduce the notion of access to justice as a norm under international law, an argument to which we will return throughout this book.

This chapter is intended to present the above materials as background to the issues that will be explored further throughout this book, not as an in-depth analysis of the interaction between the rules contained in these instruments and the needs of international lawyers and their clients. Many of these instruments, particularly the GATS, will be referred to again when these issues are addressed in greater depth in later chapters. This chapter is premised on the understanding that it is essential to get a sense of the overall framework by which services generally are regulated under international law to bring out the key tensions that exist between liberalization, and with it the free flow of legal services as an aid to commercial progress and indeed the rule of law itself, and the need to safeguard the interests of consumers. Rather than developing these arguments, this chapter will lay the foundation in terms of the key legal principles that underpin the international regulatory regime covering trade in legal services, such as non-discrimination, market access, and mutual recognition. These concepts, which will be introduced in discussing the foundational global agreement GATS, reappear throughout the regional and bilateral instruments. They represent the central conceptual framework by which international legal services are governed.

It must be emphasized from the outset that while the international instruments discussed in this chapter tend variously to refer to measures or laws and regulations enacted by national governments, international law also directly affect laws enacted at the subnational level, such as those made by states, provinces, and even local governments. This is vitally important for the regulation of international trade in legal services because so many of the rules that govern the practice of law are enacted at these levels. It would be invidious and certainly ineffectual if treaty signatories or

WTO members were able to evade their international obligations on the liberalization of services if they were to claim that only national or federal level laws that govern services were subject to discipline by these regimes. Indeed, as was mentioned in Chapter 1, it is often precisely because a wide range of subnational governments regulate the practice of law that commitments to liberalize this sector of economic activity have been so problematic at the international level.

2.2 Multilateral Instruments

This chapter begins by familiarizing the chief instruments with the chief multilateral instruments that govern the delivery of legal services. The term "multilateral" connotes participation by all (or near all) of the states in the world, and multilateralism is often viewed as the most advanced and indeed the most effective system of governance in economic relations because it precludes the need for hundreds or thousands of bilateral arrangements that can cause confusion due to complexity, duplication, and in some cases contradiction among legal regimes. Of course, there are no fully multilateral institutions in the world; even the most global organizations fall short of complete membership of the world's 190-plus sovereign states.

In international economic relations, the WTO is the most important and most widespread institution for the regulation of all services, chiefly through its services agreement, the GATS. As of 2018, the WTO comprised 164 member states, two thirds of which are developing countries; for these countries, trade in services, including legal services, constitutes a minor form of economic activity. The WTO was established in 1995, but its chief regulatory instrument setting out rules for trade, the General Agreement on Tariffs and Trade (GATT), dates back to the 1940s. The GATT contains no disciplines on services whatsoever, in no small part because cross-border supply of services did not achieve economic significance until the latter part of the twentieth century. The WTO founders turned their attention to services at the institution's inception in 1995 through the GATS; however, other spheres of WTO regulation have neglected to engage with services, notably the Agreement on Subsidies and Countervailing Measures (ASCM), which to this day addresses governmental assistance in the provision of goods only. With many of the chief barriers to trade in goods, notably tariffs, now resoundingly defeated by the WTO (and other liberalization initiatives), the neglect of services liberalization, including legal services, remains a distinct weakness of the WTO regime, failings that will be examined in more detail in Chapters 3 and 4. Yet newly acceding members of the WTO (after its creation in 1995) demonstrated a willingness to make commitments on services on a par with the world's most advanced economies, typically on a phase-in basis.[3]

Progress in this sphere through the WTO appears to be unlikely, given the shift in trade negotiations away from the multilateral arena towards the regional or megaregional level, where identifying common ground and achieving consensus seem to be more feasible in the modern era of trade policy.

2.2.1 The General Agreement on Trade in Services

The GATS is the WTO's agreement covering trade in services and the only substantial instrument administered by the WTO that addresses services. The GATS is also the world's chief instrument for regulating international services trade, as there is currently no other discipline governing services at the multilateral level. As such, the GATS represents the major legal framework for legal services at the international level. The way in which its provisions affect international trade in legal services in various forms will be considered more closely throughout this book. For now, it is essential to provide an overview of how the GATS works and to consider the ways in which it could touch upon the practice of law across national borders. In many respects, the GATS serves as the blueprint for international services disciplines at the regional and bilateral levels.

The GATS does not define "services" but instead creates for categories of "trade in services", which it defines as the supply of a service:

(a) from the territory of one Member into the territory of any other Member;
(b) in the territory of one Member to the service consumer of any other Member;
(c) by a service supplier of one Member, through commercial presence in the territory of any other Member;
(d) by a service supplier of one Member, through presence of natural persons of a Member in the territory of any other Member.

These four modes of supply of services are an ingenious creation of the GATS and have been duplicated in a number of other international instruments governing services. These modes, which may be categorized as

[3] Adlung, "Trade in Services in the WTO" at 380.

(1) cross-border supply, (2) consumption abroad, (3) commercial presence, and (4) movement of natural persons, will be examined in turn throughout this book as they apply to legal services. It is important to note that the GATS specifies that "services" does not include "services supplied in the exercise of governmental authority", a limitation that arguably precludes its application to certain varieties of international legal services, as will be explored later when we broach the important subject of legal aid and its precarious nature in many jurisdictions.

As with all of the WTO-covered agreements, adherence to the GATS is compulsory for all WTO members. However, many of the commitments that are contained within the GATS remain optional. This is because GATS is structured in terms of general and specific commitments. General commitments are compulsory, as, for example, the provisions of the GATT; specific commitments are undertaken by choice. In that sense, the GATS very much embodies the principle of flexibility. This was essential at the time of the instrument's (and the WTO's) inception. If members had been forced to make extensive commitments regarding the liberalization of their services sectors, they would not have accepted the GATS, and there would have been no services commitments at all. This would have frustrated the considerable economic gains associated with the opening of foreign markets envisaged by the predominantly developed countries that had fought for the inclusion of services as part of the WTO regime. The GATS was established as a consequence of the rapid growth in services that took place in the latter part of the twentieth century. The exponential expansion of services (aided by the Internet and telecommunications), which is expected to continue in the twenty-first century, suggests that the importance of the GATS will increase commensurately.

The general commitments of the GATS essentially consist of the Most Favoured Nation (MFN) guarantee and the promise of transparency. MFN is a familiar concept to international trade lawyers that has existed for a century or more. It is found in the GATT and many other international instruments, including those at the regional and bilateral levels. MFN obliges member states of the WTO to treat foreign services and services suppliers no less favourably than they would treat the equivalent service or service supplier from any other member state. In other words, members of the WTO must not discriminate against their trading partners on the basis of the nationality of origin of the service or the supplier that provides it. As a nondiscrimination guarantee, MFN requires a comparison between two services and services suppliers, assessing whether there is equality of opportunity among trading partners. WTO tribunals interpreting these provisions have drawn upon the jurisprudence of the GATT for guidance.[4] As a general obligation, MFN applies to all services, whether or not the member state wishes to make this commitment; however, there are some temporary exemptions that are contemplated under the agreement. The chief of these is that of preferential trading arrangements. WTO members are permitted to provide better treatment for services or services suppliers that originate from countries with which preferential trade agreements have been established. These exemptions are temporary and cannot be enlarged. There are five countries that have listed MFN exemptions for legal services under Article II:2: Brunei Darussalam, Bulgaria, the Dominican Republic, Lithuania, and Singapore, with the exemption generally covering the requirement to assess legal practitioners on a case-by-case basis.

Under the GATS, National Treatment is a specific (optional) commitment. Member states do not have to promise to treat services or services suppliers from other members at least as well as they treat domestic equivalents, but if they do so, then this commitment is binding and enforceable under the WTO Dispute Settlement System, like any other obligation. GATS nondiscrimination extends to both the service and the service supplier, reflecting the inseparability of the two. This is particularly apposite in the context of legal services, for which consumer interests are protected not by regulations regarding the minimum standard of the service, but with license requirements for the supplier. For National Treatment, WTO members are required to enter the sector and record the level of liberalization to which they are prepared to adhere. The fact that some countries, such as Brazil, have not made any commitments for legal services does not mean that foreign lawyers cannot practice there; it simply means that such countries are not bound under WTO law to maintain this level of access should they choose to rescind it or enlarge it. As with MFN, the National Treatment guarantee ensures that service suppliers from other countries have equal competitive opportunities within the domestic market of the relevant member state. They are able to compete on an equal footing on the basis of the quality and price of the service they are providing rather than as a consequence of any advantages that accrue from the way in which they

[4] See, e.g., EC Bananas III – Appellate Body Report, WT/DS27/AB/R (adopted 26 September 1997) at [233], which establishes that the prohibition on discrimination covers both de jure and de facto discrimination, the latter of which would be particularly easy to devise in the context of services.

are regulated. A comparison test is called for here as well, which has been assessed by the WTO panels and Appellate Body.[5]

WTO members list their National Treatment commitments (by sector and mode of supply) in their schedule of specific commitments. Services schedules consist of two parts: horizontal commitments, which apply to all sectors included in the schedule, and sectoral commitments, which are commitments made regarding specific services sectors or subsectors. Legal services are included under "business services". Services schedules comprise four columns. The first column identifies the services sector or subsector that is the subject of the commitment, the second and third columns indicate conditions or limitations on Market Access and National Treatment, respectively, and the fourth column contains additional undertakings.

This positive list or *à la carte* format of specific commitments is also adopted for Market Access, an obligation that, if undertaken, requires members not to place numeric or quantifiable limits on the total number of service suppliers within that sector. The relevant part reads as follows:

> [A] Member shall not maintain or adopt ...:
> (a) limitations on the number of service suppliers whether in the form of numerical quotas, monopolies, exclusive service suppliers or the requirements of an economic needs test;
> (b) limitations on the total value of service transactions or assets in the form of numerical quotas or the requirement of an economic needs test;
> (c) limitations on the total number of service operations or on the total quantity of service output expressed in terms of designated numerical units in the form of quotas or the requirement of an economic needs test;
> (d) limitations on the total number of natural persons that may be employed in a particular service sector or that a service supplier may employ and who are necessary for, and directly related to, the supply of a specific service in the form of numerical quotas or the requirement of an economic needs test;
> (e) measures which restrict or require specific types of legal entity or joint venture through which a service supplier may supply a service; and

[5] See, for example, China – Publications and Audiovisual Products, WT/DS363/AB/R (adopted 19 January 2010).

(f) limitations on the participation of foreign capital in terms of maximum percentage limit on foreign shareholding or the total value of individual or aggregate foreign investment.[6]

These restrictions prevent WTO members that have made such commitments from controlling the size and composition of legal services providers and thus play a key role in structuring the nature of the legal services market within their territories. The types of restrictions on legal services that would fall within the scope of the market access rules are nationality requirements, quotas on foreign provision/economic needs tests, restrictions on legal form, restrictions on partnership with locally licensed professionals, restrictions on the hiring of local professionals, and restrictions on the movement of employees. The extent to which these rules affect the foreign element of the provision of legal services will be explored throughout this book, notably in Chapter 5, which will examine restrictions on the setting up of law firms in other countries. These criteria do not relate to either the quality of the service supplied or the ability of the supplier to supply the service. For example, the requirement for lawyers to have specific professional qualifications may interfere with trade in services, but it is not a market access barrier within the meaning of Article XVI:2 of the GATS. It is worth noting that Article XVI does not take into account policy objectives, a fact that some commentators have criticized.[7]

Generally speaking, the specific commitments made by WTO members for legal services under the GATS (both National Treatment and Market Access) have been weak. Mode 4 commitments have been the least forthcoming, owing to the sensitivities associated with the presence of foreign individuals in many countries. Mode 2 (consumption abroad) has been subjected to the least restrictions, most likely because governments are not worried about their citizens consuming services abroad or realize that it is impractical to enforce such restrictions.[8] Modes 1 and 2 are widely regarded by WTO members as unpoliceable and therefore not worth restricting. Given the many restrictions that WTO members have been eager to maintain on various modes of service delivery, the GATS may be seen as somewhat of a disappointment, particularly in relation to autonomous liberalization commitments undertaken by WTO members

[6] Article XVI.

[7] F. Ortino, "Treaty Interpretation and the WTO Appellate Body Report in US-Gambling: A Critique", 9:1 *Journal of International Economic Law* 117 (2006).

[8] P. van den Bossche and W. Zdouc, *The Law and Policy of the World Trade Organization* (Cambridge University Press, 2012) at 530.

in bilateral or regional instruments.[9] Because the key legal obligations within the GATS are optional, there are very few measures that a government could implement that could not be maintained under the GATS. It is worth noting that the US had originally requested that the GATS contain an Annex on Legal Services that would be binding on all members and would contain some minimum level of access for their legal markets, but ultimately, this was rejected in favour of treating legal services like any other kind of service requiring specific scheduling.[10]

The GATS contains vital provisions regarding domestic regulation that control the way in which WTO members are able to enact regulations governing particular services sectors, such as professional requirements and qualifications for lawyers. In sectors where member states have made specific commitments, the GATS obliges them to "ensure that all measures of general application affecting trade in services are administered in a reasonable, objective and impartial manner".[11] As Chapter 7 will explore, this requirement has, or should have, a profound impact on the way in which foreign lawyers are licensed. Article VI:4 goes on to state that qualification requirements relating to the delivery of services must not "constitute unnecessary barriers to trade in services". This may be achieved by ensuring in particular that these requirements are:

(a) based on objective and transparent criteria, such as competence and the ability to supply the service;
(b) not more burdensome than necessary to ensure the quality of the service.

These rules, effectively comprising a necessity test, represent the fundamental principles under which disciplines governing international trade in legal services must be designed and implemented. To a degree, these rules reiterate the principle of transparency that is found in GATS Article III and elsewhere in WTO agreements and is arguably a principle of customary international law.[12] While ambiguous to an extent (the concepts of reasonableness and necessity), these provisions significantly curtail a country's capacity to enact barriers to the delivery of legal services across international borders for illegitimate (protectionist) or even legitimate (e.g., quality control) purposes. These issues will be explored

[9] Adlung, "Trade in Services in the WTO" at 370.
[10] Chapman and Tauber, "Liberalizing International Trade in Legal Services" at 963.
[11] Article VI:1.
[12] See, e.g., A. Bianchi and A. Peters eds. *Transparency in International Law* (Cambridge University Press, 2013).

in more detail throughout the book. At this time, it should be observed that Article VI:6 states: "In sectors where specific commitments regarding professional services are undertaken, each Member shall provide for adequate procedures to verify the competence of professionals of any other Member." This provision softens the obligations noted above, permitting governments to enact regulations that safeguard consumers or, in the case of legal services, clients who may be adversely affected when the level of quality of a foreign supplier is inadequate.

Because qualifications play a crucial role in the professional opportunity of lawyers and other legal practitioners, the ability of lawyers to provide services outside the country in which they obtained their qualifications cannot be underestimated. In this regard, the GATS emphasizes: "[A] Member may recognize the education or experience obtained, requirements met, or licenses or certifications granted in a particular country. Such recognition, which may be achieved through harmonization or otherwise, may be based upon an agreement or arrangement with the country concerned or may be accorded autonomously."[13] The word "may" conveys an idea of optionality, but there is a strong sense that this is the course of conduct that the WTO wishes members to take. Harmonization of legal services (to the extent to which commitments have been made in this sector) is very much an aim of the GATS. This section goes on to specify that such arrangements shall be organized in a manner that encourages the participation of other countries.[14] In other words, the nexus of harmonization agreements should be cast as wide as possible. Countries should not be excluded from negotiating mutual recognition whenever possible. The many problems associated with the recognition of foreign legal education qualifications will be analysed later in this book.

Underlining the point about members' best efforts to recognize each other's qualifications, Article VII goes on to state:

> A Member shall not accord recognition in a manner which would constitute a means of discrimination between countries in the application of its standards or criteria for the authorization, licensing or certification of services suppliers, or a disguised restriction on trade in services.

This provision captures the WTO's ethos of inclusion and the establishment of a global community wherein participation in trade is as near universal as possible. This is clearly a noble goal, but it is one that is fraught with problems when we consider the broad disparities in quality of

[13] Article VII:1.

[14] Article VII:2.

training available in different countries. The final section in the GATS on mutual recognition is as follows:

> recognition should be based on multilaterally agreed criteria. In appropriate cases, Members shall work in cooperation with relevant intergovernmental and non-governmental organizations towards the establishment and adoption of common international standards and criteria for recognition and common international standards for the practice of relevant services trades and professions.

This statement is key because it aspires to global standards for professional services, a reality that seems problematic in the context of legal services because, as was suggested earlier, legal expertise is inherently jurisdiction specific. In Chapter 7, it will be argued that international standards for many varieties of legal services are achievable in part because of common themes of ethical behaviour. This kind of multilateral approach in standard setting is well within reach of the international community, possibly by revisiting the idea of an Annex on Legal Services under the GATS.

The concept of "disguised restriction on trade" alluded to in the Recognition section of the GATS is found in the General Exceptions of the GATS and in a very real sense captures the fundamental tension at the heart of services liberalization and a members state's legitimate interest in ensuring beneficial regulation of services – a balancing act between maximizing market access, and with it commercial opportunities, and ensuring that consumers are not disadvantaged by service providers that are unfit to serve them. GATS General Exceptions permit member states to enact regulations that would otherwise violate their commitments under the agreement, including their specific commitments in certain services sectors, because of a series of important policy goals. These are specified in Article XIV of the agreement in the following manner (in relevant part):

> Subject to the requirement that such measures are not applied in a manner which would constitute a means of arbitrary or unjustifiable discrimination between countries where like conditions prevail, or a disguised restriction on trade in services, nothing in this Agreement shall be construed to prevent the adoption or enforcement by any Member of measures:
>
> (a) necessary to protect public morals or to maintain public order;
> (b) necessary to protect human, animal or plant life or health;
> (c) necessary to secure compliance with laws or regulations which are not inconsistent with the provisions of this Agreement including those relating to:
>   (i) the prevention of deceptive and fraudulent practices or to deal with the effects of a default on services contracts;

(ii) the protection of the privacy of individuals in relation to the processing and dissemination of personal data and the protection of confidentiality of individual records and accounts;

(iii) safety;

This provision discloses the WTO's recognition of the importance of non-trade or noneconomic values in that it is willing to permit laws that serve these designated goals to supersede those that promote trade, provided that these laws are genuine and are applied even-handedly. While there is limited case law under GATS General Exceptions outlining the manner in which these exceptions should be interpreted in practice[15] (in contrast to the equivalent section of the GATT), this section is expected to grow in significance in the coming years as trade in services grows, particularly for developing countries that may struggle with the competition engendered by open markets. For the international trade in legal services, the most relevant of these exceptions is Article XIV (c), more specifically fraud and privacy. The sensitivity of clients' private and financial information renders this feature of legal services highly problematic. In the modern digital era, the protection of privacy and data has grown enormously as an issue since the creation of the GATS. Most national governments have enacted extensive laws in this regard and it unquestionable that these will face scrutiny under the GATS in the coming years. Given the breadth of the concepts of public morals and public order, there may be room for measures justified under this heading to act as barriers to trade in legal services.

The GATS requires member states to publish relevant information affecting market access in their scheduled service sectors. Such rules apply only to governmental authorities and so may have a limited impact on legal services because of the volume of important information that is generated by private industry groups or professional bodies. Some regional or bilateral agreements have expanded the individuals to whom transparency rules apply to service suppliers and service suppliers associations.[16]

Finally, as with many of the WTO agreements, there are institutional features of the GATS that facilitate the administration of the agreement by the WTO for the interests of its members. The Council for Trade in

[15] See, e.g., US-Gambling, Appellate Body Report, WT/DS285/AB/R (adopted 20 April 2005) and China – Electronic Payments, Panel Report, WT/DS413/R (adopted 31 August 2012).

[16] See, e.g., Korea – Australia FTA. See further G. Muller, "Trade Agreements and Legal Services: An Anatomy of the GATS and Preferential Trade Arrangements", 9 *Global Trade and Customs Journal* 223 at 241 (2014).

Services is a body within the WTO that takes note of any mutual recognition arrangements among members and acts as an aid to the negotiation of future agreements. In that sense it fulfils the objective of transparency under the GATS that may be viewed as a cornerstone of the WTO regime.

2.2.2 *Other WTO Instruments*

In addition to the ground-breaking GATS, mention must be made of ongoing discussions about the establishment of a Services Facilitation Agreement under the WTO. In 2016, India's delegation to the WTO proposed an "Agreement on Trade Facilitation in Services" mirroring that of the highly successful Trade Facilitation Agreement launched in 2014 aimed at reducing practical barriers to goods crossing borders, such as methods of streamlining inspection processes and standardizing customs valuation procedures. This proposal expressly referenced Mode 3 services delivery (commercial presence) under the GATS and as such would help to increase foreign direct investment in services.[17] The potential for a Services Facilitation Agreement encompassing legal services to augment the provision of legal services by foreign providers in developing countries will be considered further later in this book.

As a final comment on the role of the WTO, the WTO's Trade Policy Review Mechanism (TPRM) provides extensive data on the nature of each member's services commitments, including how these are accommodated (or not) under domestic legislation. This is an invaluable source of information for trade negotiators and industry representatives such as law associations. This resource underscores the WTO's emphasis on transparency as well as its role as a disseminator of information about trade. The importance of transparency in the effective regulation of the international trade in legal services cannot be understated and will be revisited throughout this book. A similar and equally useful objective is achieved by the United Nations Conference on Trade and Development (UNCTAD), an organ of the United Nations dealing with trade, investment, and developing countries. Among other activities, UNCTAD issues the comprehensive annual World Investment Report, which outlines the trends in foreign direct investment as well as the regulatory framework governing it, including most notably International Investment Agreements, although, of course, this does not carry the force of law.

[17] WTO Working Party on Domestic Regulation, "Concept Note for an Initiative on Trade Facilitation in Services", Doc. S/WPDR/W/55, 27 September 2016.

2.3 Plurilateral: The Trade in Services Agreement

Plurilateralism is largely unexplored as a means of governance in international law. Plurilateral agreements, second cousins to multilateral treaties, are multiparty and optional. However, they aim to achieve multilateralism in that they are, in theory, open to any states that wish to be bound by their terms. The best-known example in international economic law is the Government Procurement Agreement, established through the WTO. Commentators have suggested that plurilateralism is an underappreciated approach to global economic governance that can leverage WTO membership without placing excessive burdens on state parties.[18]

In the context of services, the forthcoming but currently stalled Trade in Services Agreement (TiSA), which is not itself a WTO agreement, is poised to become significant in the near future. It has not attracted much attention, at least from the academic community, in comparison to some of the megaregionals, which will be discussed further below. The TiSA is a trade in services agreement negotiated by twenty-three member states of the WTO, including some of the world's largest economies, such as the US, the EU, Japan, Canada, and Australia. Because its focus is services, it is naturally of interest to the most developed countries, where services plays a more significant role in the economy than they do, at least for now, in the developing world. Efforts in this area reflect the understanding, noted above, that trade in services is weak relative to trade in goods and that common ground with respect to the elimination of barriers to this type of economic activity should be pursued where possible. Together, the twenty-three participating countries account for 70 per cent of global trade services.

The TiSA's structure is based on that of the GATS. It contains definitions following the four modes of supply as well as transparency obligations and GATS general exceptions. Unlike the GATS, the commitments on National Treatment across various modes of supply would be included as general obligations, for which exemptions would be specified by parties as required. This negative list approach may be more conducive to deeper liberalization across a wider range of services sectors. Market Access would remain, as in the GATS, as a specific commitment to be negotiated in a positive list format. The parties agreed that commitments should in principle reflect the parties' actual practice and that future elimination of discriminatory measures should be automatically locked unless an

[18] B. Hoekman and P. Mavroidis, "WTO 'A La Carte' or 'Menu Du Jour'? Assessing the Case for More Plurilateral Agreements", 26:2 *European Journal of International Law* 319 (2015).

exemption is listed.[19] The specific negotiating context of the TiSA, with the smaller group of economically powerful states, may be expected to result in greater commitments than were possible through the larger WTO format, as is evident in the lack of progress in the Doha Round of trade negotiations. Negotiations under the TiSA, which began in March 2013, took place in Geneva and have been chaired alternately by the US, the EU, and Australia. There is no set deadline for ending the negotiations, and it is unclear at the time of writing when they will resume.

Legal services have been included in the discussions under "professional services", and for this reason, the TiSA represents a key opportunity to liberalize trade in legal services among the world's most economically advanced countries. In light of some of the modern trends in the delivery of legal services outlined in Chapter 1, attention must be drawn to the fact that the TiSA will also contain state-of-the-art trade rules that will tackle twenty-first century challenges to the international delivery of services, including restrictions on cross-border data flows and server localization requirements that can undermine the supply of services over the Internet.[20] The importance of these elements will be explored further in Chapter 3.

As a plurilateral agreement, the TiSA is open to all WTO members that wish to join in the future. One possible scenario is that if enough WTO members sign on to the agreement, the TiSA will eventually be subsumed into the WTO as a full multilateral agreement.[21] An advantage of this strategy would be that the WTO's highly regarded dispute settlement system could be used to enforce the TiSA's obligations, which it cannot currently do, as the WTO's dispute settlement system remains exclusive to WTO members.[22] Without such institutional housing at the WTO, the TiSA would be limited to enforcement through some form of international arbitration, which may not be met with the same high levels of compliance as are seen in WTO disputes.

As it stands, the TiSA does not contain an MFN obligation. This is because it was felt that countries that did not participate in its negotiation should not benefit from the agreement without being bound by its

[19] European Union, Trade in Services Agreement at 2. See http://trade.ec.europa.eu/doclib/docs/2013/june/tradoc_151374.pdf (accessed March 2018).

[20] United States Trade Representative, Statement on TiSA Ministers Meeting, January 2016. See https://ustr.gov/about-us/policy-offices/press-office/press-releases/2016/january/statement-tisa-ministers-meeting (accessed March 2018).

[21] S. Peng, "Is the Trade in Services Agreement (TiSA) a Stepping Stone for the Next Version of GATS?", 43:2 *Hong Kong Law Journal* 611 (2013).

[22] WTO Dispute Settlement Understanding Art. 23.1.

rules. The automatic multilateralization of the agreement through MFN will likely take place when a critical mass of WTO members has joined the agreement. Until then, the TiSA will fulfil the conditions of a regional agreement specified in Article V of the GATS, discussed earlier in the chapter. Finally, the TiSA will contain an accession clause that will specify how future parties will join and provides a mechanism through which multilateralism can be achieved formally.[23]

2.4 Regional Trade Agreements

Regional rather than global trade agreements have grown in popularity in recent years. While the initial focus of such instruments may have been on the lowering of tariffs and other barriers to goods, many of these treaties now include chapters on services. As of 2017, there were 267 regional trade agreements (RTAs) that the WTO had been notified of and that were currently in force. While the proliferation of RTAs can be viewed as evidence of the fragmentation of the multilateral trading system, in fact these instruments evince a common approach, particularly in relation to disciplines on services as well as dispute settlement.[24] RTAs (like bilateral free trade agreements) that contain services disciplines are thought to be less distortive than their counterparts in goods trade (the so-called trade diversion associated with preferential partners), such arrangements may be damaging to liberalization when they impose barriers that are not present in the GATS (so-called GATS-minus agreements) in the form of carve-outs for certain sectors or "negative preferences", although thankfully few of these exist for legal services. Many concessions that have been achieved through RTAs may ultimately be extended to the global community on an MFN basis.

It should be noted that in its Economic Integration section, GATS Article V permits WTO members to grant preferential treatment for the regulation of services. These arrangements are acceptable if they have substantial sectoral coverage and provide for the absence or elimination of substantially all discrimination between or among the parties.[25] In other words, they cannot be sector specific (e.g., for legal services only) but must attempt to address economic integration generally. Moreover, such arrangements

[23] European Union, Trade in Services Agreement at 3.

[24] See comments of WTO Director General Roberto Azevedo, Book Launch: "Regional Trade Agreements and the Multilateral Trading System" (29 September 2016).

[25] Article V:1.

must not raise the overall level of barriers to trade in services within the covered sectors compared to what they were before.[26] Compliance with these conditions is monitored by the WTO's Council for Trade in Services. The extent to which the various regional and bilateral agreements covering services are actually compliant with GATS Article V is uncertain, particularly given the large number of carve-outs from such agreements for sensitive sectors such as telecommunications and financial services.

The EU represents the world's most highly integrated regional grouping of independent states, encompassing a wide range of economic and social matters across twenty-eight member states, including the UK, which at the time of writing is still a member but is due to leave formally by the end of April 2019. Trade in services is a key component of the EU's single market, although greater barriers remain in the cross-border supply of services than of goods. The core principles governing the single market for services consist of the freedom to establish a commercial presence in another EU country[27] and the freedom to supply or receive services in an EU country other than the one in which the supplier or consumer is established.[28] In 2006, the Services Directive, which covers legal services, was adopted into EU law for the purpose of facilitating trade in services across member states through the elimination or minimization of unnecessary or duplicative regulatory barriers, including those related to the establishment of offices.[29] Additionally, there are a number of EU Directives that are specific to the legal profession, including the Council Directive to Facilitate the Effective Exercise by Lawyers of Freedom to Provide Services,[30] the Directive of the European Parliament and of the Council to Facilitate Practice of the Professional Lawyer on Permanent Basis in a Member State,[31] and the Directive of the European Parliament and of the Council on the Recognition of Professional Qualifications.[32] These instruments, which generally facilitate cross-border trade in legal services within Europe, will not be explored further here because they are, strictly speaking, domestic rather than international instruments. The Directive on the Recognition of Professional Qualifications will be addressed in Chapters 3

[26] Article V:4.
[27] Article 49 TFEU.
[28] Article 56 TFEU.
[29] Directive 2006/123/EC.
[30] 77/249/EEC (22 March 1977).
[31] 98/5/EC (16 February 1998).
[32] 2005/36/EC (7 September 2005).

and 5 as an enlargement of GATS provisions that may be viewed as a suitable model for mutual recognition disciplines at the international level.

The Association of South East Asian Nations (ASEAN) Framework Agreement on Services (AFAS) aims to substantially eliminate restrictions on trade in services in the ASEAN region, comprising the fast-growing member states Brunei Darussalam, the Republic of Indonesia, Malaysia, the Republic of the Philippines, the Republic of Singapore, the Kingdom of Thailand, and the Socialist Republic of Vietnam. In its preamble, AFAS expressly references exceeding the liberalization that has been achieved under the GATS, a clear indication of the aspiration for greater economic integration in services (as in other sectors) at the regional rather than the multilateral level. In addition to specific commitments on nondiscrimination and improving market access through negotiation among members (structured as a positive list like the GATS), AFAS specifies that ASEAN members will seek to achieve mutual recognition for professional qualifications:

> Each Member State may recognise the education or experience obtained, requirements met, or licenses or certifications granted in another Member State, for the purpose of licensing or certification of service suppliers. Such recognition may be based upon an agreement or arrangement with the Member State concerned or may be accorded autonomously.[33]

This provision is of obvious relevance to lawyers from within one member state who are seeking to practice law in another jurisdiction within the ASEAN community and, by implication, the consumers who will be making use of such services. Eliminating unnecessary barriers to requalification should promote the internationalization of legal services, increasing consumer choice, and in so doing should act as a catalyst for economic development as well as rule of law.

The North American Free Trade Agreement (NAFTA), a regional economic integration agreement between Canada, the US, and Mexico that was established in 1994, contains disciplines on cross-border trade in services as well as investment (commercial presence of service businesses). Article 1201.1 specifies the scope of the agreement's coverage of cross-border services, which includes (in relevant part):

> measures respecting:
>
> (a) the production, distribution, marketing, sale and delivery of a service;
> (b) the purchase or use of, or payment for, a service;
>
> ...
>
> (d) the presence in its territory of a service provider of another Party;

[33] Article V:1.

These provisions encompass a number of activities associated with the international trade in legal services, including provision of advice remotely, fly-in-fly-out representation, and the establishment of permanent offices, each of which will be explored in greater detail in later chapters. For now, it is useful to identify that, as with the GATS, NAFTA's services chapter extends MFN treatment[34] and National Treatment[35] to services and services suppliers from signatory states. Neither of these guarantees requires the scheduling of specific commitments as per the WTO instrument, meaning that the starting point is maximum liberalization. Because it takes effort to erect barriers rather than to liberalize, this top-down or negative list approach has been incorporated into a large majority of the bilateral agreements in the Western hemisphere encompassing services. NAFTA further specifies that there shall be no requirement for any services providers from other party states to establish or maintain a local office or to be resident in its territory as a condition for the cross-border provision of a service,[36] effectively decoupling the cross-border supply from commercial presence mode of delivery.

While the future of the twenty-five-year-old NAFTA remains in doubt as of mid-2018, pending protracted renegotiations among its signatory parties, it is worth noting that parties are required to set out their commitments to further liberalize services under Annex VI to the agreement, demonstrating the intent (at the time of drafting) for NAFTA to lay the foundations of greater liberalization between the three countries going forward. Finally, echoing the GATS, NAFTA contains sections on licensing and certification with a view to harmonization in the recognition of foreign qualifications. The relevant section reads as follows:

> 1. With a view to ensuring that any measure adopted or maintained by a Party relating to the licensing or certification of nationals of another Party does not constitute an unnecessary barrier to trade, each Party shall endeavor to ensure that any such measure:
>   (a) is based on objective and transparent criteria, such as competence and the ability to provide a service;
>   (b) is not more burdensome than necessary to ensure the quality of a service; and
>   (c) does not constitute a disguised restriction on the cross-border provision of a service.
> 2. Where a Party recognizes, unilaterally or by agreement, education, experience, licenses or certifications obtained in the territory of another Party or of a non-Party:

[34] Article 1202.
[35] Article 1201.
[36] Article 1205.

(a) nothing in Article 1203 shall be construed to require the Party to accord such recognition to education, experience, licenses or certifications obtained in the territory of another Party; and
(b) the Party shall afford another Party an adequate opportunity to demonstrate that education, experience, licenses or certifications obtained in that other Party's territory should also be recognized or to conclude an agreement or arrangement of comparable effect.[37]

While part 1 encourages mutual recognition of qualifications, part 2 indicates that this is not compulsory. Given their shared common law backgrounds, the process of requalification between Canadian and US lawyers in some key jurisdictions (New York and California) is not a difficult one, although the practice varies widely across US states, most of which decline to recognize Canadian law degrees altogether. The picture is much worse for individuals with Mexican qualifications; because Mexico is a civil jurisdiction, the qualifications there have little relevance in Canada and the US. The extent to which restrictions of this nature should be permitted will be explored in Chapters 5 and 6.

The members states of MERCOSUR, the Common Market of the South (comprising Argentina, Brazil, Paraguay, Uruguay, and Venezuela) adopted a positive list approach to liberalizing services trade within the region. MERCOSUR's Protocol of Montevideo on Trade in Services, which covers legal services, provides that annual rounds of negotiations based on the scheduling of increasing numbers of commitments in all sectors with no exclusions aims to achieve the elimination of all restrictions to trade in services among the members of the group within ten years, once the Protocol comes into force.[38] Because MERCOSUR members have a common legal heritage (based on the civil law), mutual recognition of qualifications is less problematic, reflecting the reality that regional services agreements (in contrast to goods agreements) seem to require greater levels of initial integration and commonality between constituent states to be effective.

The newly signed Comprehensive and Progressive Trans Pacific Partnership (CPTPP) is considered by many to be a blueprint or gold standard for economic integration treaties for the twenty-first century, particularly given its progressive commitments on social and environmental matters.[39] Moreover, with eleven Pacific Rim countries as signatories,

[37] Article 1210.

[38] Protocol of Montevideo on Trade in Services in the Southern Common Market (MERCOSUR) (7 December 2005).

[39] E. Luce, "US-led globalism is dying with the TPP" The Financial Times (London) 27 July 2016.

including Japan, Canada, and Australia, the CPTPP accounts for more than 15 per cent of global GDP. Should the US change its mind and decide to accede (as it had intended to do under the original TPP), the CPTPP would become the largest RTA in the world – the classic megaregional agreement that many viewed as emblematic of a new direction in international economic law.

Chapter 10 of the CPTPP governs cross-border trade in services. In terms of its scope, the chapter omits "commercial presence" from the definition of "cross border trade" and "cross border supply" of services, as it is considered foreign direct investment and therefore is governed by the investment chapter of the agreement. Like the GATS, the CPTPP excludes governmental services, potentially excluding controversial fields such as health care. A range of financial services are also excluded. There are National Treatment[40] and MFN[41] obligations that are extended generally, not via scheduled commitments. Of relevance to foreign legal services supplied in countries with multiple jurisdictions (such as the US) is the subsection within National Treatment that specifies that "with respect to a regional level of government, treatment no less favourable than the most favourable treatment accorded, in like circumstances, by that regional level of government to service suppliers of the Party of which it forms a part."[42]

The CPTPP's Market Access provisions strongly resemble those of the GATS. However, the CPTPP goes further in stating, as seen in other regional agreements, "No Party shall require a service supplier of another Party to establish or maintain a representative office or any form of enterprise, or to be resident, in its territory as a condition for the cross-border supply of a service."[43] As will be examined further in Chapter 5, this commitment would have a profound impact on the way in which legal services are provided, precluding the need for the establishment of an office within the jurisdiction by practitioners seeking clients there.

In its sections on Domestic Regulation, the text of the GATS is duplicated almost verbatim. However, the CPTPP adds that conformity with these obligations will be assessed by reference to "international standards of relevant organizations".[44] It is unclear what this could mean in the context of legal services. However, it may lend weight to some of the policy documents issued by international lawyers' associations. The CPTPP goes

[40] Article 10.3.
[41] Article 10.4.
[42] Article 10.3(2).
[43] Article 10.6.
[44] Article 10.8(3).

on to outline the requirements for signatories in terms of authorization procedures. This includes the obligations to provide clear guidelines and to respond promptly to applications by foreign service providers, echoing the well-recognized need for transparency in international law. Subsections 6 and 7 of the Article on Domestic Regulation are of particular relevance to the international trade in legal services, given this sector's reliance on certain qualifications as evidence of professional competence. They read as follows:

> 6. If licensing or qualification requirements include the completion of an examination, each Party shall ensure that:
>   (a) the examination is scheduled at reasonable intervals; and
>   (b) a reasonable period of time is provided to enable interested persons to submit an application.
> 7. Each Party shall ensure that there are procedures in place domestically to assess the competency of professionals of another Party.

These provisions would have the effect of precluding party states from creating practical difficulties in the obtaining of local qualifications by rendering the testing procedures unduly onerous not because of their inherent difficulty (in terms of challenging the candidate's ability) but by making the arranging of the test itself unfeasible. For example, and of relevance if the US joins the CPTPP, the New York Bar Exam is administered only twice a year, and foreign candidates must take it in Albany, a city that is not close to an international airport and that has limited hotel room availability during testing times.[45] Of course, regulators cannot be expected to hold examinations on a regular basis where there are not sufficient candidates to warrant this. Subsection 7 is somewhat less helpful in that the procedures that are put in place may not necessarily be straightforward or easy. The CPTPP, which also contains an Annex on Legal Services, will be considered in more detail in later chapters.

Restrictions on the delivery of services can be seen in the EU–Canada CETA, which specifies that the prohibition on nondiscrimination based on national origin (National Treatment) does not prevent a party from including requirements that service suppliers obtain a licence, registration, certification, or authorization in order to supply a service or as a membership requirement of a particular profession, such as requiring membership in a professional organization.[46] CETA also allows parties to require that service suppliers maintain a local address or maintain a

[45] Based on the personal experience of author.
[46] Article 9.3 (a).

particular type or amount of insurance[47]; both of these are relevant to legal services providers.

In light of the US withdrawal from the CPTPP, attention has shifted to the forthcoming Regional Comprehensive Economic Partnership (RCEP), which appears to represent a shift in economic geopolitical leadership from West to East. The RCEP negotiations, which have been led by China, are set to include the ASEAN countries along with Australia, New Zealand, India, Japan, and Korea. While the negotiated text of the RCEP is not yet available, it is believed to have a somewhat more modest ambition in terms of liberalization than the CPTPP, in part owing to China's more cautious approach to the opening of its own internal markets,[48] a concern that is typically more pronounced in the case of services than goods. However, the agreement is expected to include disciplines on the liberalization of services among signatory parties under all sectors and modes of supply, in compliance with the GATS, but with more inclusions.[49] Given economic growth in the Asia-Pacific region, the capacity of foreign lawyers to operate within these jurisdictions represents a key stage in the internationalization of the legal profession. Progress on the RCEP is promising and, to some, may represent the future direction of economic globalization.

While the European Convention on Human Rights (ECHR) is not, strictly speaking, a regional treaty or one that governs economic activity directly, it is important to recognize the role that it plays, at least indirectly, in the provision of legal services internationally, although in a noncommercial context. Article 6 of the ECHR, which speaks of both civil and criminal rights, guarantees the right to a fair trial. Subsection 3 of this article provides as follows:

> 3. Everyone charged with a criminal offence has the following minimum rights ... (c) to defend himself in person or through legal assistance of his own choosing or, if he has not sufficient means to pay for legal assistance, to be given it free when the interests of justice so require

The provision underscores the importance of legal representation to the upholding of basic human rights, by implication highlighting the need for adequate access to lawyers, whether domestically or internationally

[47] Articles 9.3 (b) and 9.3 (c) iii.

[48] J. Wilson, "Mega-Regional Trade Deals in the Asia-Pacific: Choosing between the TPP and RCEP?", 45:2 *Journal of Contemporary Asia* 345 (2015)

[49] Government of Australia, "Guiding Principles and Objectives for Negotiating the Regional Comprehensive Economic Partnership" (endorsed by all negotiating states). See http://dfat.gov.au/trade/agreements/rcep/Documents/guiding-principles-rcep.pdf (accessed December 2016).

sourced. Case law from the European Court of Human Rights further establishes that the right of effective access to the courts implies the right to be assisted by an *independent* lawyer, meaning one who is free from governmental influence.[50] Because independence means that the lawyer is supervised not by the state directly but rather by an autonomous professional body, it has been argued that, by extension, the freedom of a foreign lawyer to establish within a state should not be denied unless there is sufficient justification for so doing, such as quality assurance.[51] In other words, access to foreign qualified lawyers should not be impeded unless there is a strong reason to do so; otherwise, the market for genuinely independent counsel is impaired.

The entitlement to legal representation and the associated need for lawyers to be able to cross borders to deliver their services can be found in a number of other human rights instruments referencing the ability of individuals to choose the lawyer they wish. For example, Article 14 of the International Covenant on Civil and Political Rights, which has seventy-three signatories around the world, contains an entitlement similar to that of the ECHR with respect to criminal proceedings:

> In the determination of any criminal charge against him, everyone shall be entitled to the following minimum guarantees, in full equality ...
>
> (d) To be tried in his presence, and to defend himself in person or through legal assistance of his own choosing; to be informed, if he does not have legal assistance, of this right; and to have legal assistance assigned to him, in any case where the interests of justice so require, and without payment by him in any such case if he does not have sufficient means to pay for it[52]

Likewise, the American Convention on Human Rights, to which there are twenty-three parties and eleven ratifications among countries in the Western hemisphere, establishes the following:

> Every person accused of a criminal offense has the right to be presumed innocent so long as his guilt has not been proven according to law. During

[50] *Golder* v. *United Kingdom*, 4451/70, ECHR, (21 February 1975).

[51] See "CCBE Statement on the European Commission Consultation on the regulation of professions: Member States' National Action Plans and Proportionality in Regulation" (19 August 2016), in which the CCBE claimed that the refusal of the right of a lawyer's establishment must be subjected to a proportionality test. See www.ccbe.eu/NTCdocument/CCBE_statement_on_pr1_1472119481.pdf (accessed January 2018).

[52] Adopted and opened for signature, ratification and accession by General Assembly resolution 2200A (XXI) of 16 December 1966 entry into force 23 March 1976, in accordance with Article 49, Art. 14(3) (d).

the proceedings, every person is entitled, with full equality, to the following minimum guarantees

(d) the right of the accused to defend himself personally or to be assisted by legal counsel of his own choosing, and to communicate freely and privately with his counsel;
(e) the inalienable right to be assisted by counsel provided by the state, paid or not as the domestic law provides, if the accused does not defend himself personally or engage his own counsel within the time period established by law ...[53]

Again, it could be argued that for an individual to be able to obtain legal assistance of "his own choosing", there should be access to foreign-qualified or foreign-regulated lawyers. Such representation is therefore effective only if barriers to practice are not maintained by governments.

2.5 Bilateralism: Free Trade Agreements and Bilateral Investment Treaties

Bilateralism (two and only two parties) has a long history in international trade and appears to be heading towards a period of greater significance, given the stalled progress in liberalization through the WTO, although it arguably represents the least advanced form of international regulation and presents problems of complexity and confusion through overlapping commitments.[54]

2.5.1 Bilateral Free Trade Agreements

With broader objectives than simply the removal of tariffs on manufactured goods, some modern bilateral FTAs embrace economic integration at many levels and include chapters on trade in services, which are typically modelled on the GATS, in some cases containing greater commitments, in others less. Since the ratification of the Mongolia-Japan Economic Partnership Agreement in June 2016, all WTO members are now party to at least one bilateral (or regional) trade agreement. As was noted above, Article V of the GATS permits these arrangements, provided that there is substantial sectoral coverage and that they reduce trade barriers between signatories. It is important to recognize that the requirement

[53] Pact of San Jose, Costa Rica, B-32 Art. 8.2 (22 November 1969). A similar provision appears in the African Charter on Human and Peoples' Rights, Art. 7(1)c.

[54] See, e.g., J. Bhaghwati, *Termites in the Trading System: How Preferential Trade Agreements Undermine Free Trade* (Oxford University Press, 2008).

of substantial sectoral coverage would preclude a bilateral treaty aimed at liberalizing legal services on its own, as tempting as it may be among industry lobby groups to consider such an agenda at some point in the future. It is worth noting that FTAs were originally bilateral, with regionalism appearing somewhat later (NAFTA being an exception). Bilateralism is, in theory, the simplest form of negotiation. It allows a smaller number of negotiators to reach consensus on issues that are of key relevance to their particular economies and that are often underscored by shared heritage and common interests.

Among the most prominent bilateral trade agreements in recent times governing services may be found in Chapter Nine of the Comprehensive Economic and Trade Agreement (CETA), which was signed in 2016 between Canada and the EU (despite prolonged objections within the EU). This treaty contains a number of commitments aimed at liberalizing trade in services between the two signatories.[55] Chapter Nine, which encompasses legal services, covers cross-border trade in services, which includes "(a) the production, distribution, marketing, sale, and delivery of a service; (b) the purchase of, use of, or payment for, a service; and, (c) the access to and use of, in connection with the supply of a service, services which are required to be offered to the public generally."[56] These categories have broad relevance to the supply of legal services on an international basis.

Like the GATS, CETA obliges signatories to extent MFN treatment to like services and service suppliers.[57] CETA applies National Treatment to all covered services as a general obligation (no positive list of commitments as under the GATS), opting to exclude coverage in sensitive areas such as air transportation and cultural services.[58] CETA duplicates the GATS Market Access prohibitions almost verbatim, but again, because of CETA's carve-outs for sensitive sectors, these are framed as general obligations, not those that signatories adopt selectively through a positive list format.[59] Crucially, legal services are not omitted from the agreement's scope, suggesting that in the future, there may be greater scope for legal services to flow across the Atlantic and perhaps lead to the establishment of European law firms in Canada and vice versa. CETA itself has been identified as a highly progressive economic integration agreement, in part because of its innovative investment dispute settlement mechanism as well as the policy

[55] Because the European Union is a customs union, it is considered as a single state.
[56] Article 9.2.
[57] Article 9.5.
[58] Article 9.3.
[59] Article 9.6.

space it accords governments to protect domestic public policy goals, such as those relating to privacy and consumer protection.[60]

Some mention should be made of the Transatlantic Trade and Investment Partnership (TTIP), which was a proposed bilateral economic integration agreement that is no longer under negotiation between the US and the EU and is unlikely to come to fruition in the near future. The TTIP would have been the largest bilateral free trade agreement in existence in terms of the GDP of its partner states. It contained a chapter on cross-border trade in services that is of crucial relevance in that services play such a vital role in the economies of both the US and the EU. In that sense, the TTIP, at least at one point, was viewed as a representation of the potential for services liberalization going forward – a key step in a more genuinely open global market for services. Furthermore, given that the agreement enshrined principles such as the right to regulate, human rights, and sustainable development, it was viewed as setting a high standard for future trade agreements from the world's largest economic powers.[61]

Chapter III of the TTIP governed cross-border trade in legal services. It started with commitments on Market Access, which were broadly similar to those of the GATS and other agreements discussed above. National Treatment was extended generally, as was MFN, with the limitation that this treatment need not be provided with respect to "measures providing for the recognition of qualifications [or] licenses" as specified under the GATS.[62] This limitation acknowledged differences that exist (or at least are perceived to exist) in qualifications such as those obtained by professionals such as lawyers, some of whom undergo years of training and others of whom who do not. The chapter also contained provisions on the continuing review of commitments made under the treaty by the parties with a view to deepening the levels of liberalization over time,[63] reflecting the potential for inferior qualification procedures to be improved at a later stage.

[60] A. Bonfanti, "Domestic Policy Space and the Settlement of Trade Disputes under the EU-Canada Comprehensive Economic and Trade Agreement", 1 *Transnational Dispute Management* (2016).

[61] P. Delimatsis, "Negotiating Services Liberalization within TTIP – The EU External Trade Policy at Crossroads", TILEC Discussion Paper, DP 2016-013 at 6, referring to Article 21. ISSN 2213-9419 http://ssrn.com/abstract=2801524 (accessed December 2016).

[62] Articles 3–4.

[63] Articles 3–6.

The TTIP contained an annex that contains guidelines on Mutual Recognition Agreements for professional qualifications, or MRAs, which is highly relevant to international legal services. It specified the nature of the information that should be provided in an MRA, with an emphasis on clarity and consistency. This was achieved through a Four-Step process that is worth repeating in its entirety because it set out a highly precise and systemic way of approaching the regulation of professional services:

> Step One: Verification of Equivalency: Each negotiating entity should verify the overall equivalence of the scopes of practice or qualifications of the regulated profession in each Party's host jurisdiction. The examination of qualifications should entail the collection of all relevant information pertaining to the scope of practice rights related to a legal competency to practice or to the qualifications required for a specific regulated profession in the respective jurisdictions. Consequently, each negotiating entity should:
>
> (a) identify activities or groups of activities covered by the scope of practice rights of the regulated profession; and
> (b) identify the qualifications required in each host jurisdiction. These may include the following elements:
>   (i) the minimum level of education required, for example, entry requirements, length of study, subjects studied;
>   (ii) the minimum level of experience required, for example, location, length and conditions of practical training or supervised professional practice prior to licensing, or the framework of ethical and disciplinary standards;
>   (iii) examinations passed, especially examinations of professional competency;
>   (iv) the extent to which qualifications from one jurisdiction are recognised in the other jurisdiction; and,
>   (v) the qualifications which the Relevant Authorities in each host jurisdiction are prepared to recognise, for instance, by listing particular diplomas or certificates issued, or by reference to particular minimum requirements to be certified by the Relevant Authorities of the jurisdiction of origin, including whether the possession of a certain level of qualification would allow recognition for some activities of the scope of practice but not others (level and length of education, major educational focuses, overall subjects and areas). There is an overall equivalence between the scope of practice rights or the qualifications of the regulated profession if there are no substantial differences in this regard between jurisdictions.
>
> Step Two: Evaluation of Substantial Differences: There exists a substantial difference in the scope of qualifications required to exercise a regulated profession, in cases of:

(a) important differences in the essential knowledge; or (b) significant differences in the duration or content of the training between the host jurisdictions. There exists a substantial difference in the scope of practice if

(a) one or more professional activities do not form part of the corresponding profession in the jurisdiction of origin; (b) these activities are subject to specific training in the host jurisdiction; and, (c) the training for these activities in the host jurisdiction covers substantially different matters from those covered by the applicant's qualification.

Step Three: Compensatory Measures: If each negotiating entity determines that there is a substantial difference in the scope of practice rights or of formal qualifications between the host jurisdictions, they may determine compensatory measures to bridge the gap. Compensatory measures should be proportionate to the substantial difference which they seek to address. Each negotiating entity should evaluate any practical professional experience obtained in the jurisdiction of origin to see whether this experience is sufficient to remedy, in whole or in part, the substantial difference in the scope of practice rights or formal qualifications between the host jurisdictions, prior to determining a compensatory measure. A compensatory measure may also take the form of, among other things, an adaptation period or, if required, an aptitude test.

Step Four: Identification of the Conditions for Recognition. Once the assessment of the overall equivalency of the scopes of practice rights or qualifications of the regulated profession is completed, each negotiating entity should specify in the MRA:

(a) the legal competency required to practice the regulated profession; (b) the qualifications for the regulated profession; (c) whether compensatory measures are necessary; (d) the extent to which professional experience may compensate for substantial differences; (e) a description of any additional compensatory measure, including the use of any adaptation period or aptitude test, to the extent needed.[64]

This Annex goes on to specify that parties should establish points of contact for all issues relevant to authorization of professional qualifications.[65]

This was a highly methodical exercise for assessing qualifications that should be viewed as a high water mark for transparency and objectivity in the international regulation on services such as those provided by legal practitioners. These features of the defunct TTIP illustrate the importance to the US and the EU of opening services for the purposes of economic progress when possible but also emphasizes the need for parties to maintain

[64] Annex X-A, 4.

[65] Annex X-A, 5.

regulatory, due process type disciplines on domestic regulations, as seen in GATS Article VI.[66]

Finally, in the interests of presenting specimens of bilateral services agreements from a range of different geographical and legal traditions, we mention the Australia-Korea Free Trade Agreement. Signed in 2014, it contains services commitments that are substantially the same as those of the GATS. However, the Annex on Professional Services of this agreement, which is broadly similar to that of the TPP, does not include legal services. The omission of legal services is unusual and likely reflects the sharp differences that exist between Anglo-American common law and Asian civil law systems, an arguably natural barrier to cross-border trade in legal services. The Australia-Korea FTA does indicate that parties should establish a working group to consider "professional services generally" and, in so doing, to consider:

procedures for fostering the development of mutual recognition arrangements between relevant professional bodies of the Parties;

the feasibility of developing model procedures for the licensing and certification of professional service suppliers;

measures maintained at the central or regional level of government that would prevent the development of a mutual recognition arrangement or prevent a service supplier of a Party from receiving the benefits of such an arrangement; and

other issues of mutual interest relating to the supply of professional services.

The Australia-Korea FTA therefore leaves room for the future inclusion of legal services within its Annex on professional services.[67] Still, commentators warn that provisions relating to future negotiations or even regular meetings, which are common in regional and bilateral services instruments, are often not followed through, casting doubt on the effective impact of RTA (regional and bilateral) provisions on actual services liberalization.[68] Other bilateral instruments will be considered throughout this book.

[66] Delimatsis, "Negotiating Services Liberalization within TTIP".

[67] Annex 7-A (4).

[68] P. Latrille and J. Lee "Services Rules in Regional Trade Agreements: How Diverse and How Creative as Compared to GATS Multilateral Rules?", WTO Staff Working Paper ERSD-2012-19, 31 October 2012.

2.5.2 *Bilateral Investment Treaties*

While international investment law forms part of FTAs and RTAs (for example, there are investment chapters in TPP and TTIP), it has historically been regulated through a distinct bilateral treaty regime. International investment is quite rightly regarded as a distinct field of economic activity apart from trade, but in the context of services, this separation becomes somewhat more problematic. Bilateral Investment Treaties (BITs), of which several thousand have been concluded among countries at all different states of economic development, provide certain guarantees for foreign economic agents against noncommercial interference. These protections notably include guarantees against expropriation without compensation as well as the wide-ranging Fair and Equitable Treatment standard that prevents host states from engaging in many kinds of unfair or egregious behaviour towards foreign enterprises. Such protections are not found in the GATS or the services chapters of FTAs; in that sense, the BITs are more comprehensive and far-reaching.[69]

BITs are narrower than that of most of the services treaties noted above, however, because although these instruments cover "commercial presence" to use the language of GATS Mode 3 service delivery, few BITs are aimed at liberalization of services. They protect investments only once they have been established in the host state; they do not grant a right of entry to foreign enterprises, and in that sense, they do not truly create new markets. Still, the definition of "investment" in BITs is typically sufficiently broad to embrace a wide range of property rights and forms of foreign ownership[70] that could certainly encompass legal services that have already been established in host states. BITs normally contain MFN and National Treatment guarantees, and because BITs affect trade in services, the MFN obligation of the GATS also applies (when the parties are WTO members). These protections are highly relevant for international law firms that have established or wish to establish a branch or office overseas. These issues will be explored in greater depth in Chapter 5.

BITs, or investment chapters in free trade agreements (sometimes collectively referred to as International Investment Agreements or IIAs),

[69] See further D. Collins, *An Introduction to International Investment Law* (Cambridge University Press, 2016). These protections are typically contained in investment chapters of FTAs.

[70] For example, Article 1 of the US Model BIT of 2012 defines "investment" as "every asset that an investor owns or controls, directly or indirectly, that has the characteristics of an investment, including such characteristics as the commitment of capital or other resources, the expectation of gain or profit, or the assumption of risk."

also provide for a direct means of redress against host state governments through neutral international arbitration. Investment arbitration is now a well established sphere of dispute settlement, with more than 800 recorded arbitration decisions and a body of reasonably coherent arbitral jurisprudence. While many claims have been brought in investor state arbitration in services as a sector,[71] no recorded disputes have been brought on the basis of the provision of legal services. Given the expansion of investor-state dispute settlement as a forum for the resolution of commercial disputes under international law, in part because of its inclusion within international investment treaties and FTAs, it is surely only a matter of time before a legal services-oriented dispute is addressed through this mechanism. While the international investment law system has its critics, it has the notable advantage (over trade remedies through a forum such as the WTO Dispute Settlement System) of providing monetary remedies rather than mandating changes to legislation. In that sense, it is often a popular choice for aggrieved enterprises that seek compensation for interference due to excessive regulation by foreign governments.

As was noted above, unlike FTAs with investment chapters, few investment treaties offer liberalization of services, as these agreements tend to cover only investments that have already been admitted into the host state. The US and Canada do offer market access through their investment agreements, and in that sense, they are more "invasive" than EU member state BITs. These treaties also tend to incorporate country-specific exceptions in the form of negative or positive lists delineating the scope of the national and MFN treatment with respect to specific sectors or activities.[72] Most countries tend to restrict investment in certain sectors through their domestic legislation. Sectoral controls, often on services such as finance and media, appear to be the most common type of legal restriction on foreign investment. The justification for such controls tends to be that certain levels of governmental oversight are required in particular sectors because of important national interests.[73] Bilateral investment treaties will be examined again later in this book.

[71] In 2016, 7 per cent of ICSID cases dealt with Financial Services, 7 per cent with Transportation, and 7 per cent with Information Services. See ICSID 2016 Annual Report at 34. Many of the claims brought against Argentina, for example, concerned the provision of utilities services, e.g., *CMS* v. *Argentina*, ICSID Case No. ARB/01/8 Award (12 May 2005).

[72] C. Titi, "International Investment Law and the European Union: Towards a New Generation of International Investment Agreements", 26:3 *European Journal of International Law* at 639, 643 (2015).

[73] J. Salacuse, *The Three Laws of International Investment Law* (Oxford University Press, 2013) at 92.

2.6 Soft Law

Not all sources of international legal rules are binding, but many are persuasive and are accorded respect from the international community in part because of the sources from which they originate. This so-called soft law comprises policy statements and guidelines issued by non-state actors. These international organizations have considerable impact on the way in which the international trade in legal services is conducted.

First among these are guidelines, policy documents, and position statements issued by the many professional regulatory bodies that govern lawyers and legal practitioners throughout the world. Although these are not governments, they do have the power to regulate lawyers and thus play a key role in the authorization of international legal services. Most of these regulatory bodies are organized at the jurisdictional level, such as the SRA in England and Wales or the Law Society of Upper Canada in the province of Ontario. Perhaps equally influential in terms of the development of soft law are the professional associations of lawyers that also engage in policy work, typically to promote the rule of law and to further the interests of legal practitioners. These bodies also tend to be organized at the national level, such as the prominent American Bar Association (ABA), a voluntary association of lawyers that has more than 400,000 members and issues model rules for professional conduct and certifies law schools as meeting certain quality standards.[74] Because this chapter and this book focus on international regimes, these organizations will not be discussed here.

The International Bar Association (IBA) is the world's leading organization of international legal practitioners, and it has a mandate to influence the development of international law as well as initiating reforms to the legal profession and promoting the rule of law around the world. It has vast resources and significant policy influence globally with special consultative status before the UN General Assembly and the UN Economic and Social Council. The IBA issued a Global Cross Border Legal Services Report as well as a number of resolutions of relevance to the international trade in legal services. Among the most significant and recent of these is the Resolution of the IBA Council on Transfer of Skills and Liberalization of Trade in Legal Services. This document, adopted by the IBA in 2008, draws attention to the fact, noted above, that few WTO members

[74] www.americanbar.org/aba.html (accessed January 2018).

made commitments respecting trade in legal services under the GATS. Accordingly, the Resolution recommends the following:

> Countries that so far have not been willing to open their legal services market to Foreign Lawyers, or that have done so to a limited extent only as regards the scope of practice rights or rights of association with Local Lawyers, may wish to grant Foreign Lawyers access to their legal services market, or to reduce or remove any existing restrictions on such access ...[75]

This granting of rights may be made subject to continuing legal education requirements or ongoing mentoring by a domestically qualified lawyer.[76] However, such conditions must be transparent, not unreasonably burdensome, extended on an MFN basis, and, perhaps most important, not adopted or designed for the purpose of constituting an obstacle to the establishment of foreign lawyers in the host jurisdiction.[77] These latter restrictions mirror the key principles of the GATS and the ethos of the WTO.

The IBA and the OECD have also identified the importance of the role of lawyers in combating corruption, an acute problem in many parts of the developing world. In 2016, the OECD and the IBA held an Anti-Corruption Summit, agreeing to form a task force to develop professional conduct standards and practice guidance for lawyers involved in establishing and advising on international commercial structures and recommended actions for governments.[78] This agenda is relevant because the capacity of lawyers to preventing corruption through, for example, rules on money laundering and tax evasion may be compromised by the lack of appropriate qualifications or screening for individuals who act as legal advisers.

Reflecting the extent of the cohesion of the legal profession across EU Member states, which is uncommon in many regional economic groups, the Council of Bars and Law Societies of Europe (CCBE) acts as an industry lobby group on behalf of the professional regulatory bodies for legal practitioners in forty-five countries, including all EU member states. In addition to promoting the rule of law as a vital ingredient of democracy, the CCBE works closely with the European Commission in establishing laws that govern the way in which lawyers can practice in other EU member states by way of temporary services, commercial presence, or

[75] www.ibanet.org (adopted 18 October 2008) at 1.

[76] At 1 (A) and (B).

[77] At 1 (C).

[78] "OECD and IBA join forces to develop practice guidance to equip lawyers in fight against corruption" (12 December 2016). See www.oecd.org/corruption/oecd-and-iba-join-forces-to-develop-practice-guidance-to-equip-lawyers-in-fight-against-corruption.htm (accessed January 2018).

requalification. The CCBE has issued a number of position papers on the regulation of the legal profession, which, generally speaking, have advocated measures aimed at facilitating the provision of legal services across EU borders, in line with the objectives of open competition, enhancing access to justice, and market integration.[79]

The ASEAN Law Association is another industry association of lawyers with international dimension; it has an objective of advancing rule of law and the harmonization of law (including professional regulation of lawyers) in the ASEAN region. With respect to the latter goal, one of the ASEAN Law Association's major achievements has been the publication of the ASEAN Legal Systems report, which outlines the key features of each member state's legal systems with a view to fostering mutual understanding, and presumably (although this is not stated in the materials) facilitating the cross-border delivery of legal services within the region.[80] Likewise, the Commonwealth Lawyers Association (CLA) is an organization for professional lawyers, academics, and students practising within the Commonwealth that seeks to uphold the rule of law and human rights by encouraging exchanges between members of the profession through various activities. Because the Commonwealth itself is mostly composed of developing countries, the CLA has a vital role in ensuring the spread of rule of law and democratization in areas with limited capacity. It also aims to promote uniformity in the standards of professional ethics for lawyers and encourages improvements in the standards of education for lawyers,[81] both of which may be viewed as goals that further the internationalization of legal services. While neither the ASEAN Law Association nor the CLA issues legally binding statements, the mission statements of these organizations as well as their broad membership, which includes lawyers, judges, and law teachers, demonstrate the significance of these non-state actors' views as a means of shaping how legal services should be regulated at the international level.

2.7 Other Sources of Law

There are many other sources from which rules governing the international trade in legal services may be drawn. The often-cited provision of

[79] See, e.g., "CCBE Statement on the European Commission Consultation on the regulation of professions".

[80] www.aseanlawassociation.org/legal.html (accessed December 2017).

[81] www.commonwealthlawyers.com/Objectives (accessed December 2017).

the Statute of the International Court of Justice declaring the sources of international law speaks not only of treaties, as discussed above, but also of customary international law and general principles of law.[82] Customary international law and general principles of law are not as readily identifiable as treaties. They come about not on the basis of express consent, as in the case of treaties, but as a consequence of years of state practice or in some cases implicitly, by not imposing an emerging custom. Yet these forms of law may be enforceable as legal obligations in international and national courts. They deserve attention in terms of their constructing a framework by which international legal services (like other forms of economic activity) may be said to be governed, even if informally. With respect to general principles of law, the rules governing the legal profession issued by national and subnational governments, typically in conformity with international obligations, should be mentioned. These will not be explored closely in this book because it would be impossible to examine all or even many of these laws in one volume. Still, considering the extent to which common themes emerge in these many domestic laws, this book will derive key principles concerning how international legal services should be approached, notably in relation to the emerging norm of access to justice, which is of particular importance in the noncommercial context and in developing countries. The extent to which the rule of law – and alongside it the role of lawyers – has contributed to the international legal order cannot be underestimated.[83] Legal counsel plays a vital role in the drafting and negotiation of treaties, as well as in the functioning of many international organizations, not to mention domestic ones.[84] It is in a sense paradoxical that there could not be an international framework of laws by which lawyers are governed if lawyers themselves were not there to create and enforce it. Of course, lawyers play a central role in many aspects of society, including commerce and politics, and the lawyer as an agent of justice has cultural significance in many countries.[85]

The United Nations Basic Principles on the Role of Lawyers (BPRL) are the most authoritative set of rules on the position of lawyers as agents of human rights. In that sense, they may be said to contribute to the

[82] Article 38(1). The provision also mentions judicial decisions and the writings of highly qualified publicists as subsidiary sources of international law.

[83] See, e.g., T. Bingham, *The Rule of Law* (Penguin, 2010) Chapter 10.

[84] J. Klabbers, *An Introduction to International Organizations Law* (Cambridge University Press, 2015).

[85] See, e.g., S. Sheppard, "The American Legal Profession in the 21st Century" 62 *American Journal of Comparative Law Supplement* 241 at 241–242 (2014).

establishment of international norms for how lawyers should be treated with a view to the preservation of the rule of law. They were adopted by the United Nations Congress on the Prevention of Crime and the Treatment of Offenders in 1990. The BPRL establish that all people have the right to seek the assistance of a lawyer at all stages of criminal proceedings. This involves the assurance that governments will provide sufficient funding for legal aid and that legal professionals will have adequate legal training, an obligation that extends to professional organizations as well as educational establishments.[86] While entry into the legal profession may not be restricted on the basis of age, race, religion, or other prohibited grounds, this does not include national origin, permitting regulatory bodies to insist that legal qualifications may be extended only to nationals of the country concerned.[87] This document highlights the importance placed by the UN on the ability of individuals to enter the legal profession and the obligation of governments to ensure the quality of lawyers whom they validate but also their right to exclude lawyers from the practice of law who are not nationals, a crucial barrier to international trade in services that underpins restrictions found in many jurisdictions. Although the BPRL were not explicitly endorsed by the UN General Assembly, these principles are rightly viewed by lawyers' associations as norms under international law.[88] However, while some aspects of the principles may arguably lead to the liberalization of trade in legal services, others could represent barriers to trade that may be exploited for illegitimate or protectionist purposes.

2.8 Conclusion

Efforts to liberalize trade in legal services through international treaties have taken a number of forms, chief among which is the multilateral GATS. However, this agreement has been largely unsuccessful because many WTO member states have made limited commitments for legal services, a phenomenon that will be explored in more detail in Chapters 3 and 4 in relation to specific modes of delivery. For their part, RTAs and FTAs, a handful of which were mentioned here for the purposes of illustration, tend to adopt a format similar to that of the GATS with respect

[86] Articles 1–3.

[87] Article 10.

[88] See the statement of the International Association of Young Lawyers: www.aija.org/basic-principles-on-the-role-of-lawyers/ (accessed December 2016) and statement of Lawyers for Lawyers. See www.advocatenvooradvocaten.nl/basic-principles/ (accessed December 2016).

to its scope and coverage. These have shown somewhat more promise in this area, as does the CPTPP. Despite truculence observed in multilateral negotiations through the WTO, political considerations appear to play an even larger role in the negotiation of services schedules in the regional or bilateral context than at the multilateral level. This is precisely why progress made at the decentralized level is believed to be a good indicator of commitments that countries should be willing to make ultimately through the GATS[89] or perhaps eventually the TiSA. Furthermore, inconsistencies in the approaches taken by states at the regional level (such as negative or positive lists and carve-outs for certain sectors) are more likely to restrain than to promote the search for global solutions[90] and the utopian idea of a truly global market for international legal services. BITs and investment chapters in FTAs appear to have reduced obstacles to the establishment of foreign offices of law firms overseas. However, as will be shown later, many ownership restrictions remain. At the same time, there are encouraging indications of a growing consensus within the international community of the vital role that lawyers play in upholding the rule of law, suggesting that, at least with certain forms of legal practice, international trade in legal services may have support through customary international law.

Given the importance of services to many economies and high existing barriers, continued efforts to liberalize this sector through treaties such as those introduced in this chapter will likely be more economically beneficial than would further tariff reductions for goods. This is no less true for legal services. Indeed, just as legal services face some of the most stringent barriers of all, they also present vast economic potential through their indirect role in the delivery of other productive forms of economic activity, including manufacturing and extraction as well as other services such as finance. It is also evident through the many international instruments discussed above that although regulatory cooperation in services delivery is a vital component of many states' global market access strategy, the capacity of governments to maintain control over the recognition of qualifications and various other aspects of the delivery of professional services is jealously guarded. In the case of legal services, the need for oversight is obvious. The resolution of this peculiar tension, which will be considered throughout this book, is one that must be approached with great care.

[89] C. Van Grasstek, "The Political Economy of Services in Regional Trade Agreements", OECD Trade Policy Working Paper TAD/TC/WP(2010) 32/FINAL at 45.

[90] Adlung, "Trade in Services in the WTO" at 371.

3

Import Restrictions on Trade in Legal Services

Cross-Border Supply

3.1 Introduction

The advent of internet telecommunications penetrating all parts of the globe via ultrafast connections and tremendous data transfer speeds has driven an explosion in cross-border delivery of services. The legal industry, which is fundamentally an industry founded upon the transfer of information, has been at the forefront of this new era of commerce. Although cross-border trade in legal services may once have been viewed as less significant than the classic lawyering associated with establishment or temporary movement, today it is unquestionably a vital area of concern for policy makers who are seeking to shape public international law in a manner that is conducive to economic prosperity but is also mindful of the inherent risks in the remote exchange of highly sensitive data. Indeed, Mode 1 supply of legal services is used frequently despite the fact that there is limited empirical evidence of it,[1] suggesting that it often flies under the radar of studies estimating the size of the global legal services market. Importers of cross-border legal services under Mode 1 tend to be located in relatively open developed economies that have small but advanced domestic legal services markets. Canada and Australia are good examples of the destination countries of such services, as are Argentina and Norway. The size of the market that is available to be served in these mid-sized developed countries is not large enough for international suppliers to establish themselves there, but international firms may still wish to supply their clients in these countries with specialist advice that the clients cannot obtain at home.

This chapter will explore innovations in the delivery of cross-border legal services through online providers, which appear to have grown rapidly in size and number in recent years. It will consider the legal risks raised by this new breed of legal service, followed by a brief examination of how

[1] Muller, *Liberalization of Trade in Legal Services* at 83.

public international law has approached this mode of delivery, first multilaterally by the WTO, then regionally. Attention will be paid to indirect forms of international regulation of this kind of legal services, meaning forms of regulation other than the specific commitments of nondiscrimination and market access. The key regulatory environment covering Mode 1 legal services engages squarely with international regulatory developments in relation to e-commerce and digital trade.

3.2 Technological Innovation and the Virtual Law Office

Legal services are unaffordable for a large portion of the population, even in developed countries such as the US and the UK.[2] This may be even more the case in countries with poorer economies and countries where legal services are poorly developed and supply is restricted. Moreover, transformative innovations in the delivery of legal solutions are required to address the increasing complexity of the global economy driven by multinational enterprises of all sizes.[3] It may be argued, then, that the way in which legal services are delivered should be reformed to improve access for consumers of all kinds. Online delivery of routine tasks coupled by automation is one of the primary ways in which this can be achieved. The growing importance of online delivery of legal services has attracted much attention as an alternative to traditional in-office supply. Some view this optimistically as an opportunity for legal services providers of the future because it will open new markets, potentially internationally, just as others close because of much-needed streamlining of routine legal processes.[4] Many kinds of legal work can be undertaken more efficiently by less-qualified, lower-cost people or even through computerization. Examples include document review for litigation, due diligence in large-scale litigation or corporate transactions, basic contract drafting, and even legal research.[5] These issues are relevant to the discussion of trade in legal services because such tasks could quite easily be done over the Internet across international borders.

Although it is impossible to keep track of the many new providers of digital legal services given the rapid pace of innovation, some of the key developments in the delivery of cross-border legal services will now be considered.

[2] L. Snyder, *Democratizing Legal Services* (Lexington Books, 2016).
[3] Hadfield, *Rules for a Flat World* at 222.
[4] Susskind, *Tomorrow's Lawyers* at 21.
[5] Ibid. at 21.

3.2.1 *Outsourcing (Business to Business)*

Outsourcing of legal services is perhaps the most significant form of cross-border supply of legal services in terms of monetary value. The size of the legal services outsourcing market is difficult to assess but was thought to have exceeded US $3 billion by 2016. Growth rate estimations also vary widely but are thought to be at least 25 per cent per year. One study suggests that the market for legal process outsourcing will exceed $40 billion by 2024.[6] Key legal outsourcing companies include UnitedLex, Pangea3, Integreon, Axiom Law, and Elevate Services.[7]

Outsourcing of legal work was initially concentrated on simple tasks of an administrative nature but has become increasingly sophisticated. Classic or pure outsourcing involves the conduct of legal work by a third-party provider. It is sometimes referred to as legal process outsourcing and covers routine tasks such as document review and due diligence. It typically involves low-cost locations overseas. The rationale behind this business strategy is one of cost reduction. Law firms are already beginning to question the wisdom of maintaining expensive offices in cities such as London and New York when telecommunication technologies are available to facilitate the provision of basic legal advice from lower-cost centres in Asia and elsewhere, not to mention the high salaries of qualified lawyers who have many years of postgraduate education from expensive law schools. Service providers in these nontraditional locations have lower salaries, and the office space they occupy is less expensive. The major impetus for the development of outsourcing was the onerous E-Discovery requirements in the US, which are inherently voluminous and, many would argue, excessive. Similar requirements exist in other jurisdictions, pressuring law firms to hire many qualified lawyers as document reviewers for the purposes of large-scale litigation matters on a temporary basis.[8]

When this work is done in another country, it is categorized as "offshoring". This has been commonly practiced by large banks that offshore legal activities to places such as India and Malaysia, where the banks have already located other functions, such as call centres. The legal resource remains part of the company, but establishing an expensive legal department in the host country is avoided.[9] Another popular form of outsourcing is

[6] Global Market Insights (20 May 2017).

[7] Global Market Insights (27 May 2017).

[8] The author was employed in this capacity for two years. The pay rate was reasonably high, but the work was incredibly tedious.

[9] Susskind, *Tomorrow's Lawyers* at 38.

"near-shoring", in which the legal support tasks are done elsewhere within the same country. This kind of activity precludes any trade in services problems, such as measures restricting Mode 1 delivery, although it could raise jurisdictional issues within a federal system, such as the US, when the near-shore location is in a different state. Near-shore providers tend to be more expensive than offshore providers, but they have the advantage of closer proximity to customers and cultural compatibility. Near-shore legal process outsourcing is expected to grow more rapidly than offshoring because of increasing operational costs in popular offshore locations such as India and South Africa as well as new data protection laws, such as those of the EU's new General Data Protection Regulation (GDPR).[10]

Another variety of outsourcing of legal services is subcontracting. This entails the passing of legal work to other law firms abroad that have much lower costs than those of larger firms located in expensive financial hubs.[11] Some in-house law departments in multination corporations engage in this type of outsourcing by exchanging work or knowledge between branches of the same company located in different countries. This is an often-unrealized efficiency, as few in-house legal departments take advantage of outsourcing of routine matters to professional support lawyers in the way that law firms do.[12] In some instances of outsourcing, large law firms establish their own dedicated facilities abroad. The London-based law firm Clifford Chance has done this in India, for example. Alternatively, and more commonly, law firms subcontract the services to an independent provider in another country.[13] Many law firms and in-house legal departments are establishing close relationships with their legal services outsourcing providers and are thus building "centres of excellence", which will be discussed further in Chapter 4, or "shared service centres" that deliver technology-oriented solutions for clients.[14]

The UK and the US are the largest markets for legal services outsourcing in terms of near-shoring. One study has shown that India is the most common foreign location for legal outsourcing staff, accounting for more than half of all outsourcing in the sample. Other leading locations are the Philippines, China, Hong Kong, and Singapore. India and, to a lesser extent, the Philippines have dominated the field because of their

[10] Global Market Insights (3 May 2017).
[11] Susskind, *Tomorrow's Lawyers* at 38–39.
[12] Ibid. at 74.
[13] Muller, *Liberalization of Trade in Legal Services* at 84.
[14] M. Lacity, L. Willcocks, and A. Burgess, *The Rise of Legal Services Outsourcing: Risk and Opportunity* (Bloomsbury, 2014) at 80–81.

English-language competence, process, and information technology competences as well as their experience in providing services through telecommunications to clients in developed countries.[15]

Legal outsourcing has proven to be a reliable means of reducing costs but offers more than cost savings. This includes channelling in-house legal staff to higher-value work, faster service delivery, scalability (especially in the context of document review, for which demand tends to fluctuate), improved quality, and access to innovations such as information technology systems. While the size of the legal process outsourcing market attest to its success as a business strategy, commentators caution that true cost savings of this kind of cross-border legal services may not be as high as is often thought. This is because outsourcing leads to some losses associated with knowledge transfer costs, lost productivity, and the expense of oversight by the firm that uses the service. Moreover, studies have shown a high staff turnover rate in outsourcing. This can be problematic in terms of delay and quality reduction (due to the need for new staff members to familiarize themselves with the intricacies of each project), both of which can lead to increased costs.[16] Perhaps unsurprisingly, the greatest successes in implementing outsourcing for legal services have typically involved close management of the activities, often by a high-level individual in the client firm who coordinates work and maintains close communication with the external providers.[17] Proponents of legal services outsourcing are most often in-house general counsel who are responsible to their firm for the expenditure on legal services. Unsurprisingly, those who tend to resist the use of outsourcing are the lawyers who feel that they are being deprived of work for which they can bill hours. Such lawyers have generally been more accepting of outsourcing parts of discovery and less accepting of outsourcing for due diligence matters because the former is viewed as less specialist.[18]

The services supplied by legal outsourcers may be classed into three categories based on the level of experience required. Level 1 activities can be done by generalist outsourcing providers. This will include secretarial or administrative staff who do not require any specific legal knowledge. Individuals with Level 1 skills are able to perform nonlegal and document management services. Level 2 activities require some legal knowledge and

[15] Ibid. at 183.

[16] Ibid. at 26.

[17] Ibid. at 64–70.

[18] A. Harmon, "The Ethics of Legal Process Outsourcing: Is the Practice of Law a 'Noble Profession' or Is It Just Another Business", 13 *Journal of Technology Law and Policy* 41–43 (2008).

context but do not necessitate legal qualifications for their execution. People with Level 2 skills may be qualified to draft documents and engage in commercial analysis and legal management services, depending on the complexity of the work. Level 3 outsourcing consists of high-value activities that require at least some legal qualifications to perform. Individuals with Level 3 skills are qualified to provide legal advice and to make legal decisions. These individuals will be needed to perform complex drafting and commercial analysis as well as the more advanced legal management systems, such as identifying documents for relevance in litigation. Such activities generally exclude the legal opinions that are normally provided by senior legal practitioners.[19] This competence-based categorization of legal and quasi-legal services can be readily adapted to various practice areas, such as intellectual property, and can be used to unbundle the range of services needed across a given transaction. Some believe that legal outsourcing services will "move up the value chain" over time, with more and more sophisticated (or Level 3) work being undertaken.[20] Still, the services most commonly offered among legal outsource providers is document management, followed by contract management.[21] With the possible exception of Level 1, these activities would likely fit within the definition of legal services discussed in Chapter 2.

3.2.2 Online Legal Services (Business to Client)

Technological advances in computing and telecommunications have facilitated an explosion of alternative legal services providers aimed directly at consumers. Because most of these can be adapted to an international marketplace, these activities fall within the sphere of cross-border trade in legal services under Mode 1. As with legal process outsourcing, such services are built upon the reality that many varieties of legal services are highly standardized and can be prepackaged for online delivery at a fraction of the cost of traditional in-office legal advice.

Disruptive technology firms such as Legal Zoom,[22] Rocket Lawyer,[23] Legalwise[24], and Avvo[25] (to name a few) can serve clients' needs on a wide

[19] Lacity, Willcocks, and Burgess, *The Rise of Legal Services Outsourcing: Risk and Opportunity* at 22–23.
[20] Ibid. at 178–179.
[21] Ibid. at 33–34.
[22] www.legalzoom.com, www.legalzoom.co.uk (accessed March 2018).
[23] www.rocketlawyer.co.uk (accessed March 2018).
[24] www.legalwise.ca, www.legalwise.co.za (accessed March 2018).
[25] www.avvo.com (accessed March 2018).

range of matters over the Internet, vastly reducing the cost of conventional legal services. Such firms have been cited as key causes in the decline of traditional law firms,[26] and many are better known as brands in the US and the UK than are most traditional law firms.[27] Such services have appeared in civil law markets as well, such as NetLex, which is a cloud-based legal information management that originated in Brazil and operates in Italy.[28] Because these providers, some of which boast rosters of thousands of lawyers working on a part-time basis, do not need to maintain offices in the traditional sense, they can offer lower-priced services to a greater number of clients, including clients in other jurisdictions. From the supplier's perspective, this kind of employment is advantageous because it offers flexibility and the ability to work from home.

Going one step further than these innovative lower-priced online services providers, a number of organizations offer rudimentary legal services at no charge, and because these are made available online, they may be supplied internationally. The Legal Services Corporation launched a website of free legal forms, as have some court systems.[29] Rulefinder is an online risk management tool developed by the London-based law firm Allen & Overy that has helped clients to navigate the rules and practices relating to international shareholding disclosure.[30] This service appears to have anticipated the role of computerization in pushing the ever-decreasing price of certain basic legal services (such as document review) towards zero, hoping to retain existing clients for other paid matters rather than seeing them defect to other suppliers. Barefoot Law in Uganda provides free legal advice on a range of matters, including commercial ones, addressing severe access issues in that country.[31] MetaTalk is another free legal advice platform delivered online that has attracted significant attention.[32]

Open-sourcing of legal services is the provision of a wide range of legal materials on the Internet without charging a fee. These may include materials such as standard form contracts, guidelines, procedures, opinions, and case studies. Open-source platforms may be particularly effective if

[26] Barton, *Glass Half Full* at 88.

[27] Susskind, *Tomorrow's Lawyers* at 46.

[28] www.netlexweb.com (accessed March 2018).

[29] Barton, *Glass Half Full* at 95.

[30] www.allenovery.com/Online-Services/Pages/default.aspx. Susskind, *Tomorrow's Lawyers* at 23.

[31] https://barefootlaw.org/about-us/our-model/ (accessed March 2018).

[32] B. Barton, "Technology Can Solve Much of America's Access to Justice Problem If We Let It" in S. Estreicher and J. Radice eds. *Beyond Elite Law: Access to Civil Justice in America* (Cambridge University Press, 2012) at 453.

they are organized as an online resource that users can add to and edit in the manner of Wikipedia.[33] Crowdsourcing is another phenomenon that has begun to affect cross-border legal services. In crowdsourcing, users seeking advice are able to ask questions of a community whose members provide responses and may also post questions themselves, blurring the distinction between supplier and consumer.[34] In this spirit, LawPivot, which was acquired by Rocket Lawyer, consists of an online collaborative forum in which users can submit legal questions and receive answers free of charge.[35] There may be a possibility in the future to integrate the provision of certain legal services, such as answers to discrete legal questions, with social network platforms such as Facebook or LinkedIn. In years to come, online legal question answering through computerization may become a normal feature of cross-border legal services. This could take the form of an online service that contains vast quantities of structured and unstructured data on law including primary sources and commentary that can be accessed through programs that understand spoken or written language, analyse fact patterns, and draw conclusions in the form of legal advice. Such a system could disrupt not simply international legal services but the entire edifice of the legal profession.[36]

Probono.net, in conjunction with Chicago Kent Law School's A2J project, created LawHelp Interactive (LHI), a free online repository of guided legal form drafting. Available forms cover matters such as child support and custody, domestic violence, debt collection, and divorce. Similarly, since 1992, the Legal Information Institute of Cornell University has been publishing legal materials online free of charge to increase the general public's understanding of legal issues.[37] While these services have been designed with self-represented litigants in mind,[38] it is not difficult to imagine how a legal service provider, perhaps an unregulated one located in another jurisdiction, could take advantage of them to package a work product for a client in the provider's home country or abroad.

It would be difficult to argue that these types of platforms constitute legal services of the kind envisioned by the definition outlined in Chapter 1. The distinction between the two would likely rest at the point at which the legal information platform took on an active advisory role rather than merely

[33] Susskind, *Tomorrow's Lawyers* at 40.
[34] Ibid.
[35] www.rocketlaw.co.uk (accessed March 2018).
[36] Susskind, *Tomorrow's Lawyers* at 55.
[37] Bernard, Henri
[38] Barton, *Glass Half Full* at 200.

assisting the user in locating information. Advances in search engines using artificial intelligence will make this determination a difficult one. Nevertheless, how information platforms that cover easily automatable matters can be applied to international legal services may be of limited relevance today, as this represents a minuscule element of cross-border legal services and does not appear to threaten an existing industry. However, this may change when such services become more sophisticated, leveraging machine learning and other nascent technologies and, in so doing, supplanting conventional legal services.[39] If this occurs, measures designed to restrict cross-border legal services may not offer much of a safeguard for an industry that has become largely obsolete.

3.2.3 Online Dispute Resolution

Another sphere of cross-border legal services that has been transformed by technological innovations relates to dispute resolution provided over telecommunications, in some cases to users in other countries. The importance of online dispute resolution in an era when so many goods and services are purchased online means that consumers expect all kinds of customer support to be readily accessible through their smartphones.[40] Reductions in legal aid in many countries, notably in the UK, has likewise turned the attention of governments to the provision of online dispute resolution systems that are more affordable and accessible than traditional courts.[41]

Virtual courts should become a key area for growth in cross-border supply of legal services. Low-cost teleconferencing platforms such as Skype and FaceTime mean that parties, advisors, witnesses, and adjudicators need not be in the same location for a hearing to take place. Adoption of virtual courts has been most significant in criminal cases in which there are vulnerable witnesses and for bail and remand hearings conducted via links between prisons and courts. These initiatives have reduced the duration of hearings and saved costs on transportation.[42] In some state courts in the US, it is possible to file court documents online, which can preclude the need for a lawyer. These services may be used for uncontested divorces,

[39] Ibid. at 98.

[40] Sir Geoffrey Vos, Chancellor of the High Court of England and Wales, "The Future of the UK's Jurisdiction and English Law after Brexit" at [33] (28 November 2017) www.judiciary.gov.uk/wp-content/uploads/2017/11/chc-frankfurt-presentation-nov2017.pdf (accessed January 2018).

[41] Susskind, *Tomorrow's Lawyers* at 96.

[42] Ibid. at 109.

orders for protection, and defences for debt collection.[43] Property tax appeals in British Columbia have been resolved by using an online platform, and the Dutch Legal Aid board instigated an online mediation service for family and landlord-tenant matters.[44] The UK courts recently launched Money Claim Online for citizens to initiate or respond to legal claims without the hassle of formal court procedures.[45] Commentators anticipate that online dispute resolution will become one of the legal profession's future growth areas.[46] This may explain why traditional law firms are being encouraged to begin integrating online technologies for document preparation, advice, and dispute resolution if they wish to survive.[47]

For their part, states will need to respond with flexibility in their approach to the regulation of this kind of legal activity under international treaties that cover Mode 1 delivery. Because dispute resolution tends to be provided by governments through their justice system rather than by firms, this type of legal service is arguably outside the scope of the GATS by virtue of Article I 3 (b), which excludes "services normally supplied in the exercise of governmental authority", which is further defined under subsection (c) to mean "any service which is supplied neither on a commercial basis, nor in competition with one or more service suppliers". Of course, many private organizations provide arbitration and mediation services, including some, like the London Court of International Arbitration (LCIA) or the International Chamber of Commerce (ICC), that do so on an international basis. Some urge that low-value civil claims should be resolved through online dispute settlement systems provided by the private sector to reduce the pressure on the public court system.[48]

Having been in existence now for at least twenty years, private dispute resolution services that are delivered online have grown in size and number recently and are showing signs of genuine uptake for the first time.[49] While some of the pioneers in this field, including Cybersettle, iCourthouse, and Virtual Courthouse, appear to be struggling to get clients, the success of eBay's[50] Resolution Centre services for its own customers is striking, handling more than sixty million disputes per year. Similarly, Modria is a

[43] Barton, *Glass Half Full* at 199.
[44] R. Ambrogi, "Is There a Future for Online Dispute Resolution for Lawyers?" Law Sites (11 April 2016).
[45] www.moneyclaimonline.gov.uk (accessed March 2018).
[46] Susskind, *Tomorrow's Lawyers* at 141.
[47] Barton, *Glass Half Full* at 102.
[48] Susskind, *Tomorrow's Lawyers* at 115.
[49] Ambrogi, "Is There a Future for Online Dispute Resolution for Lawyers?"
[50] https://resolutioncentre.ebay.co.uk/ (accessed March 2018).

private provider of online dispute settlement that can be used in conjunction with an existing court.[51] It uses a "fairness engine" that delivers financial as well as nonfinancial settlements for disputes. Its diagnosis module gathers relevant information, and its negotiation module summarizes areas of disagreement, which it follows with suggestions for resolution. If this does not achieve a settlement, Modria then directs users to a mediation module conducted by a neutral third party. Modria claims that the vast majority of claims are settled without need for mediation.[52] Wevorce uses an online legal architect to design the parameters of a divorce settlement. Its strategy appears to be based on the presumption that the adversarial process is unnecessary to achieve optimal solutions for clients.[53] It may be only a matter of time before these services are expanded internationally.

Predictive technology that will help to forecast the outcome of disputes is another legal service that may be readily delivered across international borders through the Internet. The importance of this innovation to the international business community has been identified by the senior judiciary of the UK[54] and is poised to become a key part of dispute settlement strategy, which in turn will influence business negotiations. The application of technology to automate and mechanize legal analysis is often described as "computational law" and was associated, in its early stage, with Stanford Law School's Codex Center for Legal Infomatics.[55] One noteworthy commercial example of this type of service is Blue J Legal, which began as a project within the University of Toronto Faculty of Law. It uses artificial intelligence and machine learning to predict legal outcomes in judicial proceedings on the basis of data entered by the client via the service's website. This "legal foresight" is designed to help clients, some of which are located abroad, to construct commercial strategies with a view to mitigating legal risks in areas such as taxation and employment.[56] Blue J Legal's Terms of Use specify that "no legal advice has been provided" and that no "solicitor-client relationship is formed" between the provider and the client. It is therefore unlikely that these types of predictive advisory services would fall under the definition of legal services used by the GATS and regional trade agreements (RTAs) covering services with a view to

[51] www.tylertech.com/solutions-products/modria (accessed March 2018).
[52] Ibid.
[53] www.wevorce.com (accessed March 2018).
[54] Vos, "The Future of the UK's Jurisdiction and English Law after Brexit."
[55] https://law.stanford.edu/codex-the-stanford-center-for-legal-informatics/ (accessed March 2018).
[56] www.bluejlegal.com/about (accessed March 2018).

facilitating their liberalization on an international scale. Still, to the extent to which such services displace the work of conventional lawyers and, in so doing, represent a threat to an existing domestic market, there may come a time when the standard definition of legal services in international treaties needs to be modernized to encompass this type of activity.

3.2.4 Problems Raised by Cross-Border Online Delivery of Legal Services

The technological advances that have begun to stimulate the growth of cross-border legal services present some legal challenges that could impede liberalization initiatives under public international law. The difficulty in crafting appropriate disciplines for online legal services is exacerbated by the nature of the Internet, which defies normal spatial understandings of jurisdiction associated with many other spheres of commercial and noncommercial activities. Some even see "cyberlaw" as emblematic of the emancipation of law from geographic boundaries because information is available on the Internet simultaneously to anyone with an internet connection.[57] Because activity undertaken on the Internet is, in a sense, jurisdiction-less, some feel that self-regulation by the community of internet users and service providers carries more legitimacy than the imposition of classic state-based regulation.[58]

Legal services companies in more open regulatory environments, such as the UK, have been able to export many varieties of legal services through cross-border trade into the more closed North American market.[59] Some bar associations seek to ensure that providers of "alternative legal services" such as those discussed earlier in the chapter should be restricted. Rather than simply denying access, many insist that foreign providers of internet-based services should be made to adhere to a code of conduct. This could be burdensome when such providers are already subject to home state ethical rules, a situation that is often referred to as the "double de-ontology" problem, which will be explored in Chapter 5. While the ABA identified the potential for technology to improve the delivery of legal services to meet the public's needs, the ABA's Report on the Future of Legal Services

[57] H. Lindahl, *Fault Lines of Globalization* (Oxford University Press, 2013) at 65.

[58] D. Johnson and D. Post, "Law and Borders: The Rise of Law in Cyberspace", 48 *Stanford Law Review* (1995).

[59] J. O. McGinnis and R. Pearce, "The Great Disruption: How Machine Intelligence Will Transform the Role of Lawyers in the Delivery of Legal Services", 82 *Fordham Law Review* 3041 at 3057 (2014).

prepared between 2014 and 2016 identified the need to encourage new models for regulating legal services in order to harness these innovations.[60]

Outsourcing raises many considerations for the legal practitioners who are involved. Among these are ethical issues regarding the adequacy of supervision of the processes taking place in other jurisdictions. If the individuals undertaking various tasks lack sufficient skills, their work output may be inadequate, placing clients at risk. Of course, the charge that outsourcing represents a derogation of a lawyer's ethical duty to provide the best service to the client may be challenged on the grounds that most partners or senior associates at law firms engage in analogous conduct when they delegate due diligence or document review duties to junior associates or trainees. Enhanced supervision involving qualified senior practitioners could address this problem and, as was noted earlier in the chapter, may be commercially viable, as some of the most successful examples of outsourcing employ tighter management. Measures enacted to prevent legal services outsourcing on the basis of inadequate supervision of outsourcing would likely be disingenuous. Perhaps more problematic, many of the online services discussed earlier, including outsourcing but also business-to-client services, could conceivably result in insufficient regard for client confidentiality in terms of sensitive business or in some cases personal information and trade secrets, as well as conflicts of interest. While this outcome would not be expected in countries with strong professional regulatory regimes, if the jurisdiction in which the legal advisor is located takes place lacks rules regarding confidentiality or conflicts of interest, very serious transgressions of foreign clients' rights could ensue. The extent to which domestic regulators should have authority over work that is outsourced is unclear, particularly if it is outsourced to another country.[61] International professional regimes could provide a partial answer. In this regard, the IBA's Principles on Conduct for the Legal Profession, which is intended to act as guidance for legal professionals throughout the world, specifies that the lawyer has a duty to maintain client confidentiality.[62]

The independence of lawyers may be under threat when they work in conjunction with other types of service provider, perhaps in the context of outsourcing or other online forms of assistance. Some bar associations'

[60] www.americanbar.org/groups/centers_commissions/commission-on-the-future-of-legal-services.html (accessed March 2018).

[61] E.g., UK Solicitors Regulation Authority, "SRA Consultation on Handbook Amendments Relating to International Practice" (14 March 2013), online: www.sra.org.uk/sra/consultations/international-practice.page (accessed March 2018).

[62] Principal 4 (adopted 28 May 2011).

rules of professional conduct, such as those of the ABA, require lawyers to remain independent, precluding fee sharing with non-lawyers. Adherence to this rule is why customers who use services such as Legal Zoom (which offers legal services in conjunction with other services such as accounting) may have a fragmented experience that can be dissatisfying.[63] In jurisdictions that enforce restrictions on multidisciplinary practices, such limitations could prevent the growth of online services delivered across borders from jurisdictions where the legal profession is more tightly regulated, such as the US. While jurisdictions that allow multidisciplinary services can offer an enhanced package to their clients both at home and abroad, there is a risk that this type of collaboration could place lawyers under pressure. This could undermine their ability to offer advice and representation that is in the best interests of their clients rather than of their employers or managers. Furthermore, these types of arrangements run the risk that non-legal experts will end up performing some of the work for which legal expertise is required, the determination of which is itself complicated because of the administrative nature of many tasks undertaken by modern lawyers, such as document review.[64]

In addition to confidentiality issues that are unique to the legal profession, virtual legal assistance by some of the innovative providers discussed earlier raises many troublesome issues with respect to data protection and privacy, which may be viewed as confidentiality obligations of a more general nature. The use of cloud computing for information technology functions drastically reduces information technology costs for smaller legal services providers, advantaging consumers.[65] However, storing client information on remote servers rather than on the lawyer's own computer leaves this information outside the direct control of the legal services provider. In most jurisdictions around the world, lawyers have the duty to safeguard confidential client information, including protecting that information from unauthorized disclosure and protecting clients' property from destruction, degradation, or loss, whether from system failure, natural disasters, or the dissolution of the professional's business. Moreover, lawyers have the continuing need to be able to retrieve clients' data in a form that is usable beyond the form in which it is kept in a vendor's

[63] Snyder, *Democratizing Legal Services* at 41.

[64] J. H. Matheson and P. D. Favorite, "Multidisciplinary Practice and the Future of the Legal Profession: Considering a Role for Independent Directors", 32 *Loyola University of Chicago Law Journal* 577 at 582 (2001).

[65] L. Tuthill, "Cross-Border Data Flows: What Role for Trade Rules?" in P Sauve and M Roy eds. *Research Handbook on Trade in Services* (Edward Elgar, 2016) at 360.

software product.[66] Because servers storing information may be located in a different jurisdiction from that of the people who use them (the client or the legal service provider), there is arguably a role for regulation of this practice under international law. Further issues may be raised when the server on which the data is stored is outside the jurisdiction in which the legal practitioner is located, even if the service consumer is located in the same jurisdiction as the provider. This could represent an entirely different mode of services supply that is not captured by the GATS standard classification.

The Law Society of British Columbia in Canada was one of the first regulators to address the obligations of lawyers with respect to the use of cloud computing to store clients' data. It concluded that each practitioner must conduct proper due diligence on new technology service suppliers, including those involving data storage, with the recognition that there is no duty to keep data infallibly secure. The lawyer must use reasonable care to employ the mode of communication that, in light of the circumstances, will best protect confidential client data. The lawyer must further advise clients if there is reason to believe that the chosen communications presents an unreasonable risk.[67] Of course, these concerns apply equally to legal practitioners that are providing their services outside of Mode 1, but such concerns are particularly acute in the cross-border context because the entire relationship is based upon telecommunications with little or no face-to-face contact.

The ABA's Model Rules of Professional Conduct requires the lawyer to make reasonable efforts to ensure that support services provided by non-lawyers are provided in a manner that is compatible with the professional obligations of the lawyer.[68] In the context of cloud computing or other software as a service (SAAS) that may have a multijurisdictional element, the extent of this obligation will depend upon the experience, stability, and reputation of the vendor (the non-lawyer service provider). Security measures may assist in discharging the legal practitioner's duty. This could include having in the contract between the lawyer and the SAAS provisions that specify how the vendor will handle confidential client information according to the lawyer's professional responsibilities. The lawyer should ensure that if the SAAS ceases to function as a business,

[66] Kowalski, *Avoiding Extinction* at 159.

[67] Law Society of British Columbia, Report of the Cloud Computing Working Group, 15 July 2011.

[68] Rule 5.3a).

there is a method for retrieving the data in a nonproprietary format. The SAAS should be contractually bound to return or destroy the hosted data promptly at the request of the lawyer. There should be assurances that the data storage service provider has taken steps to safeguard the security and confidentiality of the data, employing techniques such as firewalls, encryption, and intrusion detection services.[69] Commentators have observed that there may even be an implied duty of lawyers to stay informed of technological advances to ensure that cloud storage system remains sufficiently advanced to protect the client's information. Clearly, legal services providers should be aware how changes to the rules of professional privilege will affect cloud-based storage services.[70]

The profound implication of data location requirements was recently recognized by the Council of Bars and Law Societies of Europe, which submitted an amicus brief in support of Microsoft in *United States* v. *Microsoft*, a US Court of Appeal case that, as of the time of writing, has been appealed to the US Supreme Court.[71] The case considers whether the US government has the authority to use a US warrant to access private communications and electronic information that is stored abroad. This raises serious concerns for legal services providers in Europe and elsewhere who deal with often highly sensitive information that belongs to their clients but that may also be of interest to governmental authorities. Legal privilege is, of course, one of the foundations of the legal profession and perhaps the strongest argument for treating it as a special kind of service unlike others. If the court rules in favour of the US government, then its governmental agencies will be able to access data stored abroad, undermining the capacity of clients to cite this privilege to safeguard their information. Not only will this significantly enlarge the extraterritorial application of US laws, it will have profound implications for the confidentiality of lawyer-client communications, which is central to the legal profession.

3.3 Multilateral Regulation of Cross-Border Trade in Legal Services

The previous section explored some of the recent developments in cross-border legal services and associated legal issues. This section considers

[69] Kowalski, *Avoiding Extinction* at 163–164.

[70] Ibid. at 172.

[71] US Ct of Appeals Second Circuit, Docket No. 14-2985 (14 July 2016) [currently on appeal to the USSC].

how this mode of legal services delivery has been approached under public international law.

3.3.1 *Cross-Border Legal Services and GATS*

GATS commitments for cross-border supply of services are generally underwhelming relative to the liberalization undertaken autonomously by many WTO members. Indeed, there are few WTO members, apart from the recently acceded ones, for whom listed GATS commitments are close to actual trading conditions.[72] This means that WTO members are free to restrict further this mode of services at will, placing services providers in a precarious position in terms of future trading. With respect to legal services, most WTO members regarded measures covering Mode 1 of legal services delivery as unenforceable, so they did not bother listing them. It would be nearly impossible to prevent a consumer within one's territory from paying for legal services offered by someone in another territory over the Internet. While stopping a provider from delivering such a service to a consumer might be within the power of a professional regulator or law society, making this type of behaviour illegal under domestic law would be impractical in terms of enforceability. The increasing digitization of services has made it difficult for governments to impose barriers to this kind of trade, so policy makers have largely ignored it.[73] The GATS controls restrictions on Mode 1 supply of services through a focus on the service itself, not the service supplier. Measures governing the supplier of the service will be more difficult to impose on the service supplier because the supplier is located abroad and therefore is not subject to the laws of the importing country. This conundrum is reflected in the fact that during the Uruguay Round of GATS negotiations, of the seventy-six members who made legal services commitments, sixty-eight made commitments under Mode 1. Still, it is often suggested that WTO members' specific commitments under the GATS should not be perceived as static or frozen in time but rather as evolving in line with modern market realities. This is especially true for Mode 1, since comments made before the internet phenomenon surely could not have predicted the future implications of the Internet and how they would affect cross-border delivery of

[72] Adlung, "Trade in Services in the WTO" at 370–371.

[73] M. Roy, "Charting the Evolving Landscape of Services Trade Policies: Recent Patterns of Protection and Liberalization" in Sauve and Roy eds. *Research Handbook on Trade in Services* at 30.

services.[74] This progressive style of interpretation was arguably conveyed by the Appellate Body in China–Audiovisual Products.[75] An "evolutive" style of interpretation may be required to adapt international law instruments crafted during a different era to suit modern-day conditions such as these.[76]

An origin-neutral restriction on services supply through the Internet, such as legal services, could discriminate against foreign suppliers in comparison to domestic suppliers who can interact in person with their consumers. There are no known restrictions of this nature that are relevant to legal services; however, a number of jurisdictions require that the client sign documents in the presence of a witness. Such transactions can be effectuated with the assistance of notaries in the member state of the consumer who can verify the authenticity of the signature and identification, which can then be transmitted electronically to the primary legal services provider in another county. It may be that an origin-neutral measure restricting cross-border supply (e.g., online law degrees are not recognized within the licensing jurisdiction) should be viewed as a breach of national treatment under the GATS only if the foreign suppliers that are so affected are unable to resort to other modes of supply, such as establishing themselves in the territory of that member state to deal with the consumer directly.[77] The logic behind this view appears to be that foreign suppliers are not wholly deprived of their competitive opportunities vis-à-vis local suppliers as long as they can feasibly resort to other modes of supply. Whether or not this view is accurate, it is worth recalling that Footnote 10 to the National Treatment obligation in the GATS explains that members do not have to compensate for any inherent competitive disadvantages that result from the foreign character of the services. This would appear to preclude an emphasis on the competitive disadvantage arising from online services provision over great distances (and possibly in different time zones). It must be assumed that foreign lawyers relying on the Internet to serve their clients will not be able to have the same kinds of relationship with their clients as will lawyers who can meet in their office in the traditional way.

[74] E. Leroux, "Twenty Years of GATS Caselaw: Does it Taste Like a Good Wine?" in Sauve and Roy eds. *Research Handbook on Trade in Services* at 200.

[75] At [398].

[76] R. Gardiner, *Treaty Interpretation*, 2nd edn (Oxford University Press, 2017) at 274.

[77] N. Diebold, *Non-Discrimination in International Trade in Services* (Cambridge University Press, 2010) at 231.

3.3.2 *E-Commerce and Digital Trade*

The limited coverage of cross-border trade in legal services under the GATS does not mean that the innovative digital services discussed earlier in the chapter are beyond the reach of international law. It is the nascent global law of e-commerce that is most relevant here. E-commerce, sometimes more expansively described as digital trade, has become one of the most important forms of economic activity for many if not most firms around the world. While e-commerce is vital for firms that manufacture and export goods, it is even more so for firms that are focused on the delivery of services, such as those discussed earlier in this chapter.

In the late 1990s, WTO members agreed not to impose customs duties on electronic transmissions, a policy that has been extended several times. The Declaration on Global Electronic Commerce was adopted shortly thereafter to ensure that trade through e-commerce among WTO members continued to flourish. Four WTO agencies currently carry out what is known as the WTO Work Programme on E-Commerce, which was adopted in 1998 during the Second Ministerial Conference. Together, these bodies examine all trade-related issues associated with global electronic commerce, including issues identified by members. Cross-border legal services fall within the definition of electronic commerce, as specified by the Work Programme: "the term 'electronic commerce' is understood to mean the production, distribution, marketing, sale or delivery of goods and services by electronic means." The Work Programme further required that various bodies within the WTO, including the GATS Council, explore all trade-related issues to global e-commerce.[78] It was established that the GATS does apply to the delivery of a service electronically through digital telecommunications, although it does not apply to the delivery of a good that was merely ordered through telecommunications.

GATS disciplines clearly extend to services that are supplied electronically, such as the innovative legal services firms noted earlier in the chapter. In the early GATS decision US-Gambling, the WTO panel report confirmed that Mode 1 supply of services covers all means of delivery, including over the Internet.[79] More recently, in the China–Audiovisual Products case mentioned earlier, the panel determined that services commitments under the GATS extend to those that are delivered in nonphysical form,

[78] Declaration on Global Electronic Commerce, WT/MIN(98)/DEC/2 (25 May 1998).

[79] Panel Report, United States – Measures Affecting the Cross-Border Supply of Gambling and Betting Services, WT/DS285/R (10 November 2004).

again such as through the Internet.[80] In this sense, it is clear that the WTO's dispute settlement system has broadened the reach of GATS commitments as they were envisioned when the agreement was concluded in 1994, before the era of global internet commerce. Still, as was noted earlier, the extent to which the GATS can accommodate new technologies that underpin cross-border services trade is unclear. For example, search engines play a central role in assisting consumers to identify services suppliers for their needs, but search engines were not in existence when the classification systems were devised. Cloud services and internet platform services are other examples of services that are difficult to fit within historic classifications, which date back to 1991.[81] This classification scheme cross-references the Provisional Central Product Classification (CPC) of the United Nations, and although the CPC has undergone a number of revisions, WTO members have not agreed to update their commitments to reflect the revised CPC, potentially creating legal problems in terms of establishing GATS compliance.[82]

There is a considerable degree of legal uncertainty regarding the important question of whether online trade engages only GATS Mode 1 or also encompasses Mode 2, which is the subject of Chapter 4. There is further uncertainty about the applicability of the "likeness" test criteria to products and services available online and off-line. Generally speaking, there has been a worrying lack of progress at the WTO regarding digital trade strategy.[83]

It would seem that more comprehensive GATS-specific commitments for digital services are required, as called for in the WTO E-commerce Work Programme. Commentators urge that members be encouraged to schedule entire services sectors at the two-digit CPC level, covering all existing services as well as anticipating new ones. This could help to foreclose disagreements about the classification of services.[84] Since the

[80] Panel Report, China – Measures Affecting Trading Rights and Distribution Services for Certain Publications and Audiovisual Entertainment Products, WT/DS363/R (12 August 2009).

[81] World Trade Organization, "Services Sectoral Classification List", MTN.GNS/W/120 (10 July 1991).

[82] M. Wu, "Digital Trade-Related Provisions in Regional Trade Agreements: Existing Models and Lessons for the Multilateral Trade System" Inter-American Development Bank and International Centre for Trade and Sustainable Development (November 2017) at 4.

[83] Panel Report, US Gambling at [3.29] and Appellate Body Report, US-Gambling at [215]; M. Burri, "Designing Future-Oriented Multilateral Rules for Digital Trade" in Sauve and Roy eds. *Research Handbook on Trade in Services* at 341.

[84] Burri, ibid., at 349.

vocabulary used in GATS classification dates is now outdated, the negotiation and scheduling of specific commitments is frustrated. Again, there remains much debate about whether certain digital services are covered by existing commitments or whether they are entirely new.[85] Progress here may be achieved more readily under the plurilateral Trade in Services Agreement (TiSA), given the advanced nature of the economies involved and the smaller number of negotiating parties. One of the major problems with Doha Round negotiations on digital services was the fact that many WTO members lack the technological capacity for this kind of commerce, rendering these discussions less urgent.

The dearth of GATS commitments on Mode 1 supply of legal services and its questionable coverage of new services technologies does not mean that the WTO regime has no relevance to this sphere of economic activity. The WTO's Agreement on Technical Barriers to Trade (TBT), which governs technical regulations and standards, is also relevant for digital trade and cross-border supply of services. Standards governing telecommunications and broadband networks, interoperability and portability across carriers and networks, and laws on encryption and security, privacy, and data storage are susceptible to control under the TBT.[86] The market access commitments of the plurilateral Information Technology Agreement, which has been signed by eighty-two WTO members, have lowered barriers to trade in the equipment that facilitates digital trade, such as laptops, tablets, and monitors.

Furthermore, the GATS covers commitments in a number of services sectors that are critical for enabling digital trade, such as the many innovative forms of legal services that were explored earlier in this chapter. The most important of these are computer and related services and telecommunications. The WTO Annex on Telecommunications requires that each WTO member allow service suppliers to use any protocol of choice in the supply of telecommunications services.[87] Members incur these obligations whether or not they have scheduled commitments in the telecommunications sector. The Annex covers access to these services by the users, not the ability to enter the market to sell the services, which is covered by a members' schedule of GATS commitments.

It is evident from the lack of progress at the Ministerial Convention in late 2017 that there is limited support across the WTO membership

[85] Tuthill, "Cross-Border Data Flows" at 375.

[86] Wu, "Digital Trade-Related Provisions in Regional Trade Agreements" at 3.

[87] WTO Annex on Telecommunications, para. 5(a)(iii).

for a comprehensive multilateral agreement on digital trade. It seems more likely that a multiparty treaty underpinning the delivery of services such as legal services across international borders will take the form of a plurilateral or optional agreement similar to the WTO's Agreement on Government Procurement or the TiSA. If so, this raises the issue of whether there are certain digital trade preferences that a given party would be prepared to extend on a preferential, non-MFN basis to the other signatories of a plurilateral agreement, as is done currently under the Agreement on Government Procurement. There will most likely be considerable differences among the 164 WTO members concerning the scope of such an agreement; therefore the number of parties to an agreement would be small and possibly insufficient to achieve critical mass. Commentators have also advocated for the creation of a Digital Economy Trade Agreement (DETA) that would address all of the issues regarding e-commerce, including access to networks, data protection, and privacy. To be successful, such an undertaking would need to be adopted by enough WTO members and would need to preserve the MFN principle. DETA may gain traction if there is a lack of progress through the TiSA, particularly if it is pursued through the WTO in a plurilateral format among members that are more willing to make relevant commitments.[88]

It may be worthwhile instead to direct multilateral negotiations toward the more modest goal of digital trade facilitation, that is, assisting developing countries in improving their technological capacity to engage in this type of commerce and, in so doing, perhaps bolstering services such as Barefoot Law. The WTO has had some success in recent years with trade facilitation (for goods), and trade facilitation for services appears to be gaining momentum. Developing countries face significant barriers to cross-border supply of business services such as legal advice. The most critical constraint on business services suppliers in developing states is a lack of suitably qualified workers, which is likely the result of weak higher education and vocational training in the home country. There are also associated problems of access to finance to obtain the necessary qualifications and materials needed to run a business over the Internet.[89] Access to legal advice is yet another barrier. Furthermore, business services suppliers in developing countries suffer from the lack of recognition of qualifications by host countries' professional licensing authorities, requirements

[88] Burri, "Designing Future-Oriented Multilateral Rules for Digital Trade" at 355.

[89] P. Sauve and N. Ward, "A Trade in Services Waiver for Least Developed Countries" in Sauve and Roy eds. *Research Handbook on Trade in Services* at 554.

to have work verified or certified by professionals in the export market, rules specifying the sharing of fees between the home and host services suppliers, requirements to work in association with professionals in the export market, requirements to register with the licensing authorities in the export market, rules that prevent nonestablished services providers from offering services in the export market, and tax laws such as the imposition of withholding taxes or double taxation on income and profits.[90] Many of these constraints apply to the legal profession in one form or another in many countries. While minimizing these impediments is a worthy goal, it is unclear what kinds of binding commitments on digital trade facilitation would be most advantageous (e.g. consumer protection, paperless trading, data flows).[91] Trade facilitation measures for services trade through Mode 1 for developing country suppliers could consist of the simplification of visa, work permit, and registration requirements as well as simplified versions of exams being offered in the home country of the service provider where access to work is tied to previous competencies. Online testing could be particularly helpful in this regard, as could greater recognition of university qualifications obtained through distance learning courses.[92] Again, these preferential measures for suppliers from developing countries may be appropriate for less sophisticated forms of legal services, such as many of the ones that are delivered in a cross-border, digital environment.

The twenty-first century digital economy has led to the enactment of a wide range of regulations that have the potential to impede trade in services such as legal services. Perhaps the most conspicuous of these regulations are the new data protection rules found in the EU's GDPR, which was designed to harmonize data protection laws across the EU and went into force in May 2018.[93] The GDPR applies to all firms that process the personal data of people residing in the EU, regardless of the firm's location and regardless of whether the processing of the personal data takes place within the EU. It also applies to the processing of personal data of people in the EU by a firm that is not established in the EU when these activities relate to offering services to EU citizens. This has the potential to significantly affect law firms elsewhere in the world who serve clients that are located in the EU.

[90] Ibid. at 554–555.

[91] Wu, "Digital Trade-Related Provisions in Regional Trade Agreements" at 28–29.

[92] Sauve and Ward, "A Trade in Services Waiver for Least Developed Countries" at 572.

[93] Regulation (EU) 2016/679 of the European Parliament and of the Council (27 April 2016).

Several WTO members have implemented regulations aimed at protecting national security and suppressing criminal activity that takes place on the Internet, including fraud, cyberattacks, and terrorism. These laws cover issues such as electronic signatures and other forms of digital authentication as well as rules on the disclosure of source code for inspection by security agencies. Other WTO members have resisted these developments, making submissions to the WTO on what they consider excessive regulation of digital trade, including measures relating to server localization, consumer protection, and intellectual property rights. The US, for example, proposed the prohibition of digital customs duties to enable cross-border data flows as well as the prohibition of localization barriers. India has suggested that many countries do not fully appreciate the implications of negotiating binding rules regarding digital trade, particularly where such rules are permanent rather than being subject to renewal on a regular basis. These issues featured prominently in the 2017 WTO Ministerial Conference.[94]

3.3.3 *GATS General Exceptions: Privacy and Confidentiality*

At this point, it is apposite to draw attention to the capacity of the GATS, as the principle multilateral treaty that covers services, to accommodate measures that could restrict trade in legal services for public policy goals, such as those that are normally cited to justify the tight regulation of the legal profession. Such restrictions would apply to members' scheduled commitments on nondiscrimination and market access across all modes of supply, including cross-border supply. As was discussed earlier in the chapter, many companies view privacy as an important means of maintaining their clients' trust. This is especially the case in the context of legal services, where client information, as protected by the law of client privilege, can affect very serious legal entitlements and liabilities can affect very serious legal entitlements and liabilities. Today's legal practitioners must also be aware that failure to maintain privacy can lead to cybercrime, including identity theft and other security breaches. States in turn seek to preserve the privacy and confidentiality of citizens by enshrining these obligations on firms in law, even when this may restrict the delivery of online services, such as those of the innovative legal providers noted earlier in the chapter.

[94] K. Suneja, "India opposes e-commerce talks at WTO; submits document" The Economic Times (India) (4 December 2017).

The relevant provisions in this regard can be found in subsection (c) of the general exceptions article of GATS Article XIV, which states:

> nothing in this Agreement shall be construed to prevent the adoption or enforcement by any Member of measures
>
> (c) necessary to secure compliance with laws or regulations which are not inconsistent with the provisions of this Agreement including those relating to:
>
> (i) the prevention of deceptive and fraudulent practices or to deal with the effects of a default on services contracts;
>
> (ii) the protection of the privacy of individuals in relation to the processing and dissemination of personal data and the protection of confidentiality of individual records and accounts.

As was noted earlier in the chapter, this part of the GATS allows members to accommodate a range of policy goals based on social values, such as the integrity of a customer's personal information. Because client confidentiality is a pillar of the legal profession, restrictions based on this value would presumably be less susceptible to challenge as a trade-distortive measure. This is at the heart of the debate regarding the need to regulate the legal professions more closely than is necessary for other kinds of services providers. Somewhat paradoxically, it is precisely the integrity of the lawyer-client relationship that may act as a barrier to the further liberalization of cross-border trade in legal services. A WTO member state, acting at the behest of a legal regulator within its territory that seeks to protect the domestic legal services industry against foreign suppliers, could point to the sanctity of client confidentiality as a plausible reason for denying cross-border legal services providers, as there may be reasons why such data is less secure than that which passes between a lawyer and their client in a wholly domestic context. Of course, as with any trade-distortive measure, there may also be a protectionist motive behind restrictions on cross-border legal services provision. GATS Article XIV offers a framework in which services trade restrictions are assessed to identify their legitimacy in this regard.[95]

The requirement of the application of a trade-restrictive measure in a manner that does not lead to "arbitrary" or "unjustifiable" discrimination or, most tellingly, a "disguised restriction" on trade in services ensures that a member's right to invoke Article XIV general exceptions such as those

[95] T. Cottier, P. Delimatsis, and N. F. Diebold, "Article XIV GATS: General Exceptions" in R. Wolfrum, P. T. Stoll, and C. Feinaugle eds. *Max Planck Commentaries on World Trade Law*, WTO-Trade in Services, vol. 6 (Martinus Nijhoff Publishers, 2008).

related to privacy and confidentiality is exercised in a reasonable fashion. This means that the policy goal must not unduly frustrate the rights of other members. These controls on the use of Article XIV exceptions emanate from the principle of good faith, a generally recognized interpretive principle of public international law, which is designed to prevent the abuse of the general exceptions provision.[96]

The privacy and confidentiality exception to the GATS was examined by the WTO Appellate Body in the Argentina–Financial Services dispute,[97] which concerned allegedly discriminatory practices employed by Argentina in taxation measures imposed on services suppliers that did not exchange information with Argentina for fiscal transparency purposes. Here, the Appellate Body stated that a measure can be said to "secure compliance" with specific laws or regulations (as specified in Article XIVc) when its design reveals that it secures compliance with such rules even if the measure cannot be guaranteed to achieve this result with absolute certainty. This view evidently grants members fairly wide latitude in using privacy and confidentiality rules as a justification to impede cross-border services. Still, there remains the issue of whether the measure can be deemed to be "necessary" to secure compliance. In other words, the relationship between the measure and the aim must be sufficiently proximate. In the case of Argentina's taxation measures, the Appellate Body agreed with the panel that the application of the measure constituted arbitrary and unjustifiable discrimination because it did not satisfy this test. In keeping with the case law under the GATS (and GATT) general exceptions, given the stringency of the necessity test, it would appear to be exceedingly difficult for a WTO member to argue that various public policy measures relating to client interests could justify trade restrictions.

3.4 Regional Regulation of Cross-Border Trade in Legal Services

In recent years, much of the focus of international economic law has shifted away from the multilateral arena to the regional one. The extent to which this approach to regulation has been applied to cross-border trade in legal services will be considered here.

[96] Gardiner, *Treaty Interpretation* at 176.

[97] Argentina – Measures Relating to Trade in Goods and Services WT/DS453/AB/R (9 May 2016).

3.4.1 Cross-Border Trade in Legal Services Commitments in Regional Trade Agreements

As with the other modes of services delivery to be explored in this book, very few RTAs contain commitments to liberalize Mode 1 of legal services beyond the level secured under the WTO. Many states may have forgone negotiation efforts in this area because of the belief that this kind of services trade would be difficult to control in practice. GATS-like RTAs that adopt a positive list approach do not make any commitments that have not been actively included by parties in specific commitments. These are normally annexed to the text of the main treaty. Some RTAs merely incorporate relevant GATS provisions into their text, as in the Legal Services chapter of the European Free Trade Association (EFTA) and the Central American States FTA.[98] This means that where commitments on cross-border supply of legal services have not been made, the relevant state would in theory be free to enact measures denying suppliers the capacity to export legal services across borders via the Internet to consumers overseas, although enforcement of such measures against suppliers or consumers seems impracticable. States using a negative list approach for the application of commitments to specific sectors agree to apply nondiscrimination and market access to each and every service sector unless expressly excluded in a list, again normally attached as an annex. Agreements adopting this method establish "standstill provisions" in that they create exceptions for existing listed restrictions for services such as legal services.[99] The North American Free Trade Agreement (NAFTA) adopts this approach. It is worth noting that this agreement led to an enormous increase in cross-border delivery of legal services among Canada, the US, and Mexico, particularly in the early years of NAFTA.[100] Because, as was noted earlier, few WTO members bothered to schedule Mode 1 commitments for legal services under the GATS in negative list treaties, cross-border legal services would be permitted by default, explaining the success of NAFTA in this regard.

Under the plurilateral TiSA, National Treatment commitments are to be scheduled by using a negative list approach, while a positive list approach is applied for Market Access commitments. Although the future of TiSA is unclear at the time of writing, it is likely that Mode 1 supply of legal services will be unrestricted (not listed for National Treatment and listed

[98] See Chapter 4.

[99] S. Moritsch, "Research Paper: Liberalization of Trade in Legal Services: FTAs and Beyond GATS Commitments" International Bar Association [undated] at 5.

[100] Chapman and Tauber, "Liberalizing International Trade in Legal Services" at 949.

for Market Access). Finally, unlike the GATS, some FTAs include a "local presence" clause forbidding parties to require respective service providers to establish or maintain a representative office or any form of enterprise, or to impose residency requirements as a condition for the cross-border provision of a service.[101]

3.4.2 E-Commerce and Digital Trade

As was noted earlier in the chapter, cross-border legal services are a form of e-commerce and therefore rely on the international laws governing this type of trade. Whereas there has been a lack of progress at the WTO with regard to e-commerce and digital trade, the situation is somewhat different at the bilateral and regional levels. These developments have the potential to enlarge the cross-border delivery of legal services. Market access for various services sectors through RTAs can affect digital trade, particularly in the context of Mode 1 supply.

Approximately half of all WTO members have at least one RTA with an e-commerce chapter. Several WTO members have included such material only in the context of RTAs negotiated through regional integration initiatives such as the Association of South East Asian Nations (ASEAN), the Caribbean Forum (CARIFORUM), or the Gulf Cooperation Council (GCC). The first RTA to include a dedicated chapter on e-commerce was the Australia-Singapore FTA of 2003. A few earlier agreements contained one or more limited provisions relating to e-commerce, including the US-Jordan FTA and the GCC. Commitments relating to e-commerce were often contained in chapters relating to specific sectors, such as financial or telecommunications services. After the Australia-Singapore FTA went into force, several other RTAs followed that contained full e-commerce chapters, including the US-Chile FTA that entered into force in 2004. As of late 2017, there were at least sixty-nine RTAs that include an e-commerce chapter or articles(s) dedicated to e-commerce. Developing countries appear to be somewhat less eager to include e-commerce commitments in their RTAs, perhaps reflecting their lack of capacity in this field of economic activity. Brazil, India, Nigeria, and South Africa have been reluctant to commit to RTAs with extensive digital trade provisions. However, the Costa Rica–Columbia FTA does include an extensive e-commerce chapter that covers issues such as consumer protection. This agreement can be contrasted with that of the EU-Vietnam FTA, which has very limited

[101] E.g., NAFTA Art. 1205 or Art. 8.5 of the Singapore-Taiwan FTA (ASTEP) of 19 April 2014.

e-commerce coverage. A number of large trade agreements that are currently under negotiation contain provisions relevant to digital trade in services, including the TiSA, the Regional Comprehensive Economic Partnership, and the Japan-EU FTA. The Comprehensive and Progressive Agreement for Trans-Pacific Partnership (CPTPP) also contains a chapter on digital trade that focuses on nondiscrimination and transparency.

The scope of e-commerce and digital trade provisions in RTAs is highly variable, with some recent RTAs addressing a wide range of digital trade issues, including data localization and the treatment of source code, and others that simply specify that there will be no customs duties for e-commerce transactions combined with cooperation between regulatory authorities. Over time, the scope of e-commerce provisions in RTAs has generally expanded to cover a broader range of issues, which is unsurprising, given the increasingly large role that digital commerce is playing in the global economy. Earlier RTAs tended not to include material that addressed data localization directly. More recent RTAs have tended to restrict the use of these types of measures. Generally speaking, RTAs involving an advanced economy are more likely to cover a broader range of digital trade issues.[102] A number of RTAs require that signatories commit to adopting or maintaining domestic laws and regulations covering electronic transactions. This typically consists of a binding commitment, although in some cases, there is only a promise to adopt these measures as soon as is practicable.[103]

Electronic authentication technologies have an important role in facilitating digital trade. This is perhaps even more the case for legal services, given the need to validate identity and nationality for many legal documents and to address concerns about money laundering. The authentication mechanism typically takes the form of an electronic signature, which is essentially the digital equivalent of the handwritten version that is needed for physical goods. While there is a pressing need to ensure that adopted technologies are secure, laws that unduly restrict the use of digital authentication can act as barriers to digital trade. One study showed that digital authentication rules can be found in approximately half of all RTAs, including some that have been concluded among developing countries.[104]

E-commerce chapters of RTAs make express reference to the need to ensure consumer protection, which is of key importance given that this

[102] Wu, "Digital Trade-Related Provisions in Regional Trade Agreements" at 7.

[103] E.g., the ASEAN–Australia–New Zealand FTA.

[104] Wu, "Digital Trade-Related Provisions in Regional Trade Agreements" at 15.

tends to be positioned as the chief justification for regulating the legal profession. A small number of RTAs contain a binding obligation that requires the government of the signatory states to adopt or maintain consumer protection laws, the implication being that e-commerce poses distinct threats to consumers who may not be able to verify the authenticity of the suppliers that they use.[105] Approximately one in three RTAs contains a provision that requires signatories to protect the personal information of users of e-commerce. For example, the Australia-Singapore FTA states that each party shall adopt or maintain a legal framework that provides for the protection of personal information while taking into account the principles and guidelines of relevant international bodies.[106] States may comply with this obligation in various ways, including comprehensive or sector-specific privacy laws, personal information or personal data protection laws, or laws that provide for the enforcement of voluntary undertakings on privacy by enterprises.[107] These types of provisions are most common in APEC countries (which have endorsed the APEC Privacy Framework).[108] Future EU RTAs may begin to contain these types of commitments, given the growing awareness of the importance of data protection and the adoption of the EU's GDPR in 2018.

Clearly, transferring data across international borders is an essential enabling technology for e-commerce and digital trade. The use of cloud-based storage by many service providers has further intensified this process. International legal commitments facilitating international data transfer have in turn become key features of RTAs. The US-Korea FTA was the first treaty to have a specific provision aimed at ensuring the free flow of data across international borders. It was phrased in terms of refraining "from imposing or maintaining unnecessary barriers to electronic information flows across borders".[109] Unfortunately, the FTA does not define a necessary restriction on information flows and therefore is essentially nonbinding. The CPTPP is somewhat more ambitious, with signatory states agreeing that each party "shall allow the cross-border transfer of information by electronic means, including personal information, when

[105] Trans-Pacific Partnership, Art. 14.7.2 and Australia-Singapore FTA, Art. 8.3.

[106] Australia-Singapore FTA, Art. 9.

[107] Australia-Singapore FTA, Chapter 14, fn. 6. Identical language can be found in the TPP Art. 9.2.

[108] Asia-Pacific Economic Cooperation, "APEC Privacy Framework", www.apec.org/Publications/2005/12/ APEC-Privacy-Framework.

[109] US-Korea FTA, Art. 15.8.

this activity is for the conduct of the business of a covered person."[110] The term "covered person" includes a covered investment as defined in the CPTPP's investment chapter, an investor of a CPTPP party other than a financial institution, or a service supplier of a party as defined by the CPTPP's services chapter.[111] Accordingly, this would apply to legal services suppliers such as traditional law firms.

The dominant approach to ensuring cross-border information flows as a view to supporting e-commerce and digital trade is simply to promote regulatory cooperation in the area. This can be seen, for example, in some of Canada's FTAs, such as those with Peru and South Korea, in which parties "affirm the importance of ... working together to maintain cross-border flows of information as an essential element in fostering a vibrant environment for electronic commerce."[112] This type of language is also common in Latin American FTAs.[113]

The EU-Korea FTA contains a key provision regarding privacy, with each party reaffirming its commitment to protect fundamental rights and freedom of individuals. This requires the parties to adopt adequate safeguards to the protection of privacy, in particular with regard to the transfer of personal data. This agreement specifically refers to OECD Guidelines on the Protection of Privacy and Transborder Flows of Personal Data as well as the Guidelines for the Regulation of Personal Data Files.[114] The US-Korea PTA was the first trade agreement to include language relating to the free flow of information. Article 15.8 specifies that "parties shall endeavour to refrain from imposing or maintain unnecessary barriers to electronic information flows across borders."

A number of recently concluded RTAs contain chapters with horizontal disciplines on e-commerce. These agreements typically consist of general principles regarding consumer protection as well as specific disciplines. A good example of an advanced e-commerce agreement can be found in the Australia-Korea RTA. This agreement requires parties to adopt or maintain measures regulating electronic commerce taking into account the UNCITRAL Model Law on Electronic Commerce as well as other international standards, guidelines, and recommendations. Parties are also obliged to maintain measures to protect consumers who are engaged in

110 Trans-Pacific Partnership, Art. 14.11.2.

111 Trans-Pacific Partnership, Art. 14.1.

112 E.g., Canada-Colombia FTA, Art. 1507; Canada-Peru FTA, Art. 1508.

113 Costa Rica–Colombia FTA, Art. 16.7; Chile-Colombia FTA, Art. 12.5.

114 These have been revised as the Revised Guidelines on the Protection of Privacy and Transborder Flows of Personal Data (OECD, Paris, 2013).

e-commerce.[115] Advances in the development of material on e-commerce in bilateral agreements have been cited as an indication of future progress in terms of developing disciplines on domestic regulation,[116] which will be explored further in Chapter 8.

Finally, it should be noted that GATS-style general exceptions can be found in many RTAs that cover cross-border services.[117] Given the evident difficulty in satisfying general exception tests under WTO case law (in particular in relation to the chapeau) and despite the fact that we are living in an era characterized by ever-intensifying concerns about privacy and confidentiality, which are foundational to the nature of the work performed by legal services providers, states will struggle to point to these matters as valid impediments to cross-border trade in legal services. As was noted in Chapter 2, some FTAs entitle parties to require that service suppliers maintain a local address,[118] which could be problematic for firms that are seeking to tap into international markets through an internet presence.

3.5 Conclusion

The modern era of "big data" coupled with gradual advances in machine learning and artificial intelligence underscores the importance of data within the context of commercial and many other relationships. This is even more so in the case of legal services, in which data can carry legal obligations and, in some cases, liability and in which duties of confidentiality are fundamental to the role of the lawyer. Several states have passed laws regulating how companies that obtain this data from citizens must handle it. This can include data localization measures requiring that the data be stored in the state's territory or not be transmitted outside of its jurisdiction. Clearly, such measures can impede the flow of services, including legal services, across international borders. Legal professionals argue that these rules raise operational costs and frustrate their capacity to deliver cost-effective services to clients located in other countries.

Cross-border trade in legal services will continue to expand in tandem with the evolution and maturation of digital trade, adopting new forms of business driven by advances in telecommunications and nascent artificial

[115] Article 15.4.
[116] M. Krajewski, "Domestic Regulation and Services Trade: Lessons from Regional and Bilateral Free Trade Agreements" in Sauve and Roy eds. *Research Handbook on Trade in Services* at 242.
[117] E.g., CETA Art. 28.3(2).
[118] E.g., CETA Art. 9.3 b).

intelligence. Many of these innovative services, such as those relating to highly routinized work requiring less expertise, will fall outside the scope of the classic understanding of legal services and will call for regulations in other spheres, such as e-commerce. For the most part, WTO members did not schedule restrictions on cross-border legal services under the GATS, leaving this sector, at least in its classic form, open to the range of innovative providers that we see today. This approach has been broadly duplicated at the regional level, with limited commitments in RTAs covering cross-border supply of legal services. With respect to the arguably more relevant e-commerce aspects of cross-border legal services through telecommunications, there appears to be a reasonably strong response, ensuring a modest level of liberalization for this burgeoning industry. Further progress is needed both bilaterally and multilaterally on key issues relating to digital trade, including the protection of privacy but also more fundamental issues concerning the promotion of open networks and ensuring interconnection for developing countries.[119]

The commodification of routine legal services will obviously be lamented by some seasoned legal practitioners who see their hold on the legal profession slipping away. Meanwhile, clients will see this as a positive development because it will enhance affordability. While the perennial concern about safeguarding clients' interests in this new environment is genuine, resistance to international suppliers and to technologies such as online delivery of legal services from within the profession has, for the most part, predominantly reflected self-interest and the fear of loss of income and prestige. Consumers and providers alike are concerned about the application of professional responsibility rules such as those regarding confidentiality to the new arena of digital trade in legal services, which exists apart from formal market access and nondiscrimination commitments under international law instruments such as the GATS. It is unclear whether the regulatory framework for privacy and data protection is fit to address these issues.

On a more optimistic note, the liberalization of international legal services markets through cross-border delivery should increase the competitive pressures on legal services suppliers, and this may foster further innovation in the nature of the legal services.[120] With law firms under tremendous pressure to maintain their client bases as a consequence of alternative business structures and the availability of rudimentary legal information on the Internet that can be adapted and delivered by

[119] Burri, "Designing Future-Oriented Multilateral Rules for Digital Trade".

[120] Hadfield, *Rules for a Flat World* at 228–230.

nonexperts, there is an increasing emphasis on business strategies such as outsourcing. Still, because many of the technological advances in the delivery of legal services across borders discussed in this chapter are conducive to significant economies of scale, they will be more feasible for larger law firms or legal services providers that can recover the fixed costs for setting up the relevant systems.[121] This could marginalize smaller suppliers, such as those from developing states that are seeking to enter global markets. Moreover, despite advances in technology and the capacity to obtain legal services from multiple jurisdictions through the Internet, many clients will continue to prefer face-to-face advice,[122] much as they prefer to go into bank branches rather than using ATMs. If the forms and advice offered through services such as Legal Zoom and others are not currently as good as a live lawyer, it is anticipated that these services will improve over time as experience leads to changes to the programs.[123] Clients' acceptance of more fluid, ad hoc interactions with their lawyers is more likely to grow alongside that of the "digital nomad" phenomenon in which self-employed individuals serve customers around the world over the Internet without a base in a particular jurisdiction.

It is important to consider the expansion of innovative, cross-border legal services in light of those in the legal profession globally. Trends suggest that the demand for law graduates is considerably below the quantity that are produced each year by law schools across the developed world.[124] Yet demographic data indicate that the world's future population growth will be concentrated in the developing world. As they modernize their economies, emerging markets may need more lawyers than their own law schools can produce. The supply of legal services across borders by lawyers in places such as the US and Europe to clients in Southeast Asia, for example, may be a vital means of sustaining the legal profession in years to come. Countries should be aware of this trend and seek to liberalize Mode 1 delivery for legal services accordingly, both directly under the GATS and RTAs (in relation to market access and nondiscrimination) and in relation to more comprehensive commitments in e-commerce and digital trade. Progress on this front has been slow, but the increasing recognition by policy makers of the importance of this matter is encouraging.

[121] Semple, *Legal Services Regulation at the Crossroads* at 168–169.

[122] Legal Services Consumer Panel (UK) "Tracker Survey 2013 Briefing Note 3: Satisfaction with Legal Services" 6 (2013).

[123] Barton, *Glass Half Full* at 212.

[124] Tamanaha, *Failing Law Schools*.

4

Consumption Abroad and Export Restrictions on Trade in Legal Services

4.1 Introduction

Businesses seeking new markets overseas will be increasingly compelled to employ legal services providers in these jurisdictions out of convenience and the credible belief that these suppliers will have greater familiarity with the laws of the state in which their operations are located. This tendency is further driven by the momentum of globalization, which obliges business to operate across jurisdictions, in many cases seeking legal advisors other than those of their home jurisdiction, who may lack sufficient expertise in an international regulatory environment. Furthermore, just as legal services providers in the future will need to form stronger bonds with their clients to survive in an environment of intense competitive pressures, clients will expect their legal services providers to maintain regular contact. While this may be achieved through the Internet to a degree, many clients will expect to deal with their legal advisors in person and will be prepared to travel do to so. Trade in legal services through Mode 2 (consumption abroad, in which the consumer travels to another jurisdiction) may be the result of differences in the quality of legal services between jurisdictions or, relatedly, the relative openness of the jurisdiction to foreign supply. Clients who require legal services but cannot obtain it in their own jurisdiction will be motivated to seek it elsewhere. Moreover, if the law of the individual's home country specifies that foreign law firms cannot provide any legal advice whatsoever, as in India, yet the quality of the domestic law firms is poor, mobile consumers will go abroad to hire legal professionals to serve their needs.

In view of these trends, this chapter will explore the ways in which states can enhance their capacity to receive legal services consumers through regulatory initiatives at the national and international levels. It will consider the phenomenon of centres of legal excellence, which have been established in several jurisdictions around the world for this purpose. The second part of this chapter will examine the related and in some respects complementary approach taken by some countries to circumscribe the outward movement of their legal professionals and inhibit the export of legal services, in some cases with a view towards better serving domestic consumers or as a consequence of a more general aversion to liberalization in legal services. This discussion necessitates an analysis of the important issue of "brain drain", meaning the detrimental migration of professionals in large numbers, which may be a potential downside to the unchecked liberalization of trade in legal services, particularly from developed countries that are experiencing labour shortages.

4.2 Importing Legal Services

One of the consequences of liberalization of trade in legal services, which has proceeded for the most part in tandem with globalization, has been an increase in the supply of lawyers. For example, the recent opening of legal markets in some countries, such as Japan and Korea, has led to an expansion in the number of domestic lawyers in these countries who are in need of clients to serve. To the extent to which this process has outstripped need at home (as may be the case in countries with stagnant economies or static population growth), many of these individuals will seek opportunities internationally. Alternatively, demand in the country where supply originates can be augmented through efforts aimed at attracting foreign consumers. Indeed, efforts to stimulate Mode 2 supply of services may be viewed as viable responses to tight restrictions on the entry of foreign legal services suppliers in other countries, particularly given that market access is not always offered on a reciprocal basis. This section will consider some of the regulatory instruments available to governments to increase Mode 2 legal services, finishing with a consideration of whether such initiatives could transgress obligations that states incur under public international law.

First, it should be stated that a measure that applies neither to a service nor to its supplier but nevertheless affects trade in services would likely be caught by GATS disciplines, requiring assessment under National Treatment, Most Favoured Nation, and other provisions. A restriction on Mode 2 trade in services would likely be one that applies to the consumer, given that the service is consumed abroad and the supplier is located outside the jurisdiction of the importing member.[1] For example, regulations might be established in such a way that the purchase of a foreign service would result in a penalty of some kind. Alternatively, Mode 2 trade of

[1] Diebold, *Non-Discrimination in International Trade in Services* at 212.

services could be restricted by laws that did not recognize foreign permits or qualifications in order to prevent a country's own citizens from consuming these qualifications abroad.[2] As with Mode 1, the impracticality of placing these types of restrictions on the movement of consumers resulted in very few Mode 2 commitments being made by WTO members under the GATS or in regional trade agreements (RTAs). Members did not schedule Mode 2 legal services because such restrictions were considered unenforceable.

4.2.1 Improvements in the Quality of Domestic Legal Services Providers

The capacity to supply services through Mode 2 to consumers in the export market is determined by factors such as the business environment and associated reputational effects as well as the availability of a suitably skilled workforce. These issues can be particularly problematic for developing countries, which face additional barriers as foreign markets because of safety and security as well as language incompatibility. Enhancing the competitiveness of services in general is a vital policy objective of many countries, and legal services are no exception. Domestic enabling factors include institutions, governance, labour skills, management and entrepreneurial skills, and trade-related infrastructure.[3] The adoption of these policies will tend to be in line with obligations that states have undertaken under international law, including treaties covering labour (such as those of the International Labour Organization) and those that promise a transparent regulatory environment free from corruption and that uphold the rule of law. These requirements are typically found in International Investment Agreements (IIAs) and are captured by standards such as those providing for fair and equitable treatment and transparency. Customary international law principles on transparency[4] will also foster these kinds of regulatory initiatives, which will help to attract foreign consumers seeking services such as legal ones.

The phenomenon of legal pluralism, in which economic actors are subjected to legal regimes imposed variously by national, subnational, and international regimes, calls for legal services that adapt to the procedural

[2] Ibid. at 213.

[3] S. Saez and D. Taglioni, "Nurturing the Competitiveness of Services Exports: Metrics and Policy Options" in Sauve and Roy eds. *Research Handbook on Trade in Services* at 148.

[4] Peters, "Towards Transparency as a Global Norm" in Bianchi and Peters eds. *Transparency in International Law*.

mechanisms and institutions that have arisen as a consequence of these overlapping legal systems.[5] Legal services must adjust to these trends, which governments in turn accommodate through reforms to their legal systems. As will be seen later in the chapter, jurisdictions that seek to become major centres of international legal practice are more likely to adopt legal rules that are favourable to foreign consumers. Because this legal framework will be viewed as advantageous, legal practitioners in the host country will aim to render legal services involving the host country's laws. It follows that rules on the scope of legal practice and on rights of association (e.g., partnership with foreign law firms) in such jurisdictions will allow such firms to supply these kinds of services. Furthermore, locations that want to attract foreign clients will tend to avoid gratuitous restrictions of a formal or procedural nature.[6] This approach is similar to that of jurisdictions that simplify procedures for starting and operating businesses with a view towards stimulating economic activity.

Given the finite but growing supply of internationally mobile clients seeking legal services, competition among jurisdictions for consumers has intensified. Implementing the policies of the kind noted earlier may not be enough. Jurisdictions must now signal their expertise as destinations for legal clients. This has resulted in an increasing emphasis on standards. To a degree, this is captured by professional licensing itself, which, as was noted in Chapter 1, has been justified on the basis of redressing information asymmetry between consumers and suppliers regarding expertise. Some jurisdictions maintain other demarcations of expertise in the provision of legal services, perhaps most notably the Queen's Council (QC) designation in the UK. Some legal process outsourcing firms, discussed in Chapter 3, have achieved ISO (International Organization for Standardization) designation, denoting the firm's proven competency in various relevant administrative skills.[7] It is not difficult to envision a time when there may be a global ranking of legal services provision similar to that of the World Bank's Doing Business index. For the time being, while the World Bank's index assesses regulatory hurdles associated with starting and maintaining a business, it does not consider the extent to which legal advice is available to deal with these issues.[8] The World Justice Project calculates a Rule of Law Index that considers access and affordability of

[5] Berman, *Global Legal Pluralism*.

[6] Cone, "Legal Services in the Doha Round" at 42.

[7] R. Burnett, *Outsourcing IT – The Legal Aspects* (Routledge, 2009) at 168.

[8] www.doingbusiness.org/rankings (accessed March 2018).

civil (as well as criminal) justice. However, it does not appear to include data on the skills or prices of legal services providers.[9]

With somewhat deficient global standardization of legal services, one of the ways in which jurisdictions may be able to attract clients to purchase legal services in their territory is through enhancing the quality of the legal training at law schools to produce graduates who have not only experience in international law, but also familiarity with the laws of other countries. Improving legal education can also help to retain talented law graduates who might otherwise choose to emigrate, possibly because they want to be exposed to other legal systems or work cultures. Enhancements of this nature would place graduates in a position in which they would be able to provide higher-quality legal assistance in relation to the laws of the client's home state, as well as in relation to laws of third states. This goal is precisely why reforms to legal education around the world have focused on the value in training lawyers with a transnational perspective.[10] A few examples from Asia are worth mentioning.

The law school of the National University of Singapore has a globally oriented curriculum that emphasizes subjects that consider Asian and Islamic perspectives on the law.[11] Taiwanese law schools have begun to respond to the need to prepare future lawyers to handle international matters and to interact with clients from different cultures by modifying their curriculum with an internationalist aim.[12] In an effort to rectify what was viewed as a severe shortage in law students capable of serving the needs of international clients, China's 600 law schools adopted a more globalized approach to their curricula.[13] Although China is not yet a leading destination for foreign clients seeking legal services, such reforms to its legal education were designed to provide law students with exposure to the legal systems of other countries within a domestic setting, in some cases through visits by foreign experts.[14] While these efforts may be designed primarily to help domestic law firms establish themselves in more competitive

[9] https://worldjusticeproject.org/our-work/wjp-rule-law-index/wjp-rule-law-index-2016/factors-rule-law/civil-justice-factor-7 (accessed March 2018).

[10] R. Lutz, "Reforming Approaches to Educating Transnational Lawyers: Observations from America", 61 *Journal of Legal Education* 449 (2012).

[11] S. Chesterman, "Doctrine, Perspectives and Skills for Global Practice", in C. Gane and R. Hui Huang eds. *Legal Education in the Global Context* (Ashgate, 2016) at 80–82.

[12] M. Shieh and Y. Chen, "Reforming Taiwan's Legal Education in the Age of Globalization" in Gane and Hui Huang eds. *Legal Education in the Global Context*.

[13] L. Xiaohong, "Cultivating High-Quality Internationalized Legal Talents under Globalization" in Gane and Hui Huang eds. *Legal Education in the Global Context*.

[14] Ibid. at 93.

environments overseas, they will also enhance the capacity of domestic firms to serve clients entering these jurisdictions from abroad. This is not to say that foreign businesses are establishing themselves in these countries for the quality of the legal services that are found there, but firms that have settled in the countries for other reasons (e.g., favourable tax environment, access to larger markets) may be more inclined to use local law firms than those in their home jurisdiction or in a third state when the quality of the legal education has produced more capable practitioners.

Distance learning programs have given law students from around the world access to high-quality education in the common law tradition, enabling students to make themselves more business-ready for international clients. These programs, which are delivered remotely over the Internet, tend not to be accredited in the sense that they do not grant degrees that are recognized by professional regulators such as law societies or bar associations. This is likely because of the traditional expectation that a law degree must involve some degree of training in oral advocacy as well as the requirement to pass written examinations that can be strictly invigilated. The American Bar Association (ABA) has not yet accredited a JD program that is delivered entirely through distance learning, although some US law schools, such as William and Mary, offer law degrees that have distance learning components along with in-class teaching. One exception to this general rule is the qualifying LLB degree at the Open University in the UK, which is taught entirely online. LLM programs, many of which have international pathways[15], are more naturally conducive to an online format because they are nonqualifying and can be better tailored to a student's career goals. Massive Open Online Courses (MOOCs), which are not yet offered for credit towards any formal legal qualification, are nonetheless highly popular, offering students an experience similar to that of a distance learning for credit program, typically without charge and often taught by world-class scholars. It may be only a matter of time before these courses will also become credit bearing and ultimately satisfy the educational requirement for qualification to legal practice. Regulators may resist this type of education, given the risks of academic misconduct on the part of students in environments where examinations cannot be administered in person and plagiarism on assignments remains a perennial problem.[16]

[15] E.g., the International Business Law Distance Learning LLM at the author's own institution: City, University of London.

[16] J. Riley, "The Challenge of Massive Open Online Courses (MOOCs) to Traditional Legal Education: The Australian Experience" in Gane and Hui Huang eds. *Legal Education in the Global Context.*

Nonaccreditation notwithstanding, the success of distance learning programs in law is testimony to the fact that nonmobile students have some expectation that these programs will serve mobile clients.

Providing a regulatory environment in which technology can enable legal services appears to be a vital tool for jurisdictions to attract clients seeking legal services. For example, Singapore launched its Future Law Innovation Program in early 2018 with a view towards encouraging local law firms to adopt innovative technology in tandem with entrepreneurs through collaborations that have been termed "lawtech" start-ups. Part of this initiative is to enhance the digitalization of the legal profession with a view towards enabling smaller law firms and sole practitioners to better serve clients from abroad.[17] In order to foster such innovations, such activities will most likely require strong protection of intellectual property. In this regard, the importance of the WTO Trade Related Aspects of Intellectual Property (TRIPs) agreement, which ensures a minimum level of protection for a wide range of intellectual property rights, should not be underestimated as an instrument of support for modern legal services. If these types of high-tech legal services do draw foreign clients into jurisdictions such as Singapore, the host countries would be well advised to pursue RTAs with strong intellectual property protections and institutions. In this regard, it is worth drawing attention to the fact that the ASEAN Framework Agreement on Intellectual Property Cooperation exceeds the obligations of TRIPS in a number of respects.[18]

4.2.2 Centres of Legal Excellence

Members of the legal profession, including the judiciary, often point out that legal systems should not be in competition with each other because this is inimical to the interests of clients. Instead, judges, as instruments of the justice system, should collaborate with one another across jurisdictions to exchange ideas to improve their respective systems and, with them, international law itself.[19] Yet just as legal services in the future will need to embrace entrepreneurialism to compete in an ever-decreasing market,[20] a degree of competitive spirit should surely also be expected of states. This is

[17] M. Cross, "Singapore Lawyers Back National IT Plan" The Law Society Gazette (15 January 2018).

[18] N. Barizah, "The Development of ASEAN's Intellectual Property Rights Law: From TRIPS Compliance to Harmonization", 1 *Indonesia Law Review* 95 (2017) at 95–97.

[19] Vos, "The Future of the UK's Jurisdiction and English Law after Brexit" at [10].

[20] Barton, *Glass Half Full* at 223.

not regulatory arbitrage but rather conceiving the judicial system itself as a kind of business that must seek customers continuously to survive.

This view reflects the reality that consumption of legal services abroad is perhaps most closely associated with the jurisdictions that seek to promote themselves as centres of legal excellence for clients from abroad, especially in relation to settlement of disputes in commercial matters. Wealthy individuals in particular are often mobile in terms of where they seek legal representation and will draft contracts in the jurisdictions of courts or tribunals that they believe will issue favourable judgments or pressure beneficial settlements. Differences in the quality of the justice system, including both efficiency and competence of judges, or fundamental weaknesses in the home state's legal system itself (poorly defined rights and obligations) could prompt clients to seek a dispute resolution system in another country. At the same time, technological improvements have made dispute settlement in foreign courts more feasible. For example, e-filing technology may reduce the time that needs to be spent in the foreign jurisdiction through advance preparation online. Computer-assisted transcription and document display systems as well as electronic presentation of evidence, which precludes the need for oral advocacy, may be able to reduce the length of hearings,[21] again saving time and expense for foreign litigants.

England and Wales have exploited this need by developing their courts and, with them, the legal infrastructure to address these unserved clients, generating revenue for domestic lawyers who advise these foreign clients. The legal services industry generates £25.7bn annually for the UK economy, and two thirds of all claims issued in the commercial court in 2016 involved at least one litigant from outside the UK.[22] In recognition of the importance of legal services to the economy, the Law Society of England and Wales and the Ministry of Justice recently launched the Global Legal Centre campaign to promote the benefits of the law of England and Wales for contracts and to encourage the choice of English and Welsh courts for settling disputes, with London as the preferred location to resolve disputes through arbitration. This initiative included outreach activities overseas.[23] In 2015, corresponding to the 900th anniversary of the signing of the Magna Carta, the UK's legal community organized the Global Law Summit

[21] Susskind, *Tomorrow's Lawyers* at 108.

[22] E. Truss, "Legal Services at the Forefront of Global Britain" The Law Society Gazette (17 January 2017).

[23] www.lawsociety.org.uk/policy-campaigns/campaigns/global-legal-centre (accessed March 2018).

event, which was designed to showcase London's status as the world's premier law centre.[24] Such outreach projects have gained urgency since the UK's decision to leave the EU, which was set for April 2019 at the time of writing. Several European jurisdictions are seeking to divert clients away from the traditional centre of London by offering dispute resolution services in English. Germany, for example, plans to open an English-speaking commercial court in Frankfurt. Attempts to attract clients for Mode 2 services into the UK through extensive marketing campaigns may therefore be viewed as an effort simply to retain global market share.

Economic globalization has enlarged the role of informal dispute settlement systems, such as arbitration and mediation. Indeed, arbitration appears to be among the most sought-after forms of dispute settlement for travelling consumers of legal services. The emphasis on arbitration has occurred primarily because of the inability of conventional domestic court systems to respond effectively to the increasing volume of litigation, particularly of a transnational nature, to which globalization has unquestionably contributed.[25] It may also reflect the reality that governments are ill equipped to address challenges facing global economic actors through publicly funded court systems that are comparatively antiquated and inflexible in their delivery and therefore are poorly suited to deal with disputes that have an international dimension. Sophisticated arbitration and mediation are therefore crucial services that states, often in conjunction with the private sector, can offer on an internationally competitive basis. For example, the New York International Arbitration Center (NYIAC), which is located in what is arguably the world's second leading legal hub, was established to advance, strengthen, and promote the conduct of international arbitration in New York City under the laws of New York State. While it does not itself administer arbitrations or publish arbitration rules, NYIAC offers world-class infrastructure to support arbitrations and promotes the use of New York laws for international commercial contracts along with New York courts and arbitral institutions as for a dispute settlement.[26]

The success of New York and London notwithstanding, developing countries that lack sufficient natural resources to draw conventional foreign direct investment are ideally suited to focus on informal dispute settlement services such as commercial arbitration to attract Mode 2

[24] See, e.g., Truss, "Legal Services at the Forefront of Global Britain".

[25] H. Patrick Glenn, "Globalization and Dispute Resolution", 19 *Civil Justice Quarterly* 136–153 (April 2000).

[26] https://nyiac.org/about (accessed March 2018).

consumers. These Competitive Law Zones, as they have been described by some commentators, enable developing countries to become globally competitive in the provision of legal services through specialization, building legal infrastructure with the purpose of cornering a niche sector of the international legal services market.[27] The Dubai International Financial Centre (DIFC) is perhaps the best-known example of such a zone; it was established in the mid-2000s to bring in legal consumers from around the world. The DIFC offers a wide range of incentives, including tax and customs duties exemptions as well as an absence of any ownership restrictions or limits on the repatriation of profits. It has its own regulatory system for financial services, its own civil and commercial laws, and its own court system, with jurisdiction over any transactions or disputes taking place in the centre or between contracting parties anywhere in the world that choose to be governed by the DIFC's laws. The centre operates in English and has written codes based on Anglo-American legal principles. Court procedures are modelled on the London commercial courts, and judges use English precedent to decide cases. The judges who serve on the courts are former senior judges from England and other Commonwealth countries. Judgments of DIFC courts are enforceable in Dubai and internationally. While the DIFC legal system is based on that of wealthy common law countries, it operates more efficiently with faster resolution of disputes and greater accessibility, with simpler filing procedures and brief written judgments issued for all matters. The DIFC recently introduced plans to set up the world's first "Court of Future" in partnership with Microsoft to harness digital technology for case filing and management as well as trials.[28] The DIFC has already performed very well in providing a high-quality service to internationally mobile consumers of legal services.[29] Clearly, one of the advantages of the DIFC is that the risk to foreign consumers that the alien system will render results that are unfair or unenforceable in foreign jurisdictions is mitigated by the DIFC's need to preserve its reputation. As long as its legal system is furthering the overall success of the DIFC as a place to do business, which is in turn generating revenue for Dubai, there is very little chance that the rulers of Dubai will interfere with its proper functioning. The companies that use the system do not have to be there; as soon as they lose faith in the legal system, they can take their business elsewhere.[30]

[27] Hadfield, *Rules for a Flat World* at 335.

[28] E. Mekay, "Dubai Moves to Disrupt Legal Culture with Future Courts" International Bar Association (2 February 2018).

[29] Hadfield, *Rules for a Flat World* at 336–337.

[30] Ibid. at 339.

While not as well established as the DIFC, India has begun actively seeking to attract clients to its legal services market with a focus on international arbitration. The Indian government intends to establish the New Delhi International Arbitration Centre (NDIAC) to expand upon the existing International Centre for Alternative Dispute Resolution with a new Arbitration Chamber designed specifically to serve international clients. This project will include the creation of an Arbitration Academy to train arbitrators in India so that they can compete with those operating within other global arbitration centres. The overall aim of the NDIAC initiative is to make India "a hub of international arbitration".[31] Closer in concept to that of Dubai, the Singapore International Arbitration Centre (SIAC) has successfully positioned itself as a global legal centre, rising to the forefront of international commercial arbitration and offering world-class services to commercial disputants.[32] Other emerging markets centres, such as Astana in Kazakhstan, are seeking to follow this approach as a means of drawing commercial activities to their regions to stimulate development. These countries augment their capacity to import legal services with the intention of ultimately strengthening their capacity to export these services, the logic being that serving foreign clients will improve domestic legal services providers' competencies.

The centre of legal excellence strategy often arises out of initiatives to establish a regional financial services hub, as in Dubai and Singapore, each of which has been able to offer legal services such as arbitration throughout their respective regions in part by exploiting the fact that other countries in the region, such as China and India, have been closed to international legal services. Growth in the re-export of legal services has been possible in these hubs because of governmental policies designed to attract foreign law firms with a view towards laying the foundations for establishing a financial and legal services industry. This has led to the export of these services regionally to large emerging markets such as India, Malaysia, Korea, Indonesia, and Israel. Generally speaking, these countries maintain barriers to international legal services by either prohibiting foreign branches of law firms or having nationality requirements on legal services suppliers, causing them to export consumers of legal services under Mode 2.[33] Some of these issues will be explored in more detail in Chapter 5.

[31] "Bill Introduced in Lok Sabha to Create a New Arbitration Institution" The Hindu Times (India) (5 January 2018).

[32] www.siac.org.sg/ (accessed March 2018).

[33] Hook, "Sectoral Study on the Impact of Domestic Regulation on Trade in Legal Services" at 10.

4.2.3 Enhancement of the Domestic Legal Service Industry and Subsidization Issues

While primarily designed for foreign consumers, centres of legal excellence projects are unquestionably intended to showcase the skills of the domestic legal profession to the domestic business community, some members of which might be considering seeking legal services abroad. The concept of "buy local" is a familiar economic policy that is adopted, usually for political aims, to favour the sourcing of goods from as close to the consumer as possible in order to assist domestic suppliers. Most such policies are economically harmful because they force consumers to overspend and perpetuate inefficient commercial activity, leading to waste in one country and lost employment in others.[34] While "buy local" policies are not normally associated with services, in part because they do not resonate with well-organized manufacturing lobbies, they may be equally conveyed in a "hire locally" mentality. To some extent, this mentality underpins the centre of legal excellence model.

In considering well-organized efforts by countries to enhance the quality of their domestic legal services market with a view towards attracting foreign consumers, some thought must be given to the potential for such measures to be construed as "buy local"-style subsidization. In one sense, financial contributions to a domestic industry (legal services) grant a competitive advantage to the domestic supplier. Still, it is unlikely that governmental assistance to the civil justice infrastructure in legal hubs such as London or Dubai would fall within the definition of subsidy under the WTO Agreement on Subsidies and Countervailing Measures (ASCM), nor would it likely satisfy the requirement of specificity.[35] Furthermore, the ASCM does not cover governmental assistance provided to services suppliers; like the concept of "buy local", it is a goods-based agreement. RTAs with subsidies disciplines based on the language of the ASCM would be similarly excluded for these reasons. Domestic subsidy and state aid rules, such as those of the EU, would be unlikely to extend to the types of projects discussed earlier in the chapter because these legal hubs do not provide assistance directly to private sector firms. Rather, they are aimed at building up the infrastructure of the legal system itself, which is better seen as a public good, albeit one that has the potential to generate revenue for the firms that operate within it. Because the GATS prohibits discrimination

[34] "Buying Local Is More Expensive Than It Looks" The Economist (25 November 2017).
[35] Articles 1 and 2.

against like services suppliers (as well as services), it should restrict members from providing competitive advantages to their own suppliers.[36] This is the reason that most WTO members scheduled subsidy-specific horizontal limitations that allow them to grant subsidies to citizens or permanent residents. There are no subsidies commitments covering legal services listed under any members' GATS schedules. But again, centres of legal excellence do not grant assistance to the suppliers themselves; rather, they provide the general infrastructure of the justice system, so they would not be subject to GATS disciplines.

While the centres of legal excellence themselves are unlikely to fall within the scope of international disciplines on subsidies, it is conceivable that a state could offer foreign legal services providers such as global law firms preferential tax rates or other incentives as a means of attracting them to the jurisdiction with a view towards reaping the economic benefits of a global network of clients coming into the territory. Such strategies could fit within existing Free Trade Zone or other incentive regimes, including the potential for better than national treatment under some IIAs.[37] Becoming an attractive Mode 2 destination for consumers may rely on the jurisdiction's ability to attract foreign suppliers under Mode 3 or 4. Offering preferential tax rates for law firms or other legal services providers would be an unusual practice. It is not clear that this strategy has been adopted anywhere. This may be because legal practitioners are typically viewed as business support services rather than generators of economic activity in their own right, so they may not be seen as deserving of investment incentives.

4.3 Export Controls: Home State Barriers to the Internationalization of Legal Practice

This section turns to the opposite of stimulation of international demand for the supply of legal services within a jurisdiction, namely, the erection of barriers to the export of legal services internationally by home states. Whereas Section 4.2 considered efforts to make the home jurisdiction

[36] Guidelines for the Scheduling of Specific Commitments under the General Agreement on Trade in Services (GATS), S/L/92 (28 March 2001) at [16]. See also P. Poretti, "Waiting for Godot: Subsidy Disciplines in Services Trade" in M. Panizzon, N. Pohl, and P. Sauve eds. *GATS and the Regulation of International Trade in Services* (Cambridge University Press, 2008).

[37] See D. Collins, *Performance Requirements and Investment Incentives under International Economic Law* (Edward Elgar, 2015).

appealing to internationally mobile consumers, the second variety of regulatory strategy comprises those that aim to make the home jurisdiction more attractive to domestic suppliers, in effect dissuading these suppliers from opening law offices overseas. This kind of regulatory activity is not captured by one of the four modes of supply. However, it is arguably linked to Mode 2, inasmuch as maintaining the domestic supply of legal services suppliers could bolster the jurisdiction's ability to entice foreign consumers, although this outcome is unlikely to be the primary regulatory aim of an export-restrictive measure.

4.3.1 Varieties of Controls on Legal Services Export

Restrictions on the capacity of legal services providers to travel abroad to serve foreign clients may be justified on the basis that it strengthens the capacity of this sector to serve local clients. This may be cast in a positive light in terms of enhancing the rule of law and access to justice. Such providers will be compelled to make their services available to local citizens rather than to foreign clients that may pay higher fees.

The liberalization of legal services domestically, such as via the elimination or reduction in reserved areas of practice for non-lawyers, is closely linked to the liberalization of international legal markets, leading to outflows of legal professionals from a given jurisdiction. In tightly controlled markets, qualified lawyers, holding a monopoly on the provision of legal services, may have little incentive to seek clients internationally because there are enough clients at home to sustain them. A heavily restricted market therefore effectively becomes an impediment to exports. In one sense, this is advantageous to domestic clients because as long as prices are high, there will be a sufficient number of lawyers to serve their needs, whereas in theory, a highly mobile profession could leave the domestic market underserved.

The prevention of export controls on goods is well established in public international law. Article XI of the GATT prohibits restrictions on export of goods as well as restrictions on their import. This is because of the distortive effect on prices associated with a reduced supply of the goods on world markets. While the prohibition of quantitative restrictions on exports has no direct analogy under the GATS, it is worth considering the language of this article of the GATT as inspiration for a possible justification for economically distortive export-oriented restrictions on legal services.

> 1. No prohibitions or restrictions other than duties, taxes or other charges, whether made effective through quotas, import or export licences or other measures, shall be instituted or maintained by any

contracting party on the importation of any product of the territory of any other contracting party or on the exportation or sale for export of any product destined for the territory of any other contracting party.

2. The provisions of paragraph 1 of this Article shall not extend to the following:
   (a) Export prohibitions or restrictions temporarily applied to prevent or relieve critical shortages of foodstuffs or other products essential to the exporting contracting party;
   (b) Import and export prohibitions or restrictions necessary to the application of standards or regulations for the classification, grading or marketing of commodities in international trade;

The concept of "critical shortages of ... products essential" to the exporting country is worth further consideration. As was discussed in Chapter 1, it is often asserted that access to justice and rule of law are essential components of a properly functioning society. Recall that the European Convention on Human Rights guarantees the right to a fair trial in criminal matters as well as the right to free legal assistance when one is charged with a criminal offence.[38] Similar rights appear in other international human rights instruments.[39] There is a reasonable degree of what might be termed global consensus on this matter, as is evinced by the United Nations Basic Principles on the Role of Lawyers, which further establish that all people have the right to seek the assistance of a lawyer in all stages of criminal proceedings.[40] Similarly, the Union Internationale des Avocates believes that lawyers occupy a central position in the administration of justice as vital intermediaries between the public and the courts.[41] Commentators have cautioned that societies in which lawyers are more fully independent and self-regulating may be more resistant to tyranny. This suggestion is often presented as a plausible justification for tightly regulating the provision of legal services.[42] This point may be equally marshalled as an argument in favour of ensuring that there is a strong domestic core within the legal profession. Indeed, it is often noted that one of the dangers of reliance on foreign investment is that in the event of rapid departure of foreign capital, the domestic economy may collapse. Likewise, if a state has accepted so many foreign legal practitioners that there are few domestic ones, there may be a danger that the function of lawyers to defend the rights of citizens

[38] Article 6(3).

[39] See, e.g., Article 14 of the International Covenant on Civil and Political Rights.

[40] Articles 1–3.

[41] S. Lahaye-Battheu, "The Case for Drafting a European Convention on the Profession of Lawyer" (14 November 2017).

[42] Semple, *Legal Services Regulation at the Crossroads* at 216.

against the state has been fundamentally compromised. Foreign lawyers will almost certainly be the first to leave if the state collapses into tyranny or if better opportunities present themselves elsewhere. Following from this, a "severe shortage" (to use the GATT language) in the availability of legal services providers, such as could occur because of migration of professionals seeking more lucrative markets overseas, may justify the enactment of prohibitions against internationalization.

A number of export-restrictive barriers arise from rules imposed by domestic legal services regulators such as bar associations or law societies. First, some jurisdictions restrict marketing used by law firms, in some cases banning such firms from being listed in international directories or from creating websites. Clearly, this can impede a local firm's ability to generate clients abroad. Many jurisdictions control the naming of legal practices. For example, some countries require that a legal practice be named for a living partner of the firm. This can be problematic for local law firms that wish to build an international reputation over time. Second, there may be severe caps on the fees that may be charged for legal services. For example, until recently, Japan had a very tightly controlled fee regime. While these rules might appear to have a bearing only on a legal practitioner's relationship with domestic clients, such market interventions, which are typically designed with consumer protection in mind, may restrict the firm's ability to generate revenue at home, which can be leveraged to support internationalization. Third, indirect tax issues specific to the legal sector can disadvantage local legal services providers in relation to their foreign counterparts, possibly undermining the former's ability to service international markets.[43] Unfriendly domestic markets are often cited as a reason for the rapid internationalization of emerging market multinationals.[44]

Finally, governments and regulators can, intentionally or otherwise, hamper the development of an internationally competitive legal sector through measures designed to protect the hegemonic control of the local profession itself. Local bar associations may do this in part out of fear that any change will weaken the profession's independence from government or its ability to be a self-governing profession. Most jurisdictions impose restrictions on the individuals with whom a lawyer can enter into partnership and share fees. Rules on who can own a law firm are also common.

[43] Hook, "Sectoral Study on the Impact of Domestic Regulation on Trade in Legal Services" at 30.

[44] D. Collins, *The BRIC States and Outward Foreign Direct Investment* (Oxford University Press, 2013) Chapter Three.

Because these rules vary by jurisdiction, an international law firm may need to establish different business entities in each country for compliance purposes. These strategies can be costly, undermining competitiveness, especially in more flexible markets.[45]

The level of legal education available in the home state can affect the international competitiveness of the domestic legal market. Shortcomings in the legal education market can be critical in shaping attitudes to international legal practice among domestic legal services providers. This situation can cause foreign lawyers to be viewed as a threat and could discourage domestic lawyers from seeking international opportunities because foreign systems are depicted as inferior or undeserving of attention from a business case standpoint. A lack of focus on foreign or international law in the curricula of law schools could contribute to a disinterest in, or a lack of capacity for the delivery of, legal services that would be of interest to clients in other jurisdictions. A number of jurisdictions, such as the US, do not recognize legal education or legal qualifications that were obtained abroad. This could discourage future lawyers from pursuing law studies internationally. This attitude may be seen as the first step away from a potential career in international practice. Moreover, some countries maintain quotas on the number of qualified lawyers, achieved through specified bar exam pass rates. Historically, Japan and Korea adopted this approach, with pass rates of less than 2 per cent of test takers. Tight control of the number of qualified legal services providers domestically reduces the number of such individuals who are able to provide services internationally. Those who do pass will have more than enough clients to choose from at home, obviating the need to go abroad for work. Finally, many countries have limited postgraduate vocational or practical training regimes. This may result in large numbers of inadequately trained lawyers. Few of these local lawyers will be able to engage in more specialized cross-border legal work.[46]

Clearly, economy-wide regulations can affect the competitiveness of the domestic legal industry, constraining its ability to export legal services. As was noted in Chapter 3, there is a growing body of commentary on the need to offer greater customer choice in the delivery of legal services through the use of technology for readily commodifiable services and by breaking the monopoly of the legal profession over many less specialist,

[45] Hook, "Sectoral Study on the Impact of Domestic Regulation on Trade in Legal Services" at 31.

[46] Ibid. at 30.

highly routinized tasks.[47] Governments effectively deny domestic legal practitioners access to international clients by regulating their economies in such a way that their own legal professionals are not able to adapt these technological innovations to seize new commercial opportunities abroad.

Chief among these restrictions may be onerous digital trade laws, which were explored in Chapter 3. Governments can enact laws prohibiting data from being transferred out of their territory, rendering cross-border supply of legal services under Mode 1 impossible. Similarly, governments can impede the flow of services out of their territory by requiring that a copy of the data be stored within their territory. This will raise costs for firms, possibly dissuading them from offering services to clients in other jurisdictions through establishment of a local office, precluding delivery through Mode 3.[48] States have sought to use trade agreements to limit the ability of their trading partners to enact measures that impose data location requirements of this nature. General language that prohibits a party from imposing unnecessary barriers to the flow of information can operate to address protectionist data localization rules.[49]

Some recent RTAs have specific disciplines designed to combat illegitimate data localization rules. For example, the provision of the Comprehensive and Progressive Agreement for Trans-Pacific Partnership (CPTPP) that deals with the location of computing facilities specifies that "no party shall require a covered person to use or locate computing facilities in that party's territory as a condition for conducting business in that territory". This provision goes on to state that "each party may have its own regulatory requirements regarding the use of computing facilities including requirements that seek to ensure the security and confidentiality of communications". In language similar to that of the GATS general exceptions, this section of the CPTPP also clarifies that measures dealing with data localization are allowed if they serve a "legitimate public policy objective, provided that the measure: a) is not applied in a manner which would constitute a means of arbitrary or unjustifiable discrimination or a disguised restriction on international trade and b) does not impose restrictions on the use or location of computing facilities greater than a required to achieve the objective".[50] This provision of the CPTPP appears in the

[47] Susskind, *Tomorrow's Lawyers* and Barton, *Glass Half Full*.
[48] Wu, "Digital Trade-Related Provisions in Regional Trade Agreements" at 23.
[49] Ibid.
[50] Article 14.13.

third revision of the Australia–Singapore FTA,[51] and similar language can be found in the Japan–Mongolia EPA.[52]

In addition to the modern burden of digital trade laws, law firms may struggle to internationalize where they lack access to domestic capital, like firms in all sectors. A number of emerging markets still place restrictions on capital outflows, which could impede the global ambitions of larger law domestic law firms.[53] It is unclear whether these policies have actually done so for law firms yet.

Rather than enacting and enforcing measures that make the provision of legal services to foreign clients illegal or costly, another method by which governments may curtail the export of legal services is by stimulating demand internally. This may be done through conventional developmental initiatives designed to generate commercial activity that requires legal assistance in the forms of business organization, contracts, and dispute settlement, for example. As long as these activities do not transgress international subsidies disciplines such as the ASCM, there may be reason to expect that this is a sound economic strategy of which the legal sector is an indirect beneficiary.

Countries that fail to include in their RTAs provisions that facilitate trade in legal services, either by volition or omission, may also suppress the export of legal services. To take one critical example, the UK's departure from the EU risks an outcome in which UK legal services professionals will lose many of their rights of practice in EU. Moreover, once the UK leaves the EU, the free trade agreements (FTAs) that were concluded between the EU and third-party states will no longer apply to the UK. If such an FTA contains provisions that allow for the opening of the legal services market, these will no longer apply to the UK either, and legal practitioners in the UK may not be able to export legal services to these countries freely. The EU-Korea FTA[54] provides for a phased and partial opening of the legal services market to foreign lawyers by allowing EU law firms to establish joint venture firms with Korean law firms within five years of the agreement's entering into force. Five UK firms from the EU have entered the Korean market on this basis. The EU also has several Association Agreements with other countries.[55] These agreements do contain provisions on professional

[51] Australia–Singapore FTA, Art. 15.

[52] Japan–Mongolia EPA, Art. 9.10.

[53] See Collins, *The BRIC States and Outward Foreign Direct Investment.*

[54] Annex 7-A.

[55] E.g., the EU-Moldova Association Agreement, the EU-Georgia Association Agreement, and the EU-Ukraine Association Agreement.

services and mobility of persons that could be relevant for trade in legal services. Likewise, the EU-Canada Comprehensive Economic and Trade Agreement (CETA) includes the provision of temporary entry of contractual service suppliers, intracorporate transferees, and independent professionals. Although CETA does not provide substantial market opening for legal services, it does contain a series of provisions that are important for services, such as regulatory cooperation, domestic regulation, and provisions regulating the temporary stay of key personnel and graduate trainees, contractual service suppliers, and independent professionals. CETA also includes guidelines for Mutual Recognition Agreements (MRAs) between professional bodies. Failure to duplicate legal commitments of this nature in its future trade agreements with either the EU or third-party states would constitute a serious obstacle to the internationalization of UK legal services. On a more general level, any state that relies upon reciprocity for market access to legal services risks undermining the export of legal services to countries from whom they do not allow the entry of foreign suppliers. As will be seen in Chapter 5, a number of countries retain highly restrictive measures of this nature.

4.3.2 Migration of Professionals and Brain Drain

Concerns about legal services exports are tied to debates on the migration of professionals and its potentially deleterious effects on the domestic economy of the source country. As was noted earlier in the chapter, not only do legal services underpin a vibrant economy, but also lawyers are often regarded as central to the healthy functioning of a democratic society governed by the rule of law. Because a shortage in the supply of lawyers might risk harming the country of origin, the host state may wish to enact controls on migration as an aid to development or to maintain the proper functioning of society.

Although the GATS does not contain language regarding restrictions on services exports, it does specify the desire "to facilitate the increasing participation of developing countries in trade in services and the expansion of their service *exports* including, *inter alia*, through the strengthening of their domestic services capacity and its efficiency and competitiveness".[56] Article IV of the GATS also notes the importance of the liberalization of market access in sectors and modes of supply of export interest to the

[56] Preamble [emphasis added].

developing country. In other words, a competitive export market is built upon a strong domestic market.

Studies have shown that many countries will experience a decline in workforce numbers in the coming years and that in other countries, the decline in growth of the productive population and availability of human resources will be problematic as the population ages. The OECD projected workforce shortages ranging from 32 million to 39 million in developed countries. Part of this is the result of demographic trends, but part is the consequence of voluntary decisions of citizens not to engage in work that is unappealing or unrewarding.[57] Importantly, it is also caused by migration patterns, where citizens have left their home country for more attractive opportunities abroad. Such labour shortages will be experienced predominantly by developed countries, including the US, the EU, and Japan. As was noted in Chapter 3, many developing countries, in particular India, have services-oriented labour surpluses. Although these imbalances offer a strong justification for greater liberalization of Mode 3 and 4 services supply, they also support policies that aim to prevent the loss of domestic workers through migration to other countries where wages are higher. It must be conceded that labour shortages in developed countries will be focused primarily in services such as health care, finance, and construction. It is unlikely that there will be a dearth of lawyers.[58] Indeed, there is every indication that there is an oversupply of lawyers in most countries. But according to a strict economic analysis, an undersupply of legal professionals is an entirely rational outcome when barriers to migration are removed and rewards are enhanced.

The effect of migration of highly educated professionals such as lawyers and legal services providers from developing to developed countries may be described as brain drain. There is widespread concern that highly educated workers generate positive externalities for society that are lost when they emigrate. Extensive empirical studies over many decades have demonstrated that skilled migration is unambiguously detrimental to those who remain in the country of origin.[59] Harms inflicted by the movement of highly skilled workers include the positive effects on the productivity of colleagues, employees, and other workers and the provision of key

[57] Chanda, "Demographics and Labour Markets: Implications of Mode 4 Trade" in Sauve and Roy eds. *Research Handbook on Trade in Services* at 416.

[58] Ibid. at 420.

[59] F. Docquier and A. Marfouk, "International Migration by Education Attainment 1990–2000" in C. Ozden and M. Schiff eds. *International Migration, Remittances and the Brain Drain* (Palgrave MacMillan, 2006).

public services, especially health care; fiscal externalities linked to the fact that the taxes that highly skilled workers pay tend to be larger than the value of the public services they consume as well as the public funds that are invested in their education. Finally, there is the concern that these individuals contribute to the debate on important social issues with a commensurate impact on policy and institutions.[60] This last point appears to be particularly relevant for lawyers, who are often viewed as public servants who have a vital role in shaping institutions of democracy such as courts and legislatures.

The issue of brain drain is most acutely relevant for middle- to low-income countries. This is because their share of tertiary educated workers, as would characterize most legal services supplies, tends to be low in comparison to the share in high-income countries.[61] This is not to say that developed countries do not struggle with these issues. There was widespread concern in Canada in the 1990s that many of the best law school graduates were being seduced by the high salaries offered by New York law firms, which recruited aggressively on the campuses of Canadian law schools. Similar apprehensions have also arisen between New Zealand and Australia. The large number of highly educated law lecturers at UK universities from eastern and southern Europe, many of whom are qualified to practice law in their home countries, also comes to mind. Latvia and Lithuania in particular have experienced striking declines in their working age populations as a consequence of migration throughout the EU.[62]

More recently, some authors have argued, on the basis of empirical findings, that the migration of skilled workers and professionals may actually foster growth in the country of origin. This is premised on the theory that, given that the gains from education are higher abroad than at home, this will enhance domestic enrolment in education. Therefore there is more investment in the development of human capital as a consequence of increased migration opportunities. This can lead to growth and better economic performance in the home state.[63] There are also researchers who have shown that the migration of skilled workers confers other benefits,

[60] "Overview" in Ozden and Schiff eds. *International Migration, Remittances and the Brain Drain* at 10.

[61] Docquier and Marfouk, "International Migration by Education Attainment 1990–2000" at 172.

[62] "Population Decline Continues in Latvia; Riga's Population Increases" Baltic News Network (30 May 2017).

[63] Docquier and Marfouk, "International Migration by Education Attainment 1990–2000" at 152.

such as increased trade, remittances, knowledge exchange, and foreign direct investment.[64] Harmful migration of professionals must be tempered by data showing that remittances flows globally have more than doubled in the past twenty years. They are now the greatest source of foreign capital for dozens of countries in the developing world, surpassing foreign aid by a wide margin. Migration of labour has also played a key role in the integration of many developing countries into the global economy in the period after World War II. Such gains may be most clearly identified when the migrant returns home, a process that has been described as "brain circulation".[65]

There is a large body of literature on the economic advantages of increased migration, most of which focuses on immigration and restriction imposed thereon by developed countries.[66] The economic benefits of skilled migration to source countries has been well received by commentators who emphasize the economic gains associated with immigration to the developed world.[67] This more positive picture has been challenged on the basis of different interpretations of data which disclose smaller gains versus overall losses. One of the additional key observations made by this latter study was that many highly skilled migrants end up working in unskilled jobs in destination countries, minimizing beneficial knowledge transfer effects upon return and reducing the incentive to acquire education in the source country before departure.[68] At the risk of playing to a stereotype, many of us have met taxi drivers with legal qualifications in their home countries.

One concern about facilitating access to foreign markets such as the market for legal services is that it will deplete talent from other countries, including those that are in a weak state of economic development. As was noted earlier in the chapter, many foreign nationals send financial remittances to their families in their home state. Although some migrants stay in the new country, many ultimately return to their home country, bringing with them augmented knowledge, skills, and experience. Even those who stay in the foreign country are able to assist indirectly in improving their

[64] C. Ozden, "Educated Migrants: Is There Brain Waste" in Ozden and Schiff eds. *International Migration, Remittances and the Brain Drain*.

[65] A. Bradford, "Sharing the Risks and Rewards of Economic Migration", 80:1 *University of Chicago Law Review* 29 (2013) at 677.

[66] E.g., M. Trebilcock, "The Law and Economics of Immigration Policy", 5:2 *American Law and Economics Review* (2003) at 271–317.

[67] Ibid. at 637.

[68] M. Schiff, "Brain Gain: Claims about Its Size and Impact on Welfare and Growth Greatly Exaggerated" in Ozden and Schiff eds. *International Migration, Remittances and the Brain Drain* at 211.

home country's economic connections with their new home. Moreover, the availability of an exit option for skilled workers may prompt their home country to implement policies that encourage talented individuals to stay and, in so doing, improve the conditions in that country for the general population.[69]

Unfortunately, there are no known studies on the effect on source countries of the migration of providers of legal services. This type of study should be feasible, given that most legal services providers are formally registered with their home country and destination country, so presumably, their numbers would be easy enough to track. Many countries maintain a list of specialized skills that are needed as an aspect of their economic development. Individuals who have these skills are required to return to their country of origin for two years after they have engaged in work or research abroad before they can do so again. China, India, and South Korea have populations with many skills; however, law and legal services have not historically featured on the list of any countries, unlike medicine, for example, in which there is a severe shortage of skilled individuals in many developing countries.

The possibility that large-scale emigration of legal services providers will inflict harm on the society of source countries might raise questions about the wisdom of the negotiating RTAs covering legal services or MRAs for professional qualifications. Instead, if outflows of workers such as lawyers are damaging to a country, it may be appropriate to craft international agreements with relevant partner countries which will result in greater inflows of qualified individuals.[70] There are a number of bilateral migration framework agreements that address labour shortages in the recipient country and impose obligations on the sending country to ensure the return and reintegration of workers. Such agreements typically include development cooperation assistance and capacity-building commitments. Under these arrangements, services providers can temporarily access opportunities for workers with a wide range of skills levels. These mobility partnerships achieve circular migration flows, addressing the issue of skills depletion by requiring the labour-sending country to commit to readmit their nationals.[71] Migration Management Agreements pursued at a bilateral level that are tailored to the individual needs of partner

[69] Amos-Stewarta, Broughton, and Schwartz, "All Talk and No Action" at 164–165.

[70] Ibid. at 165–166.

[71] N. Ward, "Facilitating Temporary Movement of Natural Persons: Economic Partnership Agreements versus Bilateral Migration Agreements and Mobility Partnerships" in R. Kunz, S. Lavenex, and M. Panizzon eds. *Multilayered Migration Governance* (Routledge, 2011).

countries may be another solution.[72] The economic and social impact of skilled migration on source countries has prompted some commentators to recommend a migration fund that would be used to compensate the home state for any adverse effects.[73]

4.4 Conclusion

The globalization of international business has facilitated competition among legal jurisdictions for clients, including, most notably, multinational enterprises that are able to craft contracts specifying choice of law and choice of forum in a manner that suits their commercial needs. Many jurisdictions have been quick to adapt to this trend, seeking to entice mobile consumers of legal services through domestic enhancements such as strong rule of law and increasingly sophisticated dispute settlement for a focusing on international arbitration. While Mode 2 legal services may not be held in the same esteem as foreign direct investment in other sectors, they are unquestionably a source of revenue for many countries, particularly countries that lack extensive natural resources such as Singapore or, like the UK, have a strong tradition of legal excellence. Efforts to stimulate this demand may solve the excess of supply of lawyers that is seen in some jurisdictions and are unlikely to transgress public international rules on subsidization. In addition to practicalities associated with controlling mobile consumers, given the economic potential for these dispute resolution centres, it is no surprise that restrictions on Mode 2 delivery of legal services are rare in FTAs and under the GATS. States that adopt negative list formats in future FTAs will most likely omit reference to Mode 2 legal services entirely, allowing this kind of trade to the fullest extent possible.

Just as many countries try to augment the inflow of clients for their domestic legal services industry, policies may be adopted that restrain the export of legal services suppliers. These include the failure to negotiate international commitments on the liberalization of legal services and conventional restrictions on outward foreign investment. Whether or not such measures were designed with the phenomenon of brain drain in mind, it is important for future trade negotiators to be aware that an outflux of legal professionals may be detrimental to the source country, given the important role of lawyers in a democratic society that is based on the rule of law. The reciprocal nature of many legal services trade commitments suggests

[72] Kunz, Lavenex, and Panizzon, *Multilayered Migration Governance*.

[73] Bradford, "Sharing the Risks and Rewards of Economic Migration".

that where the outward movement of legal professionals is restricted, the inward movement is often similarly circumscribed. Aversion to the export of legal services often stems from aversion to the liberalization of legal services generally. Likewise, a strong inward flow of foreign clients tends to correspond to markets that are open to foreign suppliers. The issue of the establishment of legal services providers in foreign jurisdictions is the subject of Chapter 5.

5

Import Restrictions on Trade in Legal Services

Commercial Presence

5.1 Introduction

Establishing a permanent presence in a foreign state is a vitally important strategy for many legal services providers, particularly larger law firms that enjoy an ongoing relationship with clients that themselves have an international footprint. The emphasis on larger firms in this mode of trade in legal services reflects the sizable commitment of capital and resources needed to penetrate effectively into the market of a foreign country where regulatory conditions are often unknown or highly idiosyncratic and where local knowledge may be the key to success over time.

Many of the legal services providers that have successfully engaged in Mode 3 (commercial presence) supply have done so through cooperation agreements between foreign and local firms; this is sometimes referred to as the federalist model. The US-based law firm Baker & McKenzie popularized this strategy in the 1990s, in some cases merging with local firms, and became the second largest law firm in the world in terms of number of offices and fee-earning lawyers. UK law firms such as Eversheds and CMS have limited their linkages with local firms to a few locations, describing themselves instead as part of a network of prestigious firms in other countries, with such arrangements becoming more formalized in the 1990s.[1] In contrast, smaller, independent firms tend to operate through a referral system in conjunction with local contacts rather than in a formal relationship with law firms in other countries. This can take the form of an ad hoc relationship or a loose network such as the Interlex Group.[2] Most legal services providers begin to establish themselves overseas through referrals; a supplier in one country refers its clients to a provider in another country, typically on the basis of personal knowledge and reciprocity with no specific administrative coordination.[3]

[1] Muller, *Liberalization of Trade in Legal Services* at 6.
[2] www.interlextgroup.com (accessed March 2018).
[3] Muller, *Liberalization of Trade in Legal Services* at 7.

Any enterprise's decision to internationalize is based on the desire to seize an opportunity in a foreign economy whose competitive viability is founded upon the application of a firm-level advantage, initially owned by a foreign firm, to sources of competitiveness that are innate to that location. In the case of many multinationals, the advantage may be lower-cost inputs or technological know-how. In terms of regulatory approach to these foreign entities, the question arises whether the potential of the project, from the point of view of the host country's needs, will be best realized if the firm-specific attributes that are needed should be acquired by a local firm from abroad or retained and implemented by the internationalization of a foreign firm (the multinational enterprise).[4]

This logic applies to the law firm. Studies have examined the "social embeddedness" in the local environment of large law firms serving primarily corporate clients and the extent to which this influences their positioning in the global legal market in tandem with increased globalization. Law firms from the UK and Germany in particular demonstrate an evolving pattern in which firms harness specific resources to modify institutional settings and ultimately improve their position as the circumstances in the host country change – for example, as the host country proceeds with economic and developmental reforms. Interestingly, German law firms that have established themselves in global markets have performed well largely because of their capacity for technical expertise as advisors that gained experience within the constraints of a predominantly state-regulated profession. This contrasted with UK firms, which have thrived because they have exhibited traits of legal entrepreneurialism and innovation.[5]

Lawyers working for multinational firms have a role to play as modernizers, equipped with the expertise and credibility engendered by their ties to clients, many of whom are leaders in international industries. Such professionals are able to deploy and, in some instances, adapt their experience to local contexts. They bring the law of New York State or England and Wales, the practice of international commercial arbitration, corporate governance principles tied to global finance, and beneficial perspectives on anticorruption – in other words, some of the vital foundations for the rule of law. The world's elite lawyers, typically working as part of large global law firms, especially those from the US, have also shown themselves

[4] R. Pearce, *The Development of International Business* (Edward Elgar, 2017) at 64.

[5] G. Morgan and S. Quack, "Institutional Legacies and Firm Dynamics: The Growth and Internationalization of UK and German Law Firms", 26:12 *Organization Studies* 1765–1785 (2005).

willing to engage in public service through pro bono initiatives aimed at improvement of local governance.[6]

Notwithstanding the innovations that were discussed in Chapter 3, law firms, especially large ones, are thought to be predominantly responsive institutions rather than proactive ones; that is, they react to clients' demands instead of supplying their own initiatives to address problems before they arise. Law firms may accordingly be viewed as classic embodiments of the "born global" theory of multinational enterprises in which firms internationalize at a rapid pace in response to the globalized economy rather than building international attributes as they mature steadily over time, as is the case with conventional multinational enterprises. Commentators hold that the charismatic and powerful leaders of modern international law firms were able to expand their firms' business overseas in large part because this served the demands of international clients that required large networks of professions with multijurisdictional experience. US and UK firms were in a stronger position to do this because Anglo-American common law enjoys global dominance, in part owing to its flexibility, in contrast to their civil code-focused counterparts.[7]

Commentators have also contrasted the development of global law firms in what has been termed a hybrid or "glocalized" manner. Rather than expanding through diffusion of legal practice (in which the foreign firm exports its approach to resolving legal issues, often by influencing reforms in the host state to support these initiatives) or through distinctiveness (in which the foreign firm adapts its methods to the local environment), the most successful US firms have implemented an intermediate strategy. This process involves bringing practices from the home state but integrating them into the practices that are used by the local profession.[8] More specifically, US firms tend to employ a large number of associates who hold local legal qualifications, whereas the number of US law graduates working overseas, including those working at US firms with offices abroad, is marginal. It is sometimes argued that this pattern reveals a strong local connection that underpins a national distinctiveness model of expansion, in contrast to the classic diffusion model associated with many

[6] Y. Dezalay and B. G. Garth, "Corporate Law Firms, NGOs and Issues of Legitimacy for a Global Legal Order", 80 *Fordham Law Review* 2309 at 53 (2012).

[7] J. Flood, "Institutional Bridging: How Large Law Firms Engage in Globalization", 54 *British Columbia Law Review* 1087 (2013).

[8] C. Silver, N. De Bruin Phelan, and M. Rabinowitz, "Between Diffusion and Distinctiveness in Globalization: U.S. Law Firms Go Glocal", 22 *Georgetown Journal of Legal Ethics* 1431 (2009).

other kinds of multinational enterprises. This suggests that US firms with a major international presence rely on local lawyers who are sensitive to the business, political, economic, and cultural environment in which the offices are located. Indeed, this model further underscores the importance of the local context in the practice of law, perhaps one of the main reasons that trade in legal services is so tightly regulated.[9] Studies have further shown that although legal markets have been shifting to a more diffuse set of suppliers, such as legal executives, law clerks, and others, the so-called elite law firms appear to have strengthened their hold on the global market share for legal services.[10] It may be that the globalized economy necessitates a globally oriented law firm.

Given these trends, this chapter will consider the nature of the regulatory barriers facing collective legal services providers that are seeking to establish in foreign states, providing an overview of the main restrictions in some of the world's leading jurisdictions as well as significant emerging markets. It will also briefly consider how such regulations interact with relevant treaty commitments pursued at the global level as well as the bilateral level. The starting point of this analysis is again the GATS, article XXVIII (d) which specifies that "commercial presence" means "any type of business or professional establishment, including through the constitution, acquisition, maintenance of a juridical person, or the creation, maintenance of a branch or representative office". Only a small number of free trade agreements (FTAs) provide for commitments in legal services in Mode 3 that go beyond the offerings under the GATS. Moreover, only a handful of GATS-plus commitments have been made in FTAs by countries that did not schedule any commitment at the WTO.[11] Most of the Mode 3 legal services commitments that were made under the GATS during the Uruguay Round of negotiations, which saw the creation of the WTO itself, related to advisory services in the home jurisdiction and international law. There have been considerably fewer commitments under Mode 3 regarding the capacity of forms to practice host state law.

It is worth noting, at least in the context of EU law, that the distinction between Mode 3 and Mode 4 (temporary movement of natural persons) does not depend exclusively on duration. Other criteria include the regularity, periodicity, and continuity of the service supply. The fact that

[9] Ibid.

[10] J. Flood, "The Re-landscaping of the Legal Profession: Large Law Firms and Professional Re-regulation", 59:4 *Current Sociology* at 507–529 (2011).

[11] S. Moritsch, "Liberalisation of Trade in Legal Services – FTAs and Beyond GATS Commitments" International Bar Association (undated) at 2.

the provision of services is temporary does not prevent the supplier from having an office in the host state if this is necessary for the delivery of the service.[12]

5.2 International Law Firms and Commercial Presence

This section will consider some of the chief regulatory barriers faced by law firms that are establishing themselves in foreign jurisdictions, followed by a discussion of the law firm as an investment, taking the matter outside the regime of conventional trade agreements and into the sphere of international investment law.

5.2.1 Host State Regulatory Issues

The law firm is the most economically significant form of commercial presence legal services in foreign countries. This presence is typically characterized by international branches of Western firms, some of which operate in association with domestic firms. As was noted earlier, international law firms have adapted to globalization by staffing their overseas offices with local lawyers or by merging with local law firms in order to be able to practice the law of the host state through those professionals.[13] Branch offices tend to be located in large financial centres, notably London, Paris, and New York, but also Asian cities such as Beijing, Hong Kong, and Singapore and regional hubs in Buenos Aires and Sydney. The expansion of legal services through offices overseas has been accompanied by an enlargement in the substantive areas of practice by Western, mostly US firms. Although these firms initially offered legal services in US law, relying on US-educated and US-qualified lawyers, they eventually began to offer services in local law. The globalization phenomenon was tied to the growth of the economies of these host states in the late 1990s and into the twenty-first century. However, the strategy was possible only when regulatory changes were undertaken in host states that allowed foreign firms to open and allowed foreign firms to hire local lawyers, as happened with US law firms operating in the UK in the early 1990s.[14]

[12] *Reinhard Gebhard* v. *Consiglio dell'Ordine degli Avvocati e Procuratori di Milano*, C-55/94, ECR-I-4165 at [27].

[13] Silver, De Bruin Phelan, and Rabinowitz, "Between Diffusion and Distinctiveness in Globalization".

[14] Muller, *Liberalization of Trade in Legal Services* at 8.

One of the most prevalent problems facing law firms that seek to establish themselves in another country is that the concept of a law firm may not exist in that target jurisdiction or it may be much less developed. As a collective form of legal services delivery, the law firm is much more entrenched in the common law world than in civil law countries. The importance that has historically been placed on the independence of lawyers and the advice they provide does not sit easily with conventional notions of employee, either at a firm or within a corporation. As a consequence of this unfamiliarity, there is often no suitable business form in which lawyers can practice collectively, pooling their expertise as well as sharing risk. Even where there is a concept of legal partnership, further limitations are often imposed through corporate law, constraining the growth of domestic law firms and in turn stunting their capacity to internationalize. Many jurisdictions have not adopted limited liability business structures, which have become popular among many Western law firms. Codes of conduct applicable to law firms, particularly those that conflict with the laws of the home state, as well as tax regimes based on types of partnerships can also undermine the way in which foreign firms establish themselves overseas.[15]

Ownership requirements on foreign law firms are correctly described as the Mode 3 counterpart to nationality and residency requirements for natural persons.[16] This type of measure is addressed under the GATS market access disciplines of Article XIV:2 (e) and (f). Such measures could also be captured by Article XVII on National Treatment. It is more likely that such restrictions would be assessed as market access barriers, since these types of claims are easier to sustain.[17] Recall that GATS National Treatment and Most Favoured Nation (MFN) obligations apply both to the service and to the supplier of the service. This is perhaps most clearly relevant in the context of Mode 3 supply, in which, by entering the jurisdiction of the consumer, the supplier itself, not just its service, becomes subject to the laws of that country.[18] If the GATS prohibited only discrimination against the service and not discrimination against the supplier, then WTO member states would be able to pursue a wide range of discriminatory measures against legal practitioners, especially under Mode 3.

[15] Hook, "Sectoral Study on the Impact of Domestic Regulation on Trade in Legal Services" at 29.

[16] Diebold, *Non-Discrimination in International Trade in Services* at 55.

[17] Ibid.

[18] M. Krajewski, *National Regulation and Trade Liberalization in Services: The Legal Impact of the General Agreement on Trade in Services (GATS) on National Regulatory Autonomy* (Kluwer Law International, 2003) at 103.

Fee sharing with a local practitioner in the context of a merged branch or hiring a local lawyer requires a higher level of domestic regulation than is needed for a firm that is operating on its own. The local regulator's code of conduct will apply regardless of the conditions under which the foreign law firm is permitted to practice. A foreign law firm that is seeking to establish an office in another country will normally have to obtain a licence to do so and then receive permission to staff that office with professionals. This process may be complicated and time consuming, often involving many steps. There may be additional requirements if the firm wishes to include domestic lawyers in its practice as either partners or employees.

Because the GATS does not require WTO members to make commitments to introduce a corporate vehicle for the practice of law where none exists under domestic law, some jurisdictions may appear to be open to international legal services, whereas in actuality they do not allow foreign legal practice, at least through a conventional law firm. States may also have de facto domestic regulatory barriers because they do not have rules that allow for the employment of one lawyer by another. This effectively prohibits the establishment of law firms. Again, such restrictions may not appear on a GATS schedule because they are captured by neither Market Access nor National Treatment rules.[19]

Regimes for licensing foreign law firms adopt a system of either integration, in which the foreign firm is subjected to a regime similar to that of the local firm, or separation, in which the foreign firm is treated differently, normally in relation to restrictions on the scope of practice and capacity to work alongside local legal professionals. Integration is less common and tends to be used by countries seeking to transfer knowledge to the local profession by encouraging joint ventures. The separation style of regulation is more common and is designed to allow the local profession the capacity to develop and become more competitive. In some cases, the style of regulation incorporates elements of both integration and separation, as in the UK, where a foreign law firm that does not include a local solicitor in its partnership is subject to very limited regulations, involving simple notifications. Such foreign firms can practice any unreserved local law as well as foreign and international law. If the foreign firm wishes to take a local solicitor into its partnership, then the multinational partnership becomes regulated by the domestic bar association, and these rules will apply to all lawyers in the firm, whether or not they are qualified domestically.

[19] Hook, "Sectoral Study on the Impact of Domestic Regulation on Trade in Legal Services" at 14–15.

Transparency of the licensing process is a widespread problem faced by international law firms that are trying to establish themselves abroad. This is especially so in countries that do not have a tradition of receiving foreign investment in professional services sectors and whose principal experience with foreign firms is in the extractive sector. In theory, failure to maintain adequate transparency would be actionable under Article III of the GATS (and equivalent sections in regional trade agreements with services chapters), even for sectors for which there are no specific commitments, as tends to be the case for legal services. Regulatory transparency is arguably also a principle of customary international law.[20]

Some countries establish rules on the forms of permitted association between lawyers. These may involve restrictions on multidisciplinary firms involving partnerships or fee sharing between lawyers and other professionals such as accountants. There may be restrictions on management, control, and ownership involving non-lawyers that could be problematic for firms from more liberal environments, such as the UK. Such rules are based on the notion that lawyers should be independent and not subject to the supervision of non-lawyers. This situation is exacerbated in countries where foreign lawyers are not classified as "lawyers", as such associations with them may be deemed multidisciplinary and therefore prohibited.

The capacity of a foreign law firm to have a limited liability structure can be severely controlled in some countries. A foreign law firm that is established as a limited liability partnership at home will often need to form a separate partnership under the local laws of the host state when establishing an office in that country. The creation of a new entity can frustrate the ability of firms that want to integrate local lawyers who are partners of that branch into the wider, international partnership. Host states can impose quantitative limits on a foreign law firm's control of the local firm with which it has formed an association. Such rules resemble those placed on foreign investment in other sectors of the economy, which tend to be more stringent in sectors that are deemed to be sensitive or in which there is a national security risk. Some countries constrain foreign firms' usage of certain names, which can undermine their competitiveness, particularly for firms that have a strong international reputation.

Establishment of an office overseas typically requires the foreign firm to commit to observation of local codes of conduct. Because these rules also apply to domestic firms, they should not place the foreign firm at a

[20] E.g., Peters, "Towards Transparency as a Global Norm" in Bianchi and Peters eds. *Transparency in International Law.*

competitive disadvantage. However, as was noted earlier, the foreign firm may also need to adhere to similar codes of conduct in its home state; this is known as double de-ontology. Problems can arise if these codes conflict with one another. While there would usually be an overriding objective of protecting the client, the jurisdictions may have different ethical approaches – for example, in relation to managing conflicts of interest, referral fees, or advertising, the rules on which can vary widely across jurisdictions.

Law firms that have offices in multiple countries must expend resources on conflict of interest assessments in order to comply with local rules as well as those of their home regulator. Rules on publicity aim to protect consumers from misleading information that could cause them to confuse a foreign firm for a local one or that may suggest that specific lawyers continue to work for the firm when they no longer do so.[21] In some situations, local rules may be more burdensome for foreign firms than for local ones. For example, some jurisdictions require that law firms communicate with their clients on stationery that lists all of the partners in the firm; this would be impossible for firms with thousands of partners around the world. In this regard, it is worth noting that the GATS does not require member states to compensate for inherent disadvantages faced by foreign service providers due to regulatory diversity.[22] Merely being able to establish itself in the foreign market is no guarantee that a foreign firm will be able to compete on an even footing with firms that are fully adapted to the local business environment. Moreover, it may be possible to address the problem of double de-ontology through a choice of law rule listed in the Additional Commitments section under GATS Article XVIII.[23]

Law firms with branches in foreign states need to staff the offices, and this requires the satisfying of immigration requirements in the home state, an issue that will be explored further in Chapter 6. In the UK, additional requirements are placed on firms if there are local solicitors in the partnership. If local solicitors are employed only by the foreign firm, the requirement is merely that the associate solicitors must have at least three years of postqualification experience under the supervision of a local solicitor. In countries that are less open to the establishment of foreign law firms, there will be additional conditions regarding the chief representative of the foreign branch, such as this person's having a certain number of years

[21] Hook, "Sectoral Study on the Impact of Domestic Regulation on Trade in Legal Services" at 22.

[22] Footnote to Art. XVII:1 (National Treatment).

[23] Terry, "From GATS to APEC" at 905.

of postqualification experience or having the status of partner. Clearly, such requirements can reduce the employment opportunities for local solicitors who want to work in the offices of foreign firms, which may have greater experience and more sophistication.[24]

Similarly, local regulations may require that any lawyers employed in the branch office must requalify as local lawyers, regardless of their original qualification or the type of legal services they are providing. This can represent a serious obstacle to the internationalization of law firms when local requalification procedures are protracted. Consumer protection would be difficult to demonstrate here; it is far from clear that there is a need for foreign lawyers to be qualified in local law when the only services they are supplying relate to their home state or international law.

Additional restrictions may be faced by in-house counsel. In-house legal departments of companies can be very large, in some cases with over a thousand lawyers. The provision of legal services within a non-legal firm is a separate category of the practice of law that is regulated differently in different countries. Civil law countries tend to hold that lawyers should not be employees because this impairs their independence, leading to a potential conflict between their duty to their client and their duty to their employer. In contrast to common law countries, some civil law jurisdictions require that in-house lawyers either will not be admitted as lawyers or must relinquish their license when they take on employment in a non-legal company. Even in some common law jurisdictions, lawyers may have trouble moving within their company to a branch overseas. For example, in some US states, providing any legal opinions even to an employer is considered the unauthorized practice of law for anyone who is not qualified in that jurisdiction. Moreover, in many jurisdictions, solicitor-client privilege is not extended to in-house lawyers because these individuals are not fully recognized as lawyers possessing the same rights as those who are locally qualified. This was the view expressed by the Court of Justice of the European Union (CJEU) in *Akso Nobel Chemicals* v. *Commission*, in which the CJEU held that in-house lawyers lack sufficient independence, are too closely tied to their employers economically, and cannot ignore their employers' commercial strategies.[25] A differential approach to this issue could be a significant impediment to international trade in legal services, frustrating the commercial activity that depends upon it.

[24] Hook, "Sectoral Study on the Impact of Domestic Regulation on Trade in Legal Services" at 10.

[25] *Akzo Nobel Chemicals Ltd and Akcros Chemicals Ltd* v. *Commission*, C-550/07 P [2010].

5.2.2 The Law Firm as a Protected "Investment"

The establishment of a legal services provider from one country in another country for the purposes of delivering services to clients in the second country may be construed as a form of investment as well as trade, taking it beyond the scope of Mode 3 coverage under the GATS or regional trade agreements. Indeed, commentators have noted that statistics on trade in legal services regularly omit those which are provided by law firms from one country which have established in another one to provide services locally because this is not considered "trade".[26] It should be acknowledged that a country that imposes restrictions on the establishment of foreign law firms may simply displace inward capital investment through Mode 3 into Mode 2 earnings for another jurisdiction. This capital may accrue to other jurisdictions because the country's own citizens must get their legal advice from abroad. As is often said, barriers to investment from one country become gains in trade to another.

To assess whether law firms may be entitled to the protections afforded by international trade law, which consists primarily of investment treaties, it is essential to ascertain whether a law firm would fall under the definition of "investor" in an international investment agreement (IIA). The treaty regime will be available only to a complainant that holds the nationality of one of the treaty parties. Other than for sole practitioners, in which case the supplier is a natural person, the issue of nationality of the investor will most likely be based on the nationality of the firm or company. Nationality is determined by the law of the jurisdiction for which nationality is asserted. Although some jurisdictions allow law firms to be incorporated (in which case questions of nationality will typically involve the place of incorporation or the location of the head office or principal place of business), most law firms are unincorporated, usually taking the form of partnerships or associations in which designated individuals (who normally hold legal qualifications) consolidate their resources to perform specified commercial activities and share profits. While unincorporated entities do not generally enjoy their own legal protections under international law,[27] most modern IIAs provide otherwise. For example, the China-India bilateral investment treaty (BIT) states than an investor is

[26] C. Silver, "Regulatory Mismatch in the International Market for Legal Services" Northwestern University School of Law, Public Law and Legal Theory Research Paper Series, Research Paper No. 03-07 (2003).

[27] R. Dolzer and C. Schreuer, *Principles of International Investment Law* (Oxford University Press, 2012) at 47.

> any national or company of a Contracting Party; (i) nationals mean persons of either Contracting Party deriving their status as nationals of that Contracting Party from its laws in force. (ii) Companies mean corporations, firms and associations incorporated or constituted or established in the territory of either Contracting Party under its laws in force.[28]

The phrase "firms and associations constituted or established" appears to be broad enough to cover conventional legal partnerships or limited liability partnership law practices as they exist in most countries around the world. Such forms of business enterprise would most likely derive their nationality in a manner similar to that of corporations, namely, the main seat of the business or *siège social*.[29] This essentially refers to the business's place of central administration. Thus the law firm Shearman & Sterling would likely be able to avail itself of a US IIA because its main office is in New York City. Whether this firm could also avail itself of a UK, French, or Australian IIA (because it has offices in London, Paris, and Sydney) is another matter, but it would certainly be plausible, given sufficient economic ties to those jurisdictions.[30] Such a strategy could be advantageous if any of these treaty regimes were more protective than others; this may involve what is known as "treaty shopping".

To assess whether a law office established in another country could avail itself of the protections contained in IIAs, this enterprise would have to satisfy the treaty's definition of "investment". There is no universal definition of "investment"; however, the definition of "investment" found in most IIAs is broad enough to cover the commercial activities of a law firm from one country that has established an office in another country. For example, the Korea-Turkey BIT defines "investment" as follows:

> every kind of asset that an investor owns or controls and that has the characteristics of an investment, including such characteristics as the commitment of capital or other resources, the expectation of gain or profit, the assumption of risk, or a certain duration.
>
> Forms that an investment may take include:
>
> (a) an enterprise;
> (b) shares, stock, and other forms of equity participation in an enterprise;
> (c) bonds, debentures, loans, and other debt instruments of an enterprise;
> (d) turnkey, construction, management, production, concession, revenue-sharing, and other similar contracts;

[28] Article 1 (a).

[29] Dolzer and Schreuer, *Principles of International Investment Law* at 47.

[30] Article 1.2 (ii) of the India Model BIT of 2016 requires that the investor has "its management and real and substantial business operations in the territory of the Host State".

(e) intellectual property rights;
(f) licences, authorizations, permits, and similar rights conferred pursuant to domestic law; and (g) other tangible or intangible, movable or immovable property, and related property rights, such as leases, mortgages, liens, and pledges.[31]

The term "enterprise" would almost certainly encompass the activities of a global law firm such as Baker & McKenzie or Allen & Overy as well as those of smaller firms, potentially including sole practitioners. It is often thought that there is an expectation that investors will contribute to the economic development of the host state.[32] This would be harder to demonstrate if the investor were a small firm with limited capacity to influence the host state's economy. However, even a small firm could help to facilitate the spread of the rule of law, particularly in a country with weak legal infrastructure. It is important to recognize also that IIA protections are often accorded only to "covered" investments, which means those that have been admitted by the host state "subject to its relevant laws, regulations and policies".[33] This principle ensures that host states can place restrictions on the types of legal enterprises that are established in their territory, such as foreign ownership limits, even when these conditions do not appear expressly in the text of the international treaty.

If law firms are indeed covered by definitions of "investment" in IIAs, they are eligible for protection from expropriation or breach of Fair and Equitable Treatment and other standards, including nondiscrimination based on national origin. Many of the regulatory burdens discussed earlier in the chapter, particularly those that are discriminatory vis-à-vis non-domestic firms, would likely be encompassed by these provisions. It should be noted that the nondiscrimination test in international investment law (for both National Treatment and MFN) tends to involve investors who are in "like circumstances"[34] rather than like services or service suppliers as in the GATS. Some older IIAs use the phrase "like situations"[35] or "similar situations"[36] or other comparable variations. The structure of the test for like circumstances under the North American Free Trade Agreement

[31] Section A 1.
[32] See e.g., *Salini* v. *Morocco*, ICSID No. ARB/00/4, decision on jurisdiction, 23 July 2001 at [52]. See also S. Subedi, *International Investment Law: Reconciling Policy and Principle* (Bloomsbury, 2016) at 149.
[33] Australia-China FTA Art. 9.1.
[34] As in NAFTA Art. 1102 (National Treatment) and Art. 1103 (Most Favoured Nation).
[35] E.g., US-Senegal BIT (1983) Art. II.
[36] Ethiopia-Turkey BIT (2000) Art. 3(1).

(NAFTA) was articulated in *Pope & Talbot* v. *Canada*[37] and subsequently confirmed by other NAFTA arbitration tribunals, and it is often cited in non-NAFTA investment arbitrations. Analysis of this concept is of an economic nature, focusing on the existence of a competitive relationship, including whether the investors are in the same sector, which also considers whether they are subject to the same regulatory regime.[38] It could accordingly be concluded that most foreign legal services practitioners would be in like circumstances with local ones, although this is debatable when one considers commercial law versus other types of legal practice, such as family law or estate planning. It may be equally possible to argue that an investor (a law firm) practicing in the law of its home state is not in like circumstances in comparison to one practicing in the law of the host jurisdiction. National Treatment tends to cover only investments that are already established in host states, precluding pre-investment expenditures as well as discriminatory requirements contained in domestic regulations, such as a maximum percentage of foreign ownership of a law firm.

Found in most IIAs, the guarantee of Fair and Equitable Treatment is a highly indeterminate principle that tends to be construed by investment arbitration tribunals in a broad manner,[39] possibly covering many of the burdens associated with foreign law offices that were noted earlier in the chapter. More specifically, the prohibition of foreign law firms from staffing their firm with lawyers from their own home countries could transgress IIA provisions on Entry and Sojourn of personnel. For example, the India–United Arab Emirates BIT specifies: "Investors of either Contracting party shall be permitted to engage top managerial and technical persons of their choice regardless of nationality".[40] Modern IIAs that acknowledge a developmental purpose in their preamble[41] may be able to justify such breaches on the basis that they ensure that the foreign investor is making a legitimate economic contribution by hiring local labour. Although there have been no known investment disputes involving legal services, this field of legal protection under public international law would appear to be available to law firms and possibly even sole practitioners that have established themselves overseas.

[37] UNCITRAL (10 April 2002) at [78].

[38] N. DiMascio and J. Pauwelyn, "Nondiscrimination in Trade and Investment Treaties: Worlds Apart or Two Sides of the Same Coin", 102 *American Journal of International Law* 48 (2008) at 48–50.

[39] Collins, *Introduction to International Investment Law* at Chapter Five.

[40] Article 12.

[41] E.g., Mongolia-Austria.

There tends to be a lack of general exceptions IIAs, unlike the GATS, suggesting that the scope for government regulators to discriminate against foreign lawyers who have established themselves in their territory is more circumscribed than is the case in the trade context. Thus, for example, a marked increase in the regulatory burden on foreign law firms resulting in a claim of breach of Fair and Equitable Treatment may not be defensible on the basis of public interest.

5.3 Specific Jurisdictions' Rules on Establishment

This section will explore the key restrictions on the establishment of legal services providers in some of the world's leading legal services jurisdictions. This information is intended for illustrative purposes and is not intended to constitute a comprehensive guide. Much of the information that is presented here was taken from the database of the IBA that is available online,[42] which itself is based largely upon the GATS schedules of the various countries. The most important Mode 3 importers of legal services have sufficiently large domestic markets to attract investment by international law firms. The US, the EU, and China are the best examples of this phenomenon. Several other countries have the potential to become more significant importers and exporters of investment in legal services via Mode 3. For example, the Brazilian and Indian legal markets are only partially integrated into the international market for legal services, with much potential for further integration in the future.

5.3.1 European Union Member States

At a general level, EU FTAs speak of the goal of "progressive liberalisation" for trade in services with limited enforceability in terms of bright line rules. The EU Commission has stressed that services are the cornerstone of the EU economy. Gradually liberalizing global trade in services is viewed as an essential component of future economic growth. On this basis, the EU Commission urged the EU members to negotiate the liberalization of trade in services with key partners, particularly where market access is poor or where EU partners have made few commitments. Liberalization of legal services along with other professional services is one of the priorities

[42] www.ibanet.org/PPID/Constituent/Bar_Issues_Commission/BIC_ITILS_Map.aspx (accessed March 2018).

of the EU Commission's new strategy for international trade.[43] The EU-Korea FTA contains a number of liberalizing commitments on legal services, including Mode 3, which exceed those of the GATS. This agreement may act as a blueprint for future agreements. Under this agreement, EU law firms can open offices in Korea to advise foreign investors or Korean clients on non-Korean law. Law firms are also able to form partnerships with Korean firms and recruit Korean lawyers to provide multijurisdictional services. The EU has achieved a considerable degree of global integration in terms of importing Mode 3 legal services. There are more than 200 US law firms in Europe, of which close to a third are in London.

There is no separate law firm-licensing regime for foreign law firms in Italy, where more than twenty foreign law firms are established, including notably firms from the UK, the US, and Germany. A foreign law firm must complete the same registration formalities as any other foreign business would when establishing in Italy. There are no provisions for non–European Economic Area (EEA) law firms regarding restrictions on legal form and shareholding requirements, nor are there provisions on forming partnerships with local lawyers, suggesting that foreign law firms may do both. Italian regulations do not contain any restrictions on names for foreign law firms.

France places no additional licensing requirements on foreign firms; however, the local bar where the lawyer is registered must be informed about the establishment. There are over sixty foreign law firms in France, most of them based in Paris. Control of law firms must be by EU/EEA lawyers, and more than 50 per cent of the capital must be held by individuals who work for the legal entity. Law firms providing services on French or EU law must have at least 75 per cent of the partners holding at least 75 per cent of the shares who are fully admitted to the bar in France. It is not possible for foreign firms to form partnerships with French avocats; moreover, lawyers from outside the EU/EEA cannot employ French avocats. Non-EU firms are not permitted to establish branch offices in France under their own names.

More than sixty foreign law firms are established in Germany, including firms from the US, UK, Canada, and China. Germany imposes licensing requirements on foreign law firms, mandating authorization by the relevant local bar association. Foreign law firms must additionally register with

[43] G. Muller, "The EU's Global Europe Strategy and the Liberalization of Trade in Legal Services: The Impact of the EU Free Trade Agreements in Asia", 14 *Journal of World Investment & Trade* 727 (2013) at 730.

the local court if they have a corporate or limited liability form. Non-EU lawyers may be established only as sole practitioners or partnerships. However, foreign law firms can form partnerships or any form of professional association with members of the legal professions from EU member states and other WTO members. It is also possible for foreign firms to employ local lawyers. The title "Rechtsanwalt" is protected, and unless foreign lawyers undergo the full national process of qualification in Germany, they may be established only under their home title listing their home country.

In Spain, foreign law firms are restricted to practicing their home country law and international law. Over thirty foreign law firms are established in Spain from a range of countries, including the US, the UK, Germany, France, and Switzerland. There are no provisions in Spanish regulations concerning partnership with local lawyers, employment of local lawyers, or requirements regarding firm names.

5.3.2 *The United Kingdom (England and Wales)*

More than 200 foreign firms from over forty jurisdictions are established in London, perhaps the most of any city in the world, making London the world's foremost legal hub. Foreign law firms do not require licences to open offices to practise law in England and Wales, provided that they are not practising in reserved areas of work (real estate, probate, oath taking) and are not fee sharing with English solicitors or barristers. Foreign law firms that want to have English and Welsh solicitor partners and to practise in reserved areas of work need to obtain a licence from the SRA, the regulatory body for solicitors in England and Wales. There are no restrictions on the business form that a foreign firm may take unless that foreign law firm becomes licensed to undertake reserved English and Welsh law work. Foreign lawyers may become partners or employees in English or Welsh law firms. There are no specific rules for the names of foreign law firms beyond the general naming provisions that govern all businesses. If a foreign firm and a local firm merge to form a multinational partnership, the resulting entity is permitted to adopt either the name of the foreign firm or the name of the English or Welsh firm. The firm also has the option of assuming an entirely new name, provided that it complies with domestic publicity regulations that prohibits misleading names.

At the time of writing, it would appear that the UK intends to pursue international trade agreements with other countries aggressively after its departure from the EU. Whether or not these will cover Mode 3 services at all, let alone legal services, is uncertain. Attracting foreign direct investment, such as investment from foreign law firms, through a robust IIA regime with strong investor protections is highly advisable.[44] One of the UK's intentions in this regard is to roll over or grandfather in agreements such as the EU-Korea FTA, which is unusual for including legal services. However, it is not clear that Korea will support this initiative, as Korea has experienced an influx of foreign law firms in recent years, a development that has placed pressure on domestic firms. The capacity of UK firms to establish themselves in the EU after Brexit is also uncertain. However, the recent decision of French regulatory authorities to allow UK limited liability partnerships to be members of a French AARPI (Association d'Avocats à Responsibilité Professionalle Individuelle) has been welcomed by the UK legal community. This could ease profit sharing and the restructuring of UK law firms in Paris.

5.3.3 The United States of America

There are approximately twenty foreign law firms operating in the US, most of which are UK firms located in New York City. This pattern of Mode 3 investment by law firms is thought to reflect the cluster effect of financial markets as well as the demand from clients to be geographically proximate to provide supporting advisory services.[45]

Negotiating trade in legal services liberalization with the United States is notoriously difficult because the practice of law is regulated at the state level, requiring commitments from both levels of government. According to US scheduled GATS commitments, in states where foreign law firms are permitted, domestic lawyers may be employed by foreign law firms, domestic lawyers and foreign lawyers can form partnerships, and foreign lawyers may be employed by domestic firms. The US has not made any other treaty commitments specifically covering trade in legal services, although it has a number of treaties covering cross-border trade services that would embrace Mode 4. These include NAFTA (currently being renegotiated) and treaties with the Dominican Republic, Central America (CAFTA), Korea, Australia, Bahrain, Chile, Colombia, Israel, Jordan, Morocco, Oman, Panama, Peru, and Singapore. These agreements tend to

[44] D. Collins, "The UK Should Adopt Investor-State Dispute Settlement in Its Post-Brexit International Investment Agreements", 14:3 *Manchester Journal of International Economic Law* 300–317 (2017).

[45] Hook, "Sectoral Study on the Impact of Domestic Regulation on Trade in Legal Services" at 11.

specify a generic interest in fostering market access for services over time through promises to endeavour to recognize professional qualifications of services providers where possible.[46] It is often specified that a local presence in the form of a representative office is not required as a condition for cross-border supply, including Mode 4.[47] Additionally, the US Model BIT of 2012 contains strong protections for foreign investors that tend to be broadly defined in terms of "every asset". Some US IIAs, such as NAFTA, extend pre-establishment national treatment to foreign firms,[48] precluding a range of discriminatory restrictions that could affect foreign firms, such as nationality of partners. Foreign investment in the US is subject to review by the Committee on Foreign Investment in the United States, which has blocked a number of takeovers in recent years in sectors that are deemed to be of risk to national security, particularly those involving Chinese companies.

There is no special licensing procedure for foreign law firms in California except that the firms must be registered with the state bar. There are no restrictions on the scope of practice that apply to foreign firms; nor are there restrictions on names. California does not impose restrictions on the ownership share of foreign lawyers in a firm. Domestic lawyers can enter into partnerships with foreign lawyers, and domestic firms can hire foreign lawyers. A large number of foreign law firms are present in California, notably firms from the UK.

Foreign law firms may establish themselves in Illinois with no additional registration requirements. The only foreign firms that are currently present in Illinois are British ones: DLA Piper, Hogan Lovells, and Dentons. According to the US GATS commitments, domestic lawyers may be employed by foreign law firms in Illinois. Domestic lawyers may enter into partnerships with foreign lawyers, and domestic law firms may employ foreign lawyers.

There are no separate requirements for foreign law firms to open offices in New York state, and foreign legal consultants (FLCs) may open offices. Pursuant to US GATS commitments, domestic lawyers may be employed by foreign law firms in New York. A New York lawyer is entitled to enter into a partnership with a foreign lawyer and may employ a foreign lawyer. Many foreign law firms are established in New York City, perhaps the world's second most important legal market.

[46] E.g., US-Australia FTA Art. 10.4.

[47] US-Australia FTA Art. 10.5.

[48] Article 1102.

Foreign law firms are allowed to establish themselves in Texas with no special registration requirements, and FLCs are entitled to open offices. Foreign firms that are present in Texas include the UK firms DLA Piper, Dentons, Norton Rose Fulbright, and Hogan Lovells.

5.3.4 *Japan*

Japan significantly reduced its regulatory barriers to the establishment of foreign law offices in the late 1980s, resulting in a more than tenfold increase in the presence of foreign lawyers, especially those from the US.[49] Foreign law offices may open in Japan either as a foreign law firm or in association with a Bengoshi, that is, a Japanese lawyer. Only one office per firm is permitted in Japan. Firm names are not restricted, provided that the name is followed with reference to Gaikoku-Ho-Jimu-Bengoshi Jimusho. Foreign lawyers acting through the foreign law firm of which they are a member are permitted to employ Japanese-qualified lawyers. Japanese law firms may employ foreign lawyers. There are roughly fifty foreign law firms in Japan from the US, the UK, China, and Australia, most of which are in Tokyo.

The GATS was the primary means of negotiation for the removal of restrictions on trade in legal services in Japan. For the most part, these took place between the US and Japan, but the result was extended to other WTO members through the MFN provision.[50] Japan has bilateral trade agreements covering services with ASEAN, Brunei, Chile, India, Indonesia, Malaysia, Mexico, Peru, Philippines, Singapore, Switzerland, Thailand, and Vietnam. None of these treaties contains commitments on Mode 3 supply of legal services that exceed the GATS commitment, although several of them indicate the intention to negotiate commitments for further liberalization of services in the future.[51] Japan was a leading proponent of the Comprehensive and Progressive Agreement for Trans-Pacific Partnership (CPTPP), which as was noted in earlier chapters, contains material relevant to commercial presence legal services.

Japan has signed forty-eight IIAs, and foreign direct investment into Japan has been essentially fully allowed since the Foreign Exchange and Foreign Trade Act was amended in 1998. In general, the only requirement

[49] R. L. Abel, "Symposium: The Future of the Legal Profession: Transnational Law Practice" 44 *Case Western Reserve Law Review* 737 at 748 (1994).

[50] Muller, "The EU's Global Europe Strategy and the Liberalization of Trade in Legal Services" at 732.

[51] E.g., Japan-ASEAN Comprehensive Economic Partnership Article 50.2.

for foreign investors entering Japan is to submit an ex post facto report to the relevant ministries.

5.3.5 Canada

There is no licensing regime in Canada that regulates foreign firms. Foreign firms are permitted to establish an office to offer advisory services in foreign and international law. As with other industries, all foreign investment in Canada is subject to a review process, which is outlined in the Investment Canada Act (ICA). The ICA provides that every foreign investor must file a notification with Industry Canada every time a non-Canadian begins a new business activity in Canada or acquires control of an existing business in Canada. Domestic lawyers may employ foreign lawyers and vice versa. The only foreign law firms in Canada are located in Toronto, where there are a small number of US firms.

Although Canada has a number of bilateral agreements covering services, none grants additional liberalization for the establishment of legal services providers exceeding that of the GATS. Canada has fifty-two IIAs in operation that accord broad protections to foreign investors, including pre-establishment national treatment in the case of NAFTA, as was noted earlier. There is no indication that commercial presence legal services are on the NAFTA negotiating table. Along with Japan, Canada was a key driver of the CPTPP.

5.3.6 Australia

Foreign firms are permitted to establish a commercial presence (a permanent office) in Australia to offer advisory services in foreign and international law. There are no specific requirements for setting up a foreign law office in Australia. Local lawyers may be employed by foreign law firms. Australian-registered FLCs may employ Australian lawyers and have them as partners. Australia's GATS Mode 3 commitments permit joint offices involving revenue sharing between foreign law firms and local law firms in New South Wales, Victoria, Queensland, Tasmania, Western Australia, the Australian Capital Territory, and the Northern Territory subject to the foreign law firms satisfying certain requirements, including those relating to liability, standard of conduct, and professional ethics. There are some international firms in Sydney and Melbourne, in particular those of Chinese and British origin.

Australia has not made any Mode 3 commitments beyond those of the GATS in any of its FTAs. It does maintain thirty-six IIAs with full investor protections for foreign firms. Australia operates the Foreign Investment Review Board to assess the effect of particular foreign investment initiatives on the Australian economy and to identify risks to national security. Australia is a signatory to the CPTPP.

5.3.7 Emerging Markets

In recent decades, the practice of law has grown exponentially in many of the more economically advanced developing states. While the embrace of trade liberalization has unquestionably played a role in the prosperity of many of these emerging markets, there remains a measured reluctance on the part of these countries to open up services to foreign competition in contrast to the more developed jurisdictions mentioned earlier, with the exception of Japan. Legal services are no exception. This section briefly considers the regimes in place governing the establishment of foreign lawyers in the four BRIC states (Brazil, Russia, India, and China). It is worth noting that developing countries may be willing to concede better conditions for commercial establishment (meaning direct investment in their territories) in exchange for acceptance by developed countries of compromises on the presence of natural persons. Of course, attracting foreign direct investment tends to be a desire held by countries at all stages of development, just as an aversion to relenting on the acceptance of foreign workers appears to be nearly universal.

Now the sixth largest economy in the world, Brazil has a vibrant legal services sector, boasting the second largest number of lawyers per capita in the world after the US and with a sectoral market size of over $US 14bn in 2012.[52] Yet Brazil has made no commitments on commercial presence of legal services suppliers under the GATS, nor do any of Brazil's bilateral trade agreements contain commitments on legal services. Brazil has signed nineteen IIAs protecting foreign investment, but none of them are in force. There are about thirty foreign law firms operating in Brazil, including a number of international US, UK, and Spanish firms. While there is no specialized licensing regime for foreign firms, these enterprises can only advise on international and home country law. Some foreign firms have cooperation arrangements with local firms, but both the foreign and local firms have to maintain their own independence. A domestic lawyer may not be employed by a foreign law firm, nor can a domestic lawyer be in

[52] Euromonitor International. (January 2014). *Legal Services in Brazil: ISIC 7411*. www.euromonitor.com/legal-services-in-brazil-isic-7411/report (accessed March 2018).

partnership with a foreign lawyer if the domestic lawyer wishes to practice Brazilian law. Domestic law firms cannot employ foreign lawyers if the domestic lawyer seeks to practice Brazilian law.

China recently became the world's second largest economy, and it is still growing at a rapid if somewhat more modest pace. Its legal services sector comprises more than 200,000 lawyers and 16,000 law firms. Revenues from the sector increased to US $8.40bn in 2014 at a yearly growth rate of almost 10 per cent since 2009.[53] However, the establishment of foreign legal services providers in China has been heavily restricted, being among the most tightly controlled sectors of the economy in recent years. Chinese law firms enjoy many regulatory advantages over their foreign competitors, allowing Chinese firms to secure an increasing share of the market. It is thought that many of the foreign firms that are operating in China are not covering their operating costs. There are approximately 170 foreign law firms with offices in mainland China, almost all of which are located in either Beijing or Shanghai. The establishment rules are limited, essentially allowing foreign representative offices only to provide clients with assistance on home country law as well as international law; to entrust Chinese law firms to deal with Chinese legal affairs on behalf of foreign clients, and to provide information on the impact of the Chinese legal environment. Foreign law firms are allowed to open more than one office in mainland China but must wait three years between opening offices; this is known as the "three-year rule".[54]

The provision of consultancy services on Chinese law remains prohibited, precluding foreign firms from officially acting as law firms when providing advice on Chinese law. This has led to many firms providing disjointed solutions to their clients, including forming complex partnerships with Chinese firms and opening highly restrictive Joint Law Ventures (JLVs).

Certain forms of JLV have been allowed for a small number of firms, allowing Chinese-licensed lawyers to work with or foreign law firms. The Swiss "Verein" scheme is one example of such a structure, which has enabled three large foreign firms to co-brand in servicing Chinese clients together with a Chinese firm. There are still limits, including financial

[53] Ibis World. (February 2015). *Attorneys in China: Market Research Report*. *Ibis World*. www.ibisworld.com/industry/china/attorneys.html (accessed March 2018).

[54] Accession of the People's Republic of China, WTO Doc WT/L/432 (2001) (Decision of 10 November 2001) Annex 9 ("Schedule of Specific Commitments on Services – List of Article II Exemptions"), incorporating by reference Report of the Working Party on the Accession of China, WTO Doc WT/ACC/CHN/49/Add.2 (2001) (Addendum – Part II: Schedule of Specific Commitments on Services – List of Article II MFN Exemptions) II(A)(a).

structures and profit sharing; foreign law firms cannot share profits with Chinese law firms. Another variety of JLV is permitted through the Hong Kong Closer Economic Partnership Arrangement (CEPA); however, this is difficult to set up and is allowed only in Hong Kong itself. A small number of JLVs have been authorized to be established through the Shanghai (China) Pilot Free Trade Zone. However, these are contractual JLVs rather than new entities, which means that Chinese lawyers need to be employed by the Chinese partner. The chief representative of the foreign law firm is not allowed to participate in the management of the JLV. Such arrangements are also very difficult to set up. Additionally, foreign law firms are subject to higher taxes in comparison to Chinese firms that carry out the same activities. Unlike local firms, foreign law firms' offices in China are treated as corporate entities even though they are not corporations; this yields two layers of tax: a corporate tax and an income tax on partners. There are also burdensome representative office registration and staff management restrictions on foreign firms that are not applicable to Chinese law firms.

Although China has a number of FTAs, including FTAs with developed countries such as New Zealand, Singapore, Hong Kong, Iceland, and Switzerland, none contain comprehensive commitments on commercial presence of legal services suppliers. China has signed 129 IIAs, of which 110 are in force, although these tend to grant protections only to investments that are already established. China made specific commitments to liberalize its market to foreign law firms as part of its accession to the WTO, in part on the understanding that foreign law firms could help China to integrate its economy with that of the rest of the world.

Given pressures placed on China to liberalize its market following WTO accession, foreign law firms are actively involved in advising on matters relating to Chinese law for their foreign clients. This has created a kind of de facto liberalization of the domestic legal services market in that country. This situation exposes a disjunction in the interpretation of the regulations governing the establishment of foreign law offices as well as the enforcement of the regulations. Unsurprisingly, Chinese law firms have lobbied their government to marginalize the activities of foreign law firms in line with strict regulations. Yet Chinese regulators appear to be willing to disregard the excesses of foreign law firms because of their key role in opening the economy. Commentators have suggested that the approach appears to be one in which regulators are allowing Chinese firms more time to become globally competitive before taking additional steps towards liberalizing trade in legal services. Paradoxically, the nonenforcement of restrictions on the scope of practice of foreign firms may have entrenched their position, given that the trend towards liberalization appears irreversible, and it is almost certain that genuine liberalization will follow.[55]

The licensing system for foreign law firms in China that have been established under the terms of WTO accession has been criticised by foreign legal professional associations, notably the Legal Working Group of the EU Chamber of Commerce in China. Among the chief complaints is that foreign law firms operating in China must obtain approval at two levels of government: the national level and the provincial level. This process can prolong the application process, which can take more than a year, increasing administrative costs.[56] Chinese regulations require that when establishing a representative office, the foreign law firm must demonstrate that there is a sound business case for them to open the office. A feasibility report on the business prospects of the proposed office must be submitted, and there are concerns that such reports could contain sensitive information about clients. China's FTA negotiations with developed country partners such as the EU (and the UK) will almost certainly seek to address these issues.

India, which is one of the world's largest and fastest-growing economies, has a sizable legal services market, thought to be worth over $US 6bn in 2013 and expanding steadily.[57] India's rules on establishment for foreign legal practitioners are as restrictive as China's, perhaps even more so. India has not scheduled any commitments on commercial presence for legal services under the GATS or in any FTAs. India is a party to sixty-six IIAs, of which fifty-six are in force.

Foreign law firms are not permitted to establish themselves in India. A foreign lawyer can be employed by an Indian lawyer or law firm but not as a lawyer, and the foreign lawyer is not allowed to practise law in India. Until 1995, foreign law firms were able to obtain licenses to operate in India through representative offices via licenses that were issued by the Reserve Bank of India, but this system no longer applies. The lack of clarity regarding the type of legal work that such firms were allowed to do led to resentment among members of the local legal profession, who asserted that foreign firms were taking work that should have been performed by them. As will be discussed in more detail in Chapter 6, a group of Indian

55 Ibid. at 153.

56 Hook, "Sectoral Study on the Impact of Domestic Regulation on Trade in Legal Services" at 16.

57 "A Balancing Act: Cost-Benefit Analysis of Reforming India's Legal Services Market" Nathan Associates, Delhi, India (May 2016) at 15.

lawyers in conjunction with local bars pursued their complaint through the Indian courts, ultimately resulting in the expulsion of foreign lawyers from India.

Many of the largest law firms in India are family owned with tightly held equity. While they might outwardly claim to espouse globalization, they are quite likely to resist liberalization reforms because this could threaten their entrenched position, which was built upon a tightly controlled market. Although India has made few commitments to liberalize its legal services market under international law, it is unlikely that it can maintain this situation indefinitely. Given the pressure of keeping up with economic globalization and its tendency towards progressive liberalization, India must eventually liberalize its legal services market and allow the entry of foreign lawyers and law firms. Commentators urge that efforts to do so should be directed at training Indian law professionals to meet the challenges of global competition.[58] A gradual approach to reforming the regulation of India's legal services sector with a view towards increasing the presence of foreign law firms has also been advocated to cushion any adverse impacts from intense competition.[59]

Russia's legal services sector has suffered from the economic sanctions that were imposed on the country after its annexation of Crimea and the ensuing crisis in eastern Ukraine. Russia still represents a highly lucrative market for foreign firms. It made modest GATS commitments under Mode 3 (commercial presence) when it acceded to the WTO in 2012. It has also entered into a number of bilateral trade agreements, particularly with Commonwealth of Independent States (CIS) including Belorussia, Georgia, Kazakhstan, Kirghizia, Tajikistan, and Ukraine. The only treaty that includes legal services is the Agreement on Trade in Services and Investments in States, which is in force between Russia, Belorussia, and Kazakhstan. Under this agreement, foreign lawyers from Belorussia and Kazakhstan may be given preferential treatment regarding the practice of law in Russia, the precise details of which are unclear. Russia has entered into seventy-nine IIAs, of which sixty-three are in force, and it has faced a number of claims through investor-state dispute settlement.

Currently, there are two types of law firm in Russia: commercial law firms and advocate entities.[60] No special license is required to open a

[58] K. Sen and R. Sahu, "Need For FLCs in India with Respect to Honouring the GATS Journal of International Trade Law and Policy", 6:2 *JITLP* 25–33 (2007).

[59] "A Balancing Act" at 2.

[60] M. Taddia, "Legal Russia: Bear Market" The Law Society Gazette (UK) (1 February 2016).

foreign law office in Russia beyond the normal registration process for commercial entities. There are nineteen geographical areas in Russia where foreigners can visit only with prior permission, and no offices of foreign firms of any kind can be established in these areas. Domestic lawyers may be employed by a foreign law firm, although Russian advocates may not be employees subject to an employment contract. However, they may be hired by a foreign lawyer or law firm under a services contract. Domestic advocates can form partnerships with foreign lawyers through cooperation contracts. Unlicensed Russian jurists may enter into any type of partnership (contractual or in a form of a legal entity) with a foreign lawyer, but if the foreign lawyer is recorded in the special Russian registry as a foreign advocate, then the rules for Russian advocates apply. Advocates can employ a foreign lawyer provided that this foreign lawyer is not recorded in the special Russian registry as a foreign advocate. There are more than fifty foreign law firms in Russia, mostly in Moscow and Saint Petersburg, including firms from the US, the UK, and Germany. An expanded presence of foreign firms is anticipated if economic sanctions are lifted or as commercial activity shifts towards practice areas that are unaffected by the sanctions, including dispute resolution.[61] The Russian government has recently considered prohibiting the direct or indirect control of an advocate or law firm practice by a foreign person or entity. If this proposal is implemented, it will severely impair the operations of foreign firms (mostly firms from the UK and the US) in Russia, prohibiting these firms from having branch offices, representative offices, or subsidiaries in Russia. Representatives of the legal profession in the UK and the US have submitted a counterproposal for a compromise model that would allow foreign firms to continue providing legal services in Russia.

5.4 Conclusion

The capacity to establish a permanent presence in the form of a law firm in a foreign state to deliver legal services is arguably the most important of all the modes of delivery of legal services for a profession that still relies heavily on in-person contact between lawyer and client and the development of a long-term relationship based on trust and familiarity with the client's individual business interests and in which sophisticated transactions require the coordination of multiple professionals within a global association. Unfortunately, Mode 3 supply of legal services is poorly

[61] Ibid.

liberalized under international law. The primary instrument for liberalization of commercial presence delivery (either through law firms or by sole practitioners setting up overseas) is the GATS, and there are very few FTAs that exceed these commitments.

One of the arguments in favour of opening Mode 3 markets (and Mode 4 markets, as will be examined in Chapter 6) is that there may not be enough suitably qualified services suppliers in the host state to serve the domestic market adequately, particularly in the context of economic expansion in conjunction with privatization. But this argument breaks down if one accepts that highly qualified individuals may not be required for a wide range of legal tasks. The technological trends noted in Chapter 3 may serve to undermine the need for further liberalization of commercial presence. Many tasks do not require the expertise of qualified lawyers and can readily be performed by other skilled and knowledgeable individuals working in the legal sector.[62]

For the time being, however, there seems to be a singular need for global law firms, and the many barriers to this type of practice that have been enacted, in particular by some of the large emerging markets, are not only frustrating the commercial potential for Western firms but also preventing some of the beneficial economic reforms that foreign-trained lawyers are well qualified to provide. At the same time, more mature markets must ensure that their idiosyncratic approaches to the regulation of law firms do not undercut the potential for foreign competition to deliver higher-quality services to more consumers. Although permanent establishment in a foreign jurisdiction may be a vital form of legal services delivery in many contexts, notably in relation to a suite of business services for an internationally minded client on a long-term basis, legal services professionals are increasingly interested in the ability to perform one-off contracts with clients overseas for the resolution of particular matters. This issue will be the focus of Chapter 6.

[62] Susskind, *Tomorrow's Lawyers* at 37.

6

Import Restrictions on Trade in Legal Services

Movement of Natural Persons

6.1 Introduction

Legal professionals operating in a foreign state on their own or through small firms rely heavily on the more flexible forms of market access, such as cross-border supply and, particularly in the case of short-term retainers, the presence of natural persons in the foreign state. This issue is closely related to Mode 3 establishment, explored in Chapter 5, because controls on the movement of lawyers have the potential to undermine the quality of the employees in foreign offices of law firms. For example, rules specifying that intracorporate transfers are limited to one year (as in Russia) would lead to a constant turnover of personnel, which would presumably disturb the effective functioning of the office.

Free movement of service suppliers involves issues relating to the practice of home state law in the host state on either a temporary or a quasi-permanent basis. It also raises issues relating to the route to full requalification, either through a truncated process because of the recognition of foreign qualifications and experiences or through full requalification in a manner identical to that required of local applicants, which may or may not require residency or nationality. Given the rising prominence of international arbitration as a means of resolving disputes, especially those of a financial nature, lawyers from one jurisdiction are increasingly called upon to represent their clients in one-off hearings in which the seat of arbitration is the jurisdiction where the legal practitioner is not admitted. This fly-in-fly-out (FIFO) practice of law is among the most pressing issues for legal services suppliers in the globalized economy. It is no surprise that a large number of free trade agreements (FTAs) include detailed provisions aimed at facilitating the temporary entry of foreign lawyers who engage in FIFO services supply.[1]

[1] S. Moritsch, "Research Paper: International Trade in Legal Services – FTAs and Beyond GATS Commitments" International Bar Association Trade in Legal Services Committee at 3.

Mode 4 of the GATS consists of services supplied "by a service supplier of one Member through the presence of natural persons of a Member in the territory or any other Member". This contemplates the temporary presence of an individual, although in practice many such individuals will work or reside in the foreign state for long periods of time. The GATS does not outline what constitutes temporality for the purposes of Mode 4. This means that it falls to every WTO member to specify in their commitment schedule the duration of stay that is allowed for natural persons.

Mode 4 is perhaps the most politically sensitive of the modes of supply of service because it affects not only the global economy, but also many national and regional issues that have both social and economic dimensions. Foremost among these is immigration, which can also touch upon issues of national security. There are also questions about the approach to the regulation of competition.[2] Mode 4 has been underrepresented in trade in services liberalization efforts. Despite its increasing importance, there are far fewer and more limited commitments regarding the mobility of workers than is the case for other modes of supply across virtually all services sectors. Even where WTO members have undertaken temporary movement of persons liberalization, conferring the right to provide legal services in domestic law remains optional and conditional on compliance with domestic regulations.[3]

Commentators have recognized that greater mobility of labour is one of the keys to addressing widespread labour shortages that have been identified throughout the world. This is particularly the case for many developed countries, which are seeing declines in their working-age populations, as was noted in Chapter 4. At the same time, many developing countries are experiencing a surge in workers, many of whom will not be able to find employment at home.[4] The temporary movement of services suppliers seems like an obvious solution to this imbalance. With open markets for temporary workers, underemployment associated with developing countries and an insufficient supply of workers in developed countries should be resolved as workers and consumers reach an international equilibrium. The actualization of these services export opportunities and the potential for mutual gains in labour availability and need across countries are contingent upon the openness to this kind of trade.[5]

[2] Amos-Stewarta, Broughton, and Schwartz, "All Talk and No Action" at 132.

[3] Ibid. at 133.

[4] Chanda, "Demographics and Labour Markets."

[5] Ibid. at 413.

In addition to addressing labour shortages directly, Mode 4 liberalization can result in further gains in terms of knowledge transfer and skills upgrading, which can in turn lead to increases in productivity. This is why, although Mode 4 constitutes the smallest share of services trade, it is thought to offer the greatest potential returns from additional services liberalization.[6] There is limited statistical evidence regarding the extent of movement of natural person for the supply of legal services. Some commentators hold that Mode 4 delivery of legal services involves primarily staff members of international law firms working abroad on short trips. Some slightly longer visits may occur when these large law firms send employees or partners overseas to staff their international offices.[7]

The GATS Council for Trade in Services elaborated on the type of service suppliers that are contemplated under Mode 4, distinguishing in particular between independent services suppliers and employees or representatives of a service supplier. Independent services suppliers are self-employed and are referred to as independent professionals. Subcategories of the employee category are business visitors, who are employees of firms and enter the host country to set up a commercial presence or to negotiate the sale of a service on their behalf; intracorporate transfers, who are natural persons who have been employed by a firm or have been a partner for a certain amount of time and are temporarily transferred into the territory of another WTO member; and graduate trainees, who are similar to intracorporate transfers except that there is a component of training in business techniques. Service suppliers as representatives are natural persons, referred to as business services sellers who represent services suppliers and enter the host state temporarily for the purposes of negotiating the sale of a service.[8] While some jurisdictions have focused their regulatory efforts on law firms, others concentrate on the individual legal services provider; this is why commitments under Mode 4 are so important. This is the case in the US, for example. With only a few minor exceptions, US regulations governing legal services place duties on individuals, not on firms.[9]

This chapter will introduce the common barriers to trade in legal services delivered by individual suppliers entering foreign states. Following the pattern of Chapter 5, it will then briefly outline how some of these barriers are manifested in some of the world's leading legal jurisdictions.

[6] Ibid. at 427.

[7] Muller, *Liberalization of Trade in Legal Services* at 86.

[8] WTO-CTS (2009) Presence of Natural Person (Mode 4), Background Note by the Secretariat, Council for Trade in Services, S/C/W/301 (15 December 2009) at 6–7.

[9] Semple, *Legal Services Regulation at the Crossroads* at 68.

It will conclude with some thoughts on the future of negotiations covering Mode 4 legal services.

6.2 Individual Legal Services Professionals

Restrictions to Mode 4 importation of services consist of both border and behind-the-border measures affecting both entry and post-entry of service professionals. The most common of these barriers are regulations and procedures concerning eligibility for an issuance of visas and work permits, quantitative restrictions on entry, recognition and qualification-related procedures, wage parity requirements, necessity tests including economic needs tests, investment-linked mobility conditions, nationality or residency conditions, government procurement practices, and discriminatory tax laws. Regulations affecting Mode 4 are often poorly articulated and excessively burdensome in terms of both duration and cost. Even short-term work permits can take weeks or months to be processed in some countries because of the cumbersome nature of the administrative requirements. Criteria for entry may be poorly articulated, failing to differentiate between short-term and permanent movement.

Regulations covering short-term movement of services suppliers tend to be biased in favour of those with higher skills and education as well as those at higher levels within organizations who move within affiliated companies. Individuals who move in a personal capacity tend to face greater obstacles in gaining entry to the host state. Processes are often designed to serve the needs of large firms that have overseas subsidiaries, tying the movement of persons to the movement of capital or to the establishment of permanent offices according to Mode 3. Such biases appear in the points-based immigration systems that are used by many developed countries that seek highly skilled individuals.[10]

For legal professionals, the greatest barriers associated with Mode 4 delivery of services are those linked to the difference between the de facto and the de jure implications of regulations regarding qualifications, many of which have been explored already in this book. Difficulties posed by licensing and qualification regulations are compounded by the fact that many jurisdictions issue qualifications for legal practitioners on a sub-federal level, requiring coordination between the state or province that regulates qualifications and the federal authority that is in charge of immigration matters. As with law firms, individuals who have been admitted

[10] Chanda, "Demographics and Labour Markets" at 428.

to practise law in two or more jurisdictions face the problem of having to conform to multiple, possibly conflicting codes of conduct. The alternative – reciprocal acceptance of a foreign ethical code – is perhaps equally problematic, given that law societies and bar associations may have different approaches to ethics.

The main barrier to Mode 4 delivery of legal services tends to be restrictive immigration policies, which apply both to natural persons who seek permanent residence and to short-term business visitors. A common restriction on the temporary provision of legal services is a residency requirement. Depending on the length of this requirement, it can operate as a major limitation on the delivery of legal advice on a casual basis. It may be common for lawyers seeking to engage in FIFO services to do so on a tourist visa to avoid complications, with difficulties arising for longer stays. Although rarely, some jurisdictions place nationality requirements on foreign lawyers before they can be admitted to practise law within the jurisdiction. Nationality requirements have been justified on the basis that the foreign lawyer must have competence in the host jurisdiction, including an understanding of the cultural context of laws. The link between domestic nationality and the fulfilment of consumer protection is far from clear, and this concern could be addressed through other means, such as liability insurance, as will be discussed further in Chapter 8. Educational requirements and examinations would also achieve this aim. There may be a further and perhaps even more tenuous argument that only someone of a particular country's nationality can have a genuine or vested interest in the duty to uphold the law in the best interests of that country's society.

In this regard, it should be noted that the GATS Annex on the Movement of Natural Persons Supplying Services under the Agreement significantly restricts the scope of the GATS in this regard. The Annex states in part:

> 2. The Agreement shall not apply to measures affecting natural persons seeking access to the employment market of a Member, nor shall it apply to measures regarding citizenship, residence or employment on a permanent basis ...
>
> ...
>
> 4. The Agreement shall not prevent a Member from applying measures to regulate the entry of natural persons into, or their temporary stay in, its territory, including those measures necessary to protect the integrity of, and to ensure the orderly movement of natural persons across, its borders, provided that such measures are not applied in such a manner as to nullify or impair the benefits accruing to any Member under the terms of a specific commitment.

An interpretive footnote goes on to add: "The sole fact of requiring a visa for natural persons of certain Members and not for those of others shall not be regarded as nullifying or impairing benefits under a specific commitment." Because these types of restrictions are outside the scope of the GATS, it would require a commitment in a regional trade agreement (RTA) on trade in services to control them.

It is not always easy to distinguish between measures that affect the right to enter or stay in a country and the right to supply a service. For example, a regulation covering work permits could be linked with entry visa. This type of restriction could arguably be attributed to either entry or supply. The member that is seeking to control the delivery of the foreign service may have to construct the trade obstacle in such a manner that it is not caught by GATS disciplines.[11] The GATS would apply to measures such as the refusal to recognize a foreign lawyer's qualification, the obligation for foreigners to pass an examination that is more difficult than the exam for national citizens in order to obtain a licence to provide legal services, or any kind of unfavourable supply conditions.

There are common visa restrictions that prohibit foreign lawyers from taking payments while in the foreign state but not from developing contacts or pursuing negotiations on behalf of clients in their home state. The purpose of this distinction appears to be grounded in both the restriction of competition and the safeguarding of consumers. Such foreign lawyers are not truly in competition with equivalent domestic legal services suppliers because they cannot take payment. They also do not pose a risk for domestic clients because they cannot represent them and thus possibly affect their legal rights adversely.

One of the main routes by which individual lawyers may establish themselves in foreign jurisdictions for the purposes of offering legal services is by becoming a Foreign Legal Consultant (FLC), a status that has gained widespread recognition throughout the world in the past several decades.[12] The FLC concept originated in New York State and has been adopted by many jurisdictions around the world. Generally speaking, FLCs are individuals who are qualified to practise law in one country and seek to be licensed to practise law in another country without being examined by an authority that regulates the legal profession in that other country. FLCs typically need to obtain a licence from the host country

[11] Diebold, *Non-discrimination in International Trade in Services* at 214.

[12] A. Pardieck, "Foreign Legal Consultants: The Changing Role of the Lawyer in a Global Economy," 3:2 Indiana Journal of Global Legal Studies Article 5 (1996).

that is based on their experience and their moral fitness. FLCs tend to be restricted in terms of the types of law they can advise on, normally being granted the right to offer advice in relation to their home state and international law but not the law of the host state. As a consequence of these tight restrictions, it has been suggested that domestic legal services providers should not form any kind of formal association with FLCs because FLCs are not truly lawyers in the sense that domestic ones are. Such alliances would therefore transgress the bans on multidisciplinary practices that many countries impose.[13]

Severely circumscribed in their capacity to provide services, FLCs are not normally viewed as impeding the practice of domestic lawyers or undermining their monopoly on the provision of legal advice in a competitive manner. Still, expertise in a foreign jurisdiction's law could be quite valuable for firms seeking advice on entry into that overseas market from a practitioner that is locally available. Moreover, given the increasing breadth of international law, itself linked to globalization, the FLC is arguably a more valuable designation today than it was when first conceived and later advanced in a model law adopted by the American Bar Association (ABA).[14]

The FLC is an international example of what has been referred to as a "subordinated paraprofessional" model of legal regulation, in which various aspects of legal services may be performed by individuals who lack the qualifications of fully licensed lawyers, such as the Law Clerk in the Canadian province of Ontario, which is also a regulated profession. The problem with this approach, it has been suggested, is that there is a conflict of interest for the legal services regulator when the regulator is composed of members of the profession (i.e., self-regulation). When this occurs, as is the case in most US states, for example, there is a danger that claims about the poorer quality of the service by the subprofessional (e.g., the FLC) may be used to restrict artificially restrict access to the market in which other professionals – namely, fully qualified lawyers – compete.[15] The fact that FLCs tend to be able to practise only the law of their home state and international law is a likely manifestation of this phenomenon.

A lack of a specific licensing or registration regime for FLCs practising their home state law can be problematic. The foreign practitioner may wish to practise only the law of their home state (and perhaps international

[13] A. Persky, "Despite Globalization, Lawyers Find New Barriers to Practicing Abroad" ABA Journal, November 2011.

[14] American Bar Association, Model Rule for the Licensing and Practice of Foreign Legal Consultants (August 2006).

[15] Semple, *Legal Services Regulation at the Crossroads* at 290.

law), but to do so, they are compelled to requalify fully by passing the relevant bar exams in the host state.[16] One of the most significant obstacles for a prospective FLC is the requirement of postqualification experience, which can vary enormously between jurisdictions. Some countries impose a requirement of reciprocity on the recognition of FLCs, although in some instances, this is done on a discretionary basis. For example, the ABA rule on reciprocity for FLC designation specifies that a lawyer's origin is a factor that regulators may take into account. While this may create uncertainty, it also adds pragmatism and flexibility to the recognition of foreign qualifications, logic that underpins the mutual recognition provisions in the GATS, as will be explored in Chapter 7.

Exhaustive application procedures for FLC status, combined in some cases with fees, act as additional soft barriers to trade in legal services by making the process more difficult than it might otherwise be. Given that ethical considerations are paramount for legal practitioners, these cumbersome processes may have the added advantage of ensuring that the foreign lawyers who apply for FLC status will do so in good faith and will behave in an ethical manner. Behavioural economics literature suggests that forms that require more effort to complete tend to be met with more honest conduct on the part of the applicant.[17] While these registration procedures may be onerous, not having an FLC designation at all is even more restrictive.

Regardless of the extent of their qualification and experience, foreign lawyers are typically excluded from at least some aspect of the practice of local law in most jurisdictions around the world. The rationale for this protracted liberalization is one of consumer (or client) protection. Since the practice of law is highly location specific, unlike most other professions, it makes sense that a legal practitioner should become fully competent in the law of the host state before representing or advising clients. However, the definition of "local law" is itself far from certain, particularly in relation to its interaction with international law and issues of conflicts of laws and *renvoi* in which local law may refer to foreign law, given sufficient connections to that jurisdiction.[18]

Some jurisdictions maintain transfer procedures for foreign lawyers, enabling them to practise local law fully and to be integrated into the local

[16] Muller, *Liberalization of Trade in Legal Services* at 118.

[17] Y. Feldman, "Behavioral Ethics Meets Behavioral Law and Economics" in E. Zamir and D. Teichman eds. *The Oxford Handbook of Behavioral Law and Economics* (Oxford University Press, 2015).

[18] Hook, "Sectoral Study on the Impact of Domestic Regulation on Trade in Legal Services" at 25.

legal profession. These are not always offered equally to lawyers from all jurisdictions, or there may be truncated procedures for lawyers from certain jurisdictions but not others. This variable treatment, which is in principle contrary to the Most Favoured Nation (MFN) obligation, is normally based on similarities of the legal systems (e.g. common law rather than civil law) and is likely defensible on that basis. In other words, the services suppliers would not be considered "like" for the purposes of Article II of the GATS. Indeed, a narrow understanding of likeness under the GATS could allow a wide range of discriminatory policies against foreign services suppliers.

Temporary admission, most often known as FIFO or, as it is labelled in the US, *pro hac vice* admission, addresses the growing need to practise across international borders (as well as interjurisdictional regional borders). This is particularly important given the international element associated with digital businesses. Local courts need to ensure that foreign lawyers who practise before them are qualified to advise their clients on local laws and to comply with local procedural formalities. This is why most courts or bar associations that administer FIFO rules require that the foreign lawyer has assistance from local counsel, who may certify the foreign lawyer's ability and help the foreign lawyer to conform to local procedural issues, and that the applicant promises to abide by the rules of the host court. Undue restrictions on this type of practice must be viewed in light of the fact that it is much easier to obtain information about another country's legal system than was the case in the past. Whereas foreign lawyers may have needed access to a law library in the target jurisdiction to serve a client in that jurisdiction, the laws of most countries are now readily available online, in some cases for free. This is partly because of the drive towards regulatory transparency instigated by the WTO. In developed countries such as the US, the availability of legal information seems to have grown commensurately with that of the Internet. Some organizations, such as the Legal Information Institute, have consolidated publicly available law in user-friendly databases.[19]

6.3 Specific Jurisdictions' Rules on Movement of Natural Persons

As was done for Mode 3 in Chapter 5, this section will consider the major barriers to Mode 4 delivery of legal services maintained by some of the world's leading jurisdictions for legal services. In contrast to Mode 3, the temporary presence of natural persons supplying legal services tends to be

[19] Barton, *Glass Half Full* at 199.

spread around the world and is often clustered in regions that have been chosen as the seat for commercial arbitration hearings. As was noted in Chapter 4, many countries seek to attract consumers of legal services by offering comprehensive legal advice centres, including those that offer dispute settlement services. The capacity to do so often rests upon that jurisdiction's willingness to allow foreign legal services professionals to practise on a temporary basis.

6.3.1 European Union Member States

The legal profession in Europe is heterogeneous in more ways than the simple multiplicity of twenty-seven jurisdictions, each of which is integrated by the unifying force of EU law at what might be described as the federal level. Legal services are delivered by a wide range of specialized legal providers with distinct training programmes, different career paths, and different professional organizations with associated codes of conduct. Legal services providers such as judges, notaries, advocates, and state attorneys may not even view themselves as lawyers in the sense that individuals do in the US, Canada, and the UK.[20]

The EU Treaty has achieved the most liberalized regime for trade in legal services in the world, going far beyond the GATS and any other RTAs. Still, there has as yet been no effort to engage in an EU-wide reorganization of legal systems in a centralized fashion; nor has there been any direct harmonization of professional rules. In its efforts to create a single internal services market, the EU instituted two directives concerning legal qualification requirements. The first authorized legal services providers to provide their services under their home country law in all other EU countries without the need to register with the host state.[21] The more recent directive was more comprehensive.[22] Adopted in 2006 and implemented by all EU member states in 2009, the Lawyer's Establishment Directive encourages member states to develop pan-European codes of conduct for the professions.[23] This

[20] A. Uzelac and C. H. van Rhee, "Introduction" in A. Uzelac and C. H. van Rhee eds. *The Landscape of the Legal Professions in Europe and the USA: Continuity and Change* (Intersentia, 2011).

[21] EC, Council Directive of 22 March 1977 to facilitate the effective exercise by lawyers of freedom to provide services, EEC 77/249, OJ L 78, 26 March 1977, at 17.

[22] EC, Council Directive 98/5/EC to facilitate the practice of the profession of lawyer on a permanent basis in a Member State other than that in which the qualification was obtained, [1998] OJ L 77; EC, Directive 98/5/EC of the European Parliament and of the Council of 16 February 1998, OJ L 77, 14 March 1998.

[23] Directive 2006/123/EC.

directive also establishes a mechanism for the mutual recognition of professional titles of migrant lawyers who seek to practise under their home country professional title in another EU member state. The Directive provides that a European lawyer must comply not only with the rules of professional conduct applicable in the home member state, but also with those of the host member state, failing which the lawyer will face disciplinary sanctions.[24]

Although registration is still required in a host EU state, legal service markets have been substantially opened. Lawyers who are registered in one EU member state are permitted to practise domestic law in another EU member state with no limits on scope of practice and no requirement to be supervised by a domestic lawyer. Their practice must be under a foreign lawyer's home title for the first three years, after which a foreign lawyer is free to practise host country law without any need to requalify in that jurisdiction. From that point onward, unlike FLCs, the European lawyer maintains the same status as domestically qualified lawyers.

The EU has comprehensive provisions covering the free movement of lawyers from European Economic Area (EEA) countries, comprising the EU along with Norway, Iceland, Liechtenstein, and Switzerland, which is in neither the EU nor the EEA. Taken together, these directives permit legal practitioners from the EEA to establish and provide legal services in host country law as well as home country law and international law and to requalify as a host country lawyer inside the territory of the EU and the EEA. The establishment of foreign lawyers (meaning lawyers from outside the EU and the EEA) is handled differently; each EU member state applies its own rules, which have varying degrees of restrictiveness.

Various provisions in EU FTAs are relevant to the movement of professionals such as lawyers. The Comprehensive Economic and Trade Agreement (CETA), for example, contains a chapter on the creation of a framework for the negotiation of a mutual recognition agreement (MRA) for professional qualifications so that professionals from Canada and Europe can practise in each other's territory, although it has very limited substance and does not deal with lawyers expressly.[25] Similarly, the EU-Ukraine FTA states the following:

> The commitments undertaken by the Parties are subject to the following conditions:
>
> (a) the natural persons must be engaged in the supply of a service on a temporary basis as self-employed persons established in the other Party and must have obtained a service contract for a period not exceeding 12 months;

[24] Ibid.

[25] Chapter 11: Mutual Recognition of Professional Qualifications.

(b) the natural persons entering the other Party must possess, at the date of submission of an application for entry into the other Party, at least six years professional experience in the sector of activity which is the subject of the contract;
(c) the natural persons entering the other Party must possess:
   (i) a university degree or a qualification demonstrating knowledge of an equivalent level (1) and
   (ii) professional qualifications where this is required to exercise an activity pursuant to the laws, regulations or other legal requirements of the Party where the service is supplied;
(d) the entry and temporary stay of natural persons within the Party concerned shall be for a cumulative period of not more than six months or, in the case of Luxembourg, 25 weeks in any 12-month period or for the duration of the contract, whichever is less;
(e) access accorded under the provisions of this Article relates only to the service activity which is the subject of the contract and does not confer entitlement to exercise the professional title of the Party where the service is provided.[26]

CETA established a similar regulatory pattern in its provision on Contractual Service Providers and Independent Professionals in the chapter on Temporary Entry and Stay of Natural Persons for Business Purposes.[27] The EU-Korea FTA contains a legal services chapter aimed at facilitating trade in legal services, some of which are relevant for Mode 4. Under this agreement, lawyers will be allowed to use their domestic job titles, such as Solicitor, Avocat, or Rechtsanwalt. France recently introduced an FLC status to ensure the implementation of this agreement's provisions. This type of arrangement may be viewed as a suitable model for foreign practice rights for UK lawyers in the EU after the UK's departure from the EU.

In many EU countries, foreign lawyers from WTO member states may practise international and home country law on a temporary basis. As with practice on a permanent basis, short-term practice under home qualification typically requires that the professional use the professional title from his or her home state, comply with the local lawyers' code of conduct, and maintain adequate professional indemnity insurance. Such individuals must also obtain a business visa. A number of EU member states, including the large markets of Italy, France, Germany, the Netherlands, and Spain, are signatories of the Schengen agreement, which allows

[26] Article 92.2.
[27] Article 10.8.

non-EEA nationals to obtain a visa to enter for business purposes for visits of up to ninety days or multiple entries over a 180-day period. Foreign lawyers from non-WTO member states must apply for permission from the relevant bar or governmental department. Individuals from outside the EEA/EFTA and Switzerland are not permitted to appear in court at all in most EU member states. Several large EU member states do not permit FIFO practice at all. This kind of delivery of legal services is allowed in France only for nationals of states that have concluded bilateral conventions with France covering this issue. The provision of temporary services in Germany by a lawyer from a non-EU member state under the lawyer's home qualification is not permitted whatsoever. Likewise, the provision of temporary services in the Netherlands by a lawyer from a non-EU member state under the lawyer's home qualification is not permitted.

The EU's agreements with Ukraine, Georgia, and Moldova contain specific provisions on movement of contractual service suppliers and independent professionals in international and foreign (meaning non-EU) law. They require parties to "allow the supply of services" by contractual service suppliers and independent professionals subject to some qualification, experience, and other requirements. CETA established a similar regulatory pattern in its Chapter X, entitled "Temporary Entry and Stay of Natural Persons for Business Purposes."

To give a sense of the extent to which the EU embraces the presence of foreign lawyers working within its borders, this section will examine some of the restrictions placed by the most economically significant EU member states on foreign lawyers' capacity to deliver services within their territory.[28]

In Italy, there are no nationality, residency, or reciprocity requirements for foreign lawyers to be admitted to hold the title of avvocato. Foreign lawyers, under their home country title, can practise in Italy the law of their home country or public international law. Non-EEA nationals must pass the full bar exam before a special Commission of the Italian National Bar Council. There is a reduced examination for individuals who have passed examinations in Italian universities or have practised the legal profession in Italy for a significant period. For those who have an Italian law degree, requalification requires only a very reduced examination on Italian ethical and professional rules.

In France, foreign lawyers may practise the law of their home country and public international law without restriction. Foreign lawyers

[28] This information is derived from a report by the Law Society of England and Wales entitled "The EU and the Legal Sector" (2015).

can requalify in France, under conditions of reciprocity, by taking the relevant equivalence examination administered by the Conseil National des Barreaux. Very few foreign lawyers have actually done this. This reciprocity requirement in theory violates the MFN rule of GATS Article II unless it could be argued that lawyers from countries for which there is no reciprocity are not "like" suppliers. Foreign lawyers must also meet educational qualifications and pass a local examination; foreign lawyers have the possibility of passing an attenuated examination based on experience. There is no residency requirement, but a professional address where clients' files are held and kept must be provided for registration. France does not yet recognize FLCs; however, it has been prepared to offer this designation to Korean lawyers following the conclusion of the EU-Korea FTA. The new foreign legal consultant status Article 109 adopted under the EU-South Korea FTA provides that "foreign lawyers admitted to a bar of non-EU member states but linked to the EU by an international treaty" are able to practise international and home state law and go into partnership with a local lawyer. It is still unclear whether the new legislation will be applicable to all countries with which the EU has FTAs (on a MFN basis) or only to those for which trade in legal services is included in the agreement.

In Germany, foreign lawyers from WTO member states may establish themselves under their home title and can practise home country law and international public law provided that the foreign lawyers exercise a profession in their home country that is comparable in education, competencies, and legal position to the position of a Rechtsanwalt in Germany. Licences for foreign lawyers are granted by local bars, but no nationality, residency, or reciprocity requirements are imposed on foreign lawyers once they have registered. Non-EEA lawyers must undertake the full national process of qualification in Germany, which consists of an educational component as well as an examination.

Lawyers of nationalities from outside the EU/EEA who want to requalify in Spain as an abogado may have their qualifications assessed by the local bar association, with limited guidance available on how this is done, suggesting a high degree of discretion on the part of the local bar association granting the licence.

6.3.2 *United Kingdom (England and Wales)*

The regulation of legal services in the UK has placed great emphasis on the expansion of competition for the purpose of addressing consumers' needs. People who would historically have been considered clients are now held in the same regard as individuals who purchase any other service or good. Accordingly, barriers to the delivery of many kinds of legal services have been lowered, most notably in relation to the sharing of fees between lawyers and non-lawyers through alternative business structures.[29] Unlike the US and Canada, where a person either is a licensed lawyer authorized to provide any and all legal services or cannot provide any legal services, the UK has multiple licensing regimes for solicitors, barristers, conveyancers, legal executives, and others.[30] The more relaxed regulatory environment in the UK has allowed for the establishment of Citizens Advice Bureaus staffed by nonqualified volunteers with relevant experience that offer legal advice on a range of issues to low-income individuals.

As of the time of writing, what the requirements will be for European lawyers to establish themselves in the UK after the UK's departure from the EU is uncertain. The UK is expected to sign its own FTAs in the coming years in an effort to diversify its economy away from reliance on access to the EU's Single Market. Presumably, such instruments will contain provisions on the liberalization of services. The inclusion of specific provisions on trade in legal services in such treaties exceeding those of the GATS is probably unlikely, as these are uncommon in modern FTAs. However, given the size of the UK's legal services market and its importance to the domestic economy, the UK is in a position to take up world leadership in the liberalization of legal services, much as it has done in modernizing the legal profession at home.

Once it leaves the EU, the UK will no longer be bound by the EU's Establishment Directive, so presumably, no special privileges will be granted in the UK to EU or EEA lawyers unless this is achieved in a new trade agreement between the UK and the EU. Currently, there is no requirement for a foreign lawyer to obtain a licence to practise as an FLC in the UK, and such individuals are entitled to practise the law of their home state and international law. To fully requalify as an English solicitor, foreign lawyers must take the Qualified Lawyers Transfer Scheme (QLTS) exam, which is a good example of autonomous recognition pursued under GATS Article V.[31] This requires the candidate to have sufficient prior experience in the practice of law in his or her home jurisdiction. A foreign lawyer who

[29] Semple, *Legal Services Regulation at the Crossroads* at 80–84 (described as "competitive-consumerist" reforms).

[30] Ibid. at 98.

[31] The author took an earlier version of the QLTS (the QLTT), and it was neither difficult nor lengthy. In the past, the transfer exam could be taken in Toronto, Sydney, and various cities in the US; it now must be taken in the UK.

seeks to become an English barrister may apply as a foreign-qualified lawyer, which requires documentation evincing experience. There is limited express guidance as to how these applications will be reviewed.

Foreign lawyers may obtain a visa to visit clients in the UK. These individuals may also obtain special "permitted paid employment" visas, which are valid for up to one month without the need to obtain a work permit. FIFO lawyers should also register with the Chamber of Advocates. Foreign lawyers are allowed to undertake mediation and arbitration, which are vital areas of professional practice in London, where there are a number of international arbitration institutions. Currently, non-EEA and Swiss lawyers can apply for a temporary call to the bar (via the Bar Standards Board) to conduct a specific case (or cases) in England and Wales. To obtain a temporary call, a candidate is required to provide the Bar Standards Board with evidence of competency, experience, and good character.

6.3.3 United States

The manner in which legal services are regulated in the US has been criticized primarily because it tends to be highly proscriptive and rules based rather than being proactive or outcome focused as in jurisdictions such as the UK and Australia.[32] The regional character of the regulation of the legal profession in the US is linked to the highly decentralized nature of government itself. The US legal system is composed of dozens of common law systems, each with its own hierarchy of judges, a degree of uniformity being achieved through treatises such as the Uniform Commercial Code. There is much universality in legal education in the ABA-approved law schools, which tend to concentrate on federal law, much as there is standardization among professional codes of ethics across the country.[33]

The three-year graduate law degree that is required to practise in all US states is often viewed as excessive, in part because there is no evidence that it leads to more competent lawyers. It is also poorly defensible in terms of the costs it imposes on law students. Such costs are inevitably passed on to clients, restricting access to justice.[34] It is further questionable whether law school curricula, particularly in graduate-style law schools in the US, are well suited to prepare students for the practice of law. Few academics

[32] Snyder, *Democratizing Legal Services* at 12.

[33] R. J. Goebel, "Legal Practice Rights of Domestic and Foreign Lawyers in the United States," 49:2 International and Comparative Law Quarterly 413–444 at 419 (2000).

[34] Semple, *Legal Services Regulation at the Crossroads* at 102.

at these law schools have practised themselves, the emphasis on faculty hiring being geared towards publishing record and in some cases a doctoral qualification.[35] The practical value of a US law school education is thrown into doubt by studies showing that a bare majority of law school graduating classes in recent years are employed full time by the following year.[36] Moreover, US law schools do not truly compete for students in a genuine market environment. Much of the demand for places in law school comes from the US government's requirement that students must graduate from an ABA-accredited law school to hold a law licence.

Each of the fifty US states plus the District of Columbia has its own licensing regime for lawyers. Almost all US states have a single licensing process for individuals who seek to provide legal services, and all individuals who are able to satisfy this process are identified as lawyers, although they are often also described as attorneys. The US is thought to be the most lawyered country in the world, with roughly one in every 260 people holding the qualification.[37] For those who do not obtain this licence to practise, attempts to provide legal services outside the supervision of a lawyer may make the person liable for unauthorized practice of law. In this sense, US lawyers have a well-established hegemony over the delivery of legal services that is maintained by state bar associations, which tend to define the boundaries of the acceptable practice of law, often in conjunction with the national ABA, further entrenching their monopoly.[38] Indeed, the intense regulation of the legal services market in the US has been described as "the triumph of the ABA" in the early twentieth century, when it carved out a broad range of lucrative services for its members through tightly controlled rules on exclusivity.[39] Regulatory reform of the tightly controlled legal profession in the US with a view towards greater liberalization is anticipated by some, in part in response to the integration of technology into the delivery of legal services.[40]

In its current form, NAFTA, for example, calls for future negotiations on MRAs among the legal professions, and lawyers are included in the

[35] C. Stolker, *Rethinking the Law School: Education, Research, Outreach and Governance* (Cambridge University Press, 2014) at 142 and J. Sonsteng, "The Unfulfilled Promise of Law Schools to Prepare Students for the Practice of Law" in Gane and Hui Hang eds. *Legal Education in the Global Context*.

[36] Barton, *Glass Half Full* at 49.

[37] "A Balancing Act" at 16, www.nathaninc.com/company/organization/nathan-india (accessed March 2018).

[38] Semple, *Legal Services Regulation at the Crossroads* at 47–48.

[39] G Hadfield, *Rules for a Flat World* (Oxford University Press, 2016) at 229.

[40] Barton, *Glass Half Full* at 19.

professional visa programme, allowing citizens of Canada and Mexico to work in the United States in legal services for US or foreign employers.[41] The US-Australia FTA calls for the creation of a working group to foster MRAs among professional bodies.[42] There is no evidence that any progress has been made in this regard under either treaty.

US law maintains a doctrine of "unauthorized practice of law", which is treated as a criminal offence in some states.[43] It can also lead to disciplinary proceedings or disqualification by state bar associations. This may explain why the practice of law by foreign-qualified individuals is tightly regulated in the US, a jurisdiction that is known for having a generally open stance towards services trade. The US Supreme Court forbade the requirement of US citizenship as a precondition for bar admission. In *Application of Griffiths*[44] it held that the equal protection clause of the US Constitution prevented a state from demanding US citizenship as a precondition for admission to the bar. The court declared that resident aliens should have equal employment rights in view of their economic contributions to society and that there was no reason to question their loyalty or their capacity to fulfil ethical and professional obligations as officers of the court because of their citizenship. For individuals over the age of twenty-five who are seeking only to practise the law of their home state and international law to the extent to which it relates to that home state law, there are FLC rules in thirty-one US states, the District of Columbia, and the US Virgin Islands. The US listed details of its FLC regime under its Additional Commitments schedule of the GATS.[45]

The US implements a "service salespersons" designation, which could be of use to legal professionals who negotiate on the behalf of other companies seeking to provide business activities in the US that are not of a retail nature, meaning that they are not aimed at the general public. Such individuals are permitted to enter the US for periods of up to ninety days. Entry for service salespeople, who cannot receive remuneration from a source in the US, is limited to a ninety-day period. A number of US states have recently modified their rules, allowing foreign lawyers to practise on a FIFO basis subject to the completion of an application and payment of a fee which is usually a few hundred dollars. In almost all US jurisdictions,

41 Article 1210.5.2.
42 Annex 10-A Professional Services.
43 California Business and Professional Code s 6126 (a) and New York Judiciary Law s 485.
44 413 U.S. 717 (1973).
45 Article XVIII, allowing members to list measures for matters including qualifications and licenses.

lawyers who appear in court on a one-off basis must do so with a local lawyer acting as local counsel. It is thought that as many as 15 per cent of all lawsuits filed in the US involve the participation of a foreign lawyer.[46]

In the US, litigation before courts in states other than the one in which a lawyer has been admitted to the bar can be achieved without difficulty through the *pro hac vice* admission process. However, courts have wide discretion in evaluating candidates and usually require association with local counsel along with the consent of the client. Extrajurisdictional legal practice in consultation, negotiation, and transactions is normal in the US. There is a risk that courts of the state in which this practice is conducted may decide that the legal work constitutes the unauthorized practice of law, potentially subject to a variety of sanctions. There is no US federal rule authorizing cross-border temporary practice of this nature.[47]

California has relatively liberal admission requirements for foreign lawyers. Foreign-trained lawyers who have been admitted to practise law in a jurisdiction outside the US are often eligible to take the bar exam in California without needing to complete any additional requirements. If the foreign-trained legal practitioner has not been admitted to practise outside the US, the applicant is still eligible to take the bar exam after completing an LLM degree program that covers four separate subjects tested on the exam, which is notoriously difficult with among the lowest pass rates in the country. Foreign law school graduates must request individual evaluation to determine legal education equivalency for the purposes of taking the California Bar Exam. Graduates from foreign law schools who are not admitted in their home state may qualify to take the California Bar Exam if they obtain an LLM degree or complete an additional one year of law study at an ABA-approved law school. In California, FLCs may practise home country law and international law provided that the FLC first obtains advice from an attorney who is licensed in that jurisdiction. FLCs who regularly supply such services must obtain a licence, to be renewed annually, and must provide an address of record. FLCs may not practise US federal law or the law of any US state, including appearing in court or preparing any documents. FLCs must have sufficient experience, be in good standing with their home country bar, and hold professional liability insurance. California permits lawyers who are licensed to practise in another US jurisdiction to practise only temporarily in California without

[46] Cornell Law School, Legal Information Institute "Pro Hac Vice", www.law.cornell.edu/wex/pro_hac_vice (accessed March 2018).

[47] Goebel, "Legal Practice Rights of Domestic and Foreign Lawyers in the United States."

registering with the state bar. Individuals who are qualified in another US state must submit information about the particular pending matter for which the *pro hac vice* permission is sought.

Reflecting a narrower approach to international trade in legal services than California's, Florida does not allow foreign applicants to become qualified attorneys. Only graduates of a three-year ABA-approved American JD program are eligible for bar admission in Florida. Similarly, foreign law firms are not permitted to establish themselves in Florida. Foreign lawyers can become FLCs in Florida. Practice in this capacity is limited to the laws of the foreign country in which the person is admitted to practise and cannot consist of any activity or service constituting the practice of the laws of the US or any US state, including appearing in court or preparing legal documents. FLCs must use the title "Foreign Legal Consultant, Not Admitted to Practice Law in Florida" alongside their home title, and they must provide clients with a letter disclosing the extent of their professional liability insurance coverage. They must maintain an office in Florida and provide an annual sworn statement to confirm that they remain in good standing with their home bar. Florida has an express rule allowing temporary practice for foreign lawyers that specifies the scope of practice in which foreign-qualified lawyers may engage, which includes a pending arbitration or mediation taking place within Florida or litigation that is undertaken in conjunction with a lawyer who has been admitted to the bar in Florida. Foreign lawyers are not included under the Florida's *pro hac vice* rule for court appearances, which covers out-of-state US lawyers only. Foreign lawyers may provide arbitration or mediation services without registration if these are in, or reasonably related to, a pending or potential arbitration or mediation.

Foreign lawyers may requalify as attorneys in Illinois by requesting permission from the Board to take the Illinois Bar Examination. To do so, the foreign lawyer must have been licensed to practise law in the country in which the law degree was conferred for a minimum of five years and must currently be in good standing. There is the additional requirement that during five of the seven years immediately prior to making the application in Illinois, the lawyer must have verifiably devoted an annual minimum of 1000 hours to the practice of the law of the country where he or she is licensed. Illinois also permits foreign lawyers to become FLCs, licensed to offer services regarding the law of their home country and international law to the extent to which it is incorporated into home country law. Illinois forbids FLCs to practise third-country law or Illinois law. FLCs must register with the Illinois state bar, abide by the state code of conduct, demonstrate experience in their area of legal expertise, and meet professional indemnity insurance requirements. Illinois allows foreign-qualified lawyers to provide, upon registration with the court, legal services on a temporary basis in Illinois for court hearings, administrative tribunals, and alternative dispute resolution proceedings. Such appearances are limited to five in one calendar year.

New York is perhaps the most popular US jurisdiction for foreign-qualified lawyers to seek establishment, in large part because New York law is widely chosen as governing law for international commercial contracts the world over. Foreign-qualified lawyers may take the New York Bar Examination if they satisfy the New York State Board of Law Examiners that they meet the legal education requirement for access to the examination in terms of both duration of study and the substance of law studies, which essentially requires that it be based on English common law.[48] An applicant who does not satisfy these requirements may obtain an LLM degree at an ABA-accredited university. The New York Board of Law Examiners has discretion to admit a foreign lawyer to practise in New York without examination if the person has been admitted to practise law in another country whose jurisprudence is based upon the principles of English common law and that country would similarly admit a New York attorney to its bar without examination. New York also allows foreign lawyers to obtain a licence to become an FLC (having originated the concept) with requirements similar to those seen earlier. FLCs in New York cannot represent clients in court or prepare any instruments that are intended to have a legal effect on behalf of clients, such as deeds for land or probate documents. FLCs cannot advise on the law of New York, the US, or any other US state and must be in good standing with their home bar. FLCs must have at least five years of experience in practising law in their home state and be of good moral character. Foreign lawyers may appear in court in New York on a case-by-case basis at the discretion of the court on the basis of the applicant's good standing in the home jurisdiction. If granted by the court, *pro hac vice* permission lasts for eighteen months. There are no specified restrictions regarding scope of practice.

Becoming qualified as an attorney in Texas requires passing the Texas Bar Exam. Eligibility to take this exam is predicated on the foreign lawyer's

[48] In the author's experience, although the New York Bar Exam is not a difficult one, it is lengthy. There are practical issues for foreign applicants who must take the exam in Albany, where there is limited overnight accommodation during exam season. There is also a requirement for an in-person interview before admission to the bar.

having graduated from a non-correspondence law school that is accredited by its jurisdiction, holding a valid licence within that jurisdiction, having practised law for five of the last seven years. Most problematically, the foreign lawyer must demonstrate that the foreign law is comparable to that of Texas or holds an LLM degree from an ABA-approved law school (not by correspondence or distance learning). The applicant must demonstrate that he or she holds the equivalent of a JD. As with New York, this requirement would preclude, for example, graduates of the UK Graduate Diploma in Law course, as it is of only one year's duration. Texas also has an FLC regime that broadly resembles that of the states discussed previously. The scope of practice permitted to FLCs includes the practice of home country law and the practice of international law to the extent to which it is incorporated in home country law. Practice of third-country law and practice of US law are not permitted. The designation FLC is available to an individual who is a member in good standing of a recognized legal profession in a foreign country and has practised law for at least three of the last five years. Good moral character and maintaining an office in Texas are also required. FLCs must further be in good standing with their home bar and abide by the home state's code of conduct. Texas permits "reputable attorneys" who reside outside of the US to seek permission to participate in legal proceedings taking place in Texas. Applications for such permission involves filing a motion with the relevant court in Texas.

6.3.4 *Japan*

Among all developed countries, Japan's regulations on establishment of foreign legal services providers are the most stringent and discriminatory, perhaps reflecting the country's restrictive approach to immigration. Foreign lawyers may register with the Japan Federation of Bar Associations as a Gaikoku-Ho-Jimu-Bengoshi (GJB), which is similar to an FLC. The scope of practice available to such individuals is limited to the law in which the individual is qualified and to international law, provided that the relevant international law is in force in the home jurisdiction. The practice of third-country law and the practice of Japanese law are disallowed. This restriction also precludes court appearances as well as preparation of legal documents unless this is undertaken in conjunction with a Japanese Bengoshi. To register as a GJB, a foreign lawyer must have practised for at least three years, at least two of which must have been in the lawyer's home jurisdiction, be in good standing in the home jurisdiction, and have the capability to compensate for damages caused to a client. While there is no requirement of a permanent presence or office for GJBs, such individuals must be resident in Japan for at least 180 days a year. In addition, once GJB registration has been obtained, the foreign qualification to practise must be maintained; otherwise, the registration will be withdrawn.

There is no special requalification route for foreign lawyers who want to become admitted in Japan as a fully qualified Bengoshi. Foreigners must follow the domestic qualification route to be admitted in Japan, requiring applicants to pursue their legal education and obtain their qualifications in Japan. Unquestionably, the need to master the Japanese language is a significant barrier for foreigners who want to undertake this process. Legal services are not covered in the agreements with Mexico and Chile, and the agreement with Switzerland covers legal services through a best efforts provision on the creation of a future MRA.[49]

There is no express rule allowing temporary practice by foreign lawyers in Japan. Japan's GATS commitments suggest that a commercial presence is required for the delivery of legal services in Japan unless such delivery is done through a local lawyer. Most Organisation for Economic Co-operation and Development (OECD) members have reciprocal visa exemptions with Japan for business visits of up to ninety days. Foreign lawyers may obtain a visa for the purpose of visiting clients or contacts in Japan but not to obtain remuneration or to accept payment. The lack of a FIFO rule in Japan, in contrast to the US, for example, can most likely be explained by practical language barriers as well as technical legal ones. It is unlikely that many non-Japanese qualified lawyers will have sufficient proficiency in Japanese to appear before courts in that country. Furthermore, the Japanese legal system is a complex mixture of Roman law, German codes, and US law from the nineteenth century. It is difficult to envision that many foreign lawyers will have this knowledge. This is also why there are very few US law students in Japan, in contrast to US law schools, where there are many Japanese students.

6.3.5 *Canada*

The Canadian legal profession has been described as one that combines the strong collective governance of the English tradition with the creativity and client responsiveness that are characteristic of US lawyers.[50]

[49] Article 49.

[50] P. Gerard, *Lawyers and Legal Culture in British North America: Beamish Murdoch of Halifax* (University of Toronto Press, 2011).

Lawyers in Canada are regulated at the provincial level, with every legal practitioner required by law to be a member of one of Canada's fourteen provincial and territorial law societies. Each of these organizations maintains its own set of rules governing its members. National mobility for lawyers began in 2001, and a new National Mobility Agreement went into effect in 2013, allowing lawyers who are qualified in one Canadian jurisdiction to practise in another upon simple registration without any additional training or educational requirements. This system of harmonization is a considerable achievement, particularly given the fact that there remain a remarkable number of barriers to economic integration across Canada's provinces. There is a single licensing process in order to provide legal services in Canada, and those who satisfy this requirement are identified as lawyers or, more formally, barristers and solicitors, reflecting Canada's British heritage. The supply of legal services without such qualification is deemed unauthorized practice of law and carries a sanction, which is typically administered by the local law society.

Canada has a FLC regime for individual legal services providers who are qualified to practise law in another country and who seek to practise only the law of their home state and international law. FLCs cannot practise the federal law of Canada or the law of any Canadian province or territory. FLC licences are granted by each provincial bar association on the basis of evidence of the practice of home country law for a designated period along with membership in the home country's bar association.

There is no nationality requirement for foreigners to become fully qualified as lawyers in Canada. The Supreme Court of Canada (SCC) ruled that the Law Society of British Columbia's citizenship requirement for admission to the bar was a form of unequal treatment, breaching constitutional rights, and could not be justified on policy grounds.[51] The SCC reasoned that citizenship alone neither achieves nor ensures familiarity with Canadian institutions and customs, nor does it demonstrate a real connection to Canada. Tellingly, the SCC also agreed with the lower court's assessment that the claim that lawyers fulfil a public function is overly broad and unduly restrictive, a noteworthy statement coming from a body composed of lawyers.

To practise law as a fully qualified barrister and solicitor in any province or territory (apart from Quebec, whose laws are based on the French civil code), foreign lawyers must apply to the National Committee on Accreditation (NCA) to have their qualifications and experience assessed.

[51] *Andrews* v. *Law Society of British Columbia* [1989] 1 SCR 143, 56 DLR (4th).

The NCA tends to perform this function in a highly discretionary, case-by-case manner, taking into account factors such as the individual's performance on his or her university course. The complicated, time-consuming, and unpredictable process of requalifying in Canada through the NCA is well known.[52] Once having passed this evaluation, the individual follows the same process for admission as domestic graduates do, typically involving completion of a bar admission course offered by the relevant law society. Provincial law societies have a monopoly on the provision of this training, in contrast to the UK and the US, where there are a range of private educational providers. As with most jurisdictions, the provincial law societies charge annual membership fees, which are among the highest in the world, even for nonresident members who are no longer in practice.[53]

Canada's GATS commitments on Mode 4 delivery of legal services are unbound, meaning that Canada has no commitments to liberalize the movement of natural persons for either market access or national treatment, with specific exceptions only where Canada has chosen to make commitments. These exemptions include business visitors, intracompany transferees, and professionals.[54] Under the GATS, business visitors are permitted to enter Canada to participate in business meetings to set up contracts or to conduct negotiations for a period of no more than ninety days. During this period, such individuals may not receive remuneration from within Canada or participate in sales or supply services directly to Canadians. Legal professionals who choose to enter Canada as business visitors are not permitted to practise law while there. Professionals are natural persons who hold academic credentials and professional qualifications for a designated field.

As was noted earlier, CETA's chapter on Mutual Recognition of Professional Qualifications creates a framework that allows Canada and the EU to recognize each other's professional qualifications through future agreements with a view towards facilitating practice in each other's territory. This involves the creation of a joint committee that will meet on a regular basis to review qualifications.[55] NAFTA likewise called for future negotiations of MRAs for the legal professions. Lawyers are included in

[52] Amos-Stewarta, Broughton, and Schwartz, "All Talk and No Action" at 151–152.

[53] Personal experience of the author.

[54] WTO, General Agreement on Trade in Services: Canada: Schedule of Specific Commitments, WTO Doc WT/GATS/SC/16, (1994), online: WTO, www.docsonline.wto.org (accessed March 2018). [WTO, Canada: Schedule of Specific Commitments].

[55] Articles 11.3–11.5.

that agreement's professional visa programme, allowing citizens of the US and Mexico to work in Canada.[56]

In Canada, FLCs qualify as professionals under the GATS, whereas lawyers and other legal professionals do not. To be an FLC, an individual is generally required to hold a Canadian law degree or its equivalent. When an individual seeks to enter a regulated profession with licensing requirements in Canada, such as law or working as an FLC, a work permit cannot be issued under the GATS unless the applicant has obtained, before arrival in Canada, a temporary or permanent licence from the appropriate province. Once the professional applicant has obtained a licence from the regulatory body and a work permit has been granted, the individual may enter Canada for ninety days or for the time it takes to complete the service contract the person is coming to Canada to fulfil, whichever ends first. Licensing requirements are primarily domestic regulations, which pose a significant barrier to accessing the legal services market in Canada.[57]

The only Canadian province that does have an express FIFO rule is British Columbia. This province allows foreign lawyers to practise on one-off occasions, not to exceed thirty days per calendar year, without a permit. Such lawyers who intend to stay for less than six months and do not plan to enter the Canadian labour market and who can demonstrate that their main place of business and source of income are located outside Canada and that the profits from their business will accrue outside Canada may obtain visas for business purposes. US and Mexican applicants having somewhat more flexibility with respect to visas under NAFTA.

Other provinces, such as Ontario, require that the foreign lawyer submit an application to practise on a temporary basis. The application process requires extensive documentation, and although there is no fee, the process can take up to fifteen business days. The lack of automatic *pro hac vice* reciprocity between Canada and the US is somewhat surprising, given that Canada has an advanced interprovincial mobility rule that allows the temporary practice of law in other Canadian provinces for periods of less than 100 days per year without registration. Furthermore, there is a high degree of integration between the economies of Canada and the US as well as similar legal systems (including the educational requirements for professional legal qualification). It may make more sense for Canadian and

[56] Article 1210.5.2.

[57] Citizenship and Immigration Canada, "Appendix D: General Agreement on Trade in Services" in FW 1, Foreign Worker Manual: Temporary Foreign Worker Guidelines (Citizenship and Immigration Canada, 2011) at 132, online: Citizenship and Immigration Canada, www.cic.gc.ca (accessed March 2018).

American lawyers to requalify in each other's jurisdictions fully when possible rather than seeking admission on a one-off basis, since dual qualification may be useful means of attracting internationally focused clients.

6.3.6 Australia

Like the UK, Australia has a dual licensing system for barristers and solicitors. The regulation of these professions, collectively known as lawyers, in Australia is done by the states and territories. This reflects the federal structure of government in that most authority for law making rests with the regions. There have been attempts to harmonize the system of licensing for lawyers on a national basis, as Canada has done; however, this has not been successful in Australia. Still, uniform principles for the assessment of foreign applications to acquire the full practising rights of Australian lawyers have been adopted by all regional admitting authorities. Reforms to the regulation of legal services in Australia have concentrated on the promotion of competition and consumer interests, much along the lines of the approach taken by the UK. Commentators have observed the activist style of consumer groups and competition authorities in instigating the emphasis on multiple legal services occupations, effectively opening up the market to suppliers beyond the traditional lawyer.[58]

Australia has an FLC regime, requiring applicants with foreign legal qualifications to obtain a licence from the state law society that allows them to practise home state law as well as international law. Licences are granted subject to experience, holding professional indemnity insurance, and, in some cases, the requirement that the foreign lawyer not hold an equivalent licence in another Australian state. A limited licence, rather than full admission as an Australian lawyer, is required in order to provide legal advisory services in foreign law and international law. A full licence is required for legal advisory and representational services in domestic law. In all Australian states and territories except South Australia, there is a general prohibition on the practice of foreign law in Australia unless the practitioner is an "Australian-registered foreign lawyer" or is an "Australian legal practitioner". An overseas-qualified foreign lawyer is exempt from the general prohibition on practising foreign law in Australia if the lawyer practises foreign law in Australia on a temporary basis (periods that do not exceed ninety days in any twelve-month period). UK solicitors have complained that they are required to take a high number of examinations (up

[58] Semple, *Legal Services Regulation at the Crossroads* at 78–79.

to eleven separate papers) at the state/territory level in order to requalify in Australia. This is thought to have a detrimental impact on the efficacy with which they can operate in the market. While clearly cumbersome, this process appears to be broadly consistent with that of Canada.

Australia included legal services covering Mode 4 in its FTAs with Chile, Malaysia, Singapore, and the US. In the agreements with Chile, the US, and Singapore, legal services are included on the basis of potential future MRAs, as in the CETA. In the Malaysian and Thai agreements, specific commitments were made on legal services, but these merely duplicated commitments that had been undertaken in the GATS. It is worth drawing attention to the fact that lawyers who are admitted in New Zealand are given special status in Australia, qualifying them for mutual recognition under the Trans-Tasman Mutual Recognition Arrangement, which took effect in 1998 and is reviewed on a regular basis.[59] New Zealand and Australia are among the most closely integrated countries in the world outside of a customs union.

6.3.7 Emerging Markets

There is thought to be a significant portion of Mode 4 trade in services taking place between developing countries that is unreported. Key barriers to temporary movement of services providers to developing countries include visa and work permit matters, the lack of recognition of qualifications and skills, prior experience rules, the imposition of withholding requirements, and the double taxation of income, nationality and residency requirements, requirements to work in association with professionals in the target country, rules specifying the need to undertake training and exams in the export market prior to work certification, reciprocity requirements, complex and expensive registration procedures, mandatory membership in professional licensing organizations in the host country, and forced and nonrecoverable contributions to host country social security and unemployment insurance programmes.[60] Many of these apply to legal professionals who seek to work overseas on a temporary basis. Unsurprisingly, developing countries have a more restrictive approach to FIFO, just as common law countries tend to be more amenable to this kind of practice than do countries with the civil law tradition, reflecting in part the common law's historic doctrine of *pro hac vice*, particularly within the US.[61]

[59] The basic provision is Article G.2 on Occupations.

[60] Sauve and Ward, "A Trade in Services Waiver for Least Developed Countries" at 571.

[61] See S. J. Goldstein, "Constitutional Law: Attorney Not Entitled to Hearing upon Denial of Admission Pro Hac Vice", 44 Missouri Law Review 772 (1979).

Brazil has a civil law legal system in which foreign lawyers who do not possess a Brazilian legal qualification may work in Brazil as FLCs (consultor de direito estrangeiro) once they have been granted authorization by the powerful Brazilian Bar Association (OAB). Such FLCs are entitled to practise only the law of their home state and international law. To obtain this designation, foreign lawyers must demonstrate that they are entitled to practise law in their home state, have a Brazilian resident visa, have good moral character without prior convictions, and have relevant experience. There is also a requirement for the applicant to demonstrate that the home jurisdiction offers reciprocal rights. This requirement appears to violate the MFN rule of GATS Article II, irrespective of the fact that Brazil has not made any specific commitments under the GATS for legal services. FLCs licences are issued for three-year periods and are renewable indefinitely.

To become qualified as a Brazilian avogado, foreign law graduates must meet all of the requirements prescribed for Brazilian lawyers, including passing the OAB Exam. Foreign degrees must be validated for this purpose, and if such qualifications are not sufficient, the candidate may be able to take additional exams to the point at which this is viewed as equivalent to a Brazilian law degree. Proof of reciprocity from the lawyer's home state is required for foreign lawyers to register. Portuguese lawyers may register at the OAB without going through the common qualification route for foreign lawyers.

The lack of international law commitments on the establishment of foreign lawyers by Brazil has created a situation where a reversal of policy could result in foreign lawyers being unprotected. Formal cooperation between foreign-trained and local lawyers was permitted, but in 2010, one of the regional bar associations ruled that such alliances were contrary to its rules. The federal bar of Brazil is still reviewing this matter, and a national policy is forthcoming.[62] There remains significant resistance to the liberalization of the legal profession to foreign entrants within the OAB, and there are fears that existing rules will be made more restrictive in the future.[63]

There is no requirement in Brazil for foreign lawyers to register in order to practise on a FIFO basis, and in that sense, Brazil treats commercial establishment under Mode 3 the same as it does temporary movement of persons under Mode 4. In other words, foreign lawyers are entitled to practise foreign law and international law once they have been granted express

[62] Muller, *Liberalization of Trade in Legal Services* at 732.

[63] M. Taddia, "The Brazilian Legal Market" Law Society Gazette (UK) (2014).

authorization by the OAB, as was mentioned in Chapter 5. Business people seeking to visit Brazil are required to apply for a short-stay business visa, which is valid for up to ninety days. There are exemptions for this visa for some countries. Brazil's approach to foreign lawyers has been the source of much debate in recent years, and it remains unclear whether the Federal Council of the OAB will review its policy.[64]

As was mentioned in Chapter 5, China maintains a tightly controlled market for legal services, including that which affects temporary movement of natural persons. China is unusual in that it allows only Chinese nationals to practise local law. The only exception to this prohibition is that residents of Hong Kong and Macao are permitted to take the Chinese bar exam and to obtain a licence to practise Chinese law. Hong Kong and Macao residents with a Chinese practising licence are able to act for clients in nonlitigation matters and in litigation cases related to Hong Kong–related or Macao-related marriage or inheritance matters. The fact that non-Chinese citizens are not permitted to take the Chinese bar exam should be contrasted with the fact that Chinese law graduates can take the QLTS and the New York Bar Exam, for example.

China's WTO accession commitments did not include a commitment to allow foreign lawyers to practise Chinese law or a commitment to allow foreign law firms to employ Chinese lawyers.[65] Foreign lawyers cannot obtain licences to establish and practise as a FLC unless they are employed by a foreign law firm's representative office in China and are registered as representatives. Such FLC representatives must obtain a business visa and must have at least two years' experience of practising law in their own jurisdiction. Foreign lawyers can obtain visas to visit clients and to engage in marketing of business activities but not to practise law. China imposes no special requirements regarding FIFO delivery of legal services. However, appearance and participation by foreign lawyers in many types of meetings involving their clients and Chinese departments are often prohibited, restricted, or permitted only under certain conditions, without transparency and on a case-by-case basis.

It is worth noting that the China-Australia FTA aims at facilitating increased mobility for Australian and Chinese lawyers, including

[64] R. Bianco, "Litigation and Enforcement in Brazil: Overview" Thomson Reuters: Practical Law (1 September 2017).

[65] A. Godwin, "The Professional 'Tug of War': The Regulation of Foreign Lawyers in China, Business Scope Issues and Some Suggestions for Reform", 33 Melbourne University Law Review 132 (2009).

professional secondments between law firms in Australia and China (intracorporate transferees). The FTA between China and Iceland (the first between China and a European country) simply encourages the parties to publish information about visa and work permit requirements.[66]

The delivery of legal services by individual lawyers is perhaps even more circumscribed in India than in China. Although Indian regulations require an advocate to be a citizen of India, the Bar Council of India may prescribe the conditions subject to which foreign qualifications in law obtained by persons other than citizens of India may be recognized for the purpose of admission as an advocate. This provision has been used for only a few special, individual cases.

As was mentioned in Chapter 5, FIFO practice in India was the subject of a court case as a consequence of complaints brought by Indian law firms that were concerned about losing work to foreign suppliers.[67] The court established that there is no barrier for foreign lawyers to visit India for a temporary period on a FIFO basis for the purpose of giving legal advice to their clients in India about foreign law or their own system of law and on diverse international legal issues. Affirming the status quo, the Supreme Court of India gave a limited concession to foreign lawyers, formally allowing them to enter India on behalf of clients and to act in international arbitration. While this decision did not advance the liberalization of international legal services in terms of establishing offices in India, it at least removed the uncertainty for fly-in-fly-out practitioners.[68] The decision is expected to affirm the status quo in which foreign lawyers flying into and out of India for short durations who advise only on matters of foreign law and international law are permitted.

All aspects of advice on Indian law must be performed by Indian advocates to whom foreign firms refer their clients or matters. These rules were designed to ensure that foreign lawyers are not a commercial threat to either Indian lawyers (from whom they might divert business) or Indian clients (to whom they might provide incompetent advice). This restriction has been praised by commentators because in addition to achieving these

[66] Moritsch, "Research Paper: International Trade in Legal Services" at 9–10.

[67] *Bar Council of India* v. *AK Balaji & Ors* (W.P. 5614/2010) (High Court of Madras) (21 February 2012).

[68] *Bar Council of India* v. *A.K. Balaji & Ors* [Civil Appeal Nos. 7875–7879 of 2015] 13 March 2018.

aims, it is thought to fulfil the government of India's objective of making the country an international hub of commerce.[69]

Russian advokatura, or advocates, who account for a small proportion of legal practitioners in Russia, are recognized and regulated by law. Only a licensed advokat can conduct criminal litigation in court and must be registered with one of the regional bar associations overseen by the Federal Chamber of Advocates of the Russian Federation. Many foreigners are surprised to discover that in Russia, lawyers practising commercial law are not regulated at all. However, although these nonadvocates, also known as legal consultants or jurists, are unregulated, there have been proposals to unite the legal profession under the regional and federal bar associations.

A foreign lawyer may practise in Russia without requiring any licence. A foreign lawyer may also seek to be recognized as a foreign advocate. A foreign lawyer may become a foreign advocate and be entered in the special Russian register maintained by the Ministry of Justice, provided that the lawyer's status in his or her home jurisdiction is similar to that of a Russian advocate, meaning that the lawyer has equivalent education and experience and has passed an examination. Foreign advocates are generally entitled to provide legal services only on the law of the lawyer's home country, much like a FLC. If the foreign lawyer is employed in this capacity in a domestic or foreign law firm, there are no restrictions on scope of practice. Foreign lawyers may qualify to become full Russian advocates by following the same process that exists for Russian nationals.

There is no requirement for foreign-qualified lawyers to obtain a licence for temporary legal practice in Russia. There is, however, a general rule that any foreigner who seeks to provide any kind of services during a temporary (or long-term) stay in Russia, must obtain immigration authorization. Exceptions may be granted to foreign lawyers on a case-by-case basis. Thus one of the main barriers to trade in legal services in Russia is one of transparency; it is difficult to know in advance the nature of the restrictions with which foreign lawyers will be faced. Foreign lawyers are able to obtain visas to visit clients or to market their work but not to practise. Subject to obtaining the permission noted earlier, foreign lawyers can provide arbitration or mediation or act as an arbitrator. There are very few restrictions on the type of proceedings in which foreign lawyers can become involved in Russia. Some criminal cases and some cases involving minors or the mentally disabled are restricted to advocates. As with established lawyers,

[69] A. Saxena and K. Bhatia, "Foreign Lawyers Can Fly In and Fly Out of India to Advise on Foreign Law but Not on Indian Law" The Asian Lawyer [undated].

FIFO legal practitioners can appear in court either as jurists or by obtaining the status of a Russian or a foreign advocate in Russia.

6.4 Pressing Issues in Mode 4 Legal Services Liberalization

Current negotiations on the temporary natural persons delivery across all services under the GATS are running into difficulties. This is in part because of the complexity of issues associated with the movement of people, as distinct from the movement of the service itself or of a company supplying it, even when this movement is temporary. Greater clarity regarding the requirements for the delivery of legal services under Mode 4, in particular what constitutes temporary movement and when it becomes establishment could help.[70] Indeed, some of the material in this chapter could arguably have been included in Chapter 5. Perhaps more important, as was suggested in Chapter 1, legal services have lacked the economic magnitude to draw much attention under the GATS, a political reality that is felt across all modes of delivery. Despite these constraints, facilitating the supply of legal services under Mode 4 is not entirely ignored on the global trading agenda.

Modest support for the Trade in Services Agreement (TiSA), which aims to enlarge on GATS Mode 4 commitments, suggests there is some willingness to drive the liberalization of movement of persons, at least among advanced economies. It will be interesting to see, when negotiations for this agreement resume, whether any progress is made under the TiSA with regard to the movement of natural persons and the provision of legal services. One of the key issues in this regard will be the distinction that some parties may seek to draw between full licensing of professionals for practising host country law and the somewhat lesser category of limited licensing for home country and international law.[71] States that have a tradition of liberalization in legal services, such as Australia, the EU, and the US, are considered most likely to negotiate for TiSA commitments involving limited licensing for FLCs in foreign and international law, including arbitration; exclusion of residency requirements; avoiding limitations on partnerships and associations between foreign and local firms; allowing foreign law firms to employ local practitioners; and facilitating FIFO.[72]

[70] Muller, *Liberalization of Trade in Legal Services* at 152.

[71] Moritsch, "Research Paper: International Trade in Legal Services" at 11.

[72] Ibid. These issues arguably embrace both Mode 3 and Mode 4.

Regulatory cooperation between home and host countries is a vital condition to enable trade in services under Mode 4. Promises to negotiate future recognition with regard to legal qualifications are rife in FTAs. Although there has been a remarkable lack of progress in terms of GATS-specific commitments under Mode 4, there are a few examples of cooperation agreements between border agencies that have been able to facilitate the movement of business people and service suppliers between contracting parties. The Asia Pacific Economic Cooperation (APEC) Business Travel Card is one such initiative.[73] It will be explored further in Chapter 7.

In one sense, Mode 4 liberalization is fundamentally about labour mobility. Mobility arrangements that have been pursued multilaterally, bilaterally, or regionally covering Mode 4 delivery of legal services need to be modified in line with the changes that are underway to the legal profession to further liberalization in this sphere. In the past, most Mode 4 GATS commitments were designed primarily to facilitate the movement of highly skilled professionals, such as business visitors, in categories linked to investment flows, such as the presence of a multijurisdictional law firm.[74] Although this may have served the needs of legal professionals in the past, practising on a FIFO basis may not be suited to these traditional forms of liberalization. Additionally, the orientation of future Mode 4 commitments for legal services must be expanded to cover a wider range of legal services providers and skill levels,[75] including document review and the routine preparation of boilerplate contracts.

Cross-border mobility through temporary arrangements between countries has been presented as a useful means of redressing labour market shortages, enabling countries with labour surpluses and countries with labour deficits to exploit their circumstances for mutual benefit. In contrast to permanent immigration programmes, temporary mobility arrangements are less prone to attracting political and social opprobrium or to incite fears about brain drain. Countries are increasingly addressing labour mobility matters under comprehensive bilateral economic cooperation and partnership agreements that exceed the commitments undertaken pursuant to the WTO and the GATS. Examples include NAFTA, the Japan-Singapore Agreement, and the Comprehensive Economic Partnership and Comprehensive Economic Cooperation agreements

[73] G. Gari, "Services Negotiations: Where Have We Been and Where Are We Heading?" in Sauve and Roy eds. *Research Handbook on Trade in Services* at 607.

[74] Chanda, "Demographics and Labour Markets" at 444.

[75] Ibid.

between India and various Asian countries. Sending countries must focus their efforts on increasing technical and vocational education as well as improving accreditation. National qualification regimes and certification systems must be developed. This may require funding for universities and domestic regulators. Sending countries must further identify target markets and align the development of their domestic capacity to address these needs overseas. Such matters may be difficult to achieve through multilateral negotiations in fora such as the WTO or plurilaterally through instruments such as the TiSA. Bilateral negotiation of these specific policy matters on a country-by-country basis may be more feasible.[76]

It is also essential that agreements for mobility of services labour pursued bilaterally should include provisions to ensure that supply capacity in the source partner country is commensurate with the demand requirements in the receiving partner country, maximizing market access opportunities. Mobility arrangements tend to be subject to requisite education and skill capacity building in the source country (seeking to essentially replicate those of the receiving country). However, many sending countries will struggle to align their institutions with the needs of target host states. Better cooperation between the partner countries, including their governments, educational providers, and regulatory bodies, could help to improve the alignment of the training and skills development in the source country with the market opportunities in the receiving country. These needs may be cyclical, just as the supply potential from the source country will fluctuate over time. Meanwhile, the GATS is structured to capture Mode 4 commitments on a permanent basis. One way to deal with this issue for the GATS or any other agreement that adopts this method is to specify that commitments are only temporary, to be reassessed contingent on market conditions.[77] While this may lead to problems in the administration or enforcement of these commitments, a degree of regularity or an indication of the types of metrics that will be used to inform changes in policy could alleviate some of the concerns.

As with Mode 1, commentators have suggested waivers for Mode 4 services suppliers from developing countries, although this could be problematic from the standpoint of quality and consumer protection in the context of traditional legal services. This would be less of a concern for more modern forms of highly routinized legal services. Trade facilitation measures for services trade through Mode 4 for developing country

[76] Ibid. at 442.

[77] Ibid. at 444.

suppliers may include the simplification of visa, work permit, and registration requirements as well as offering of simplified versions of exams in the home country of the service provider where access to work is tied to previous competencies.[78] Again, these preferential measures for suppliers from developing countries may be suitable in the context of less sophisticated legal services, such as those that characterize the bulk of much modern legal services.

The fact that few RTAs have been able to expand labour mobility beyond that of the GATS may indicate that there is an overall lack of political will for this variety of economic globalization. This resistance may be even more entrenched for legal services providers, as lawyers' services are often viewed as an unnecessary transaction cost on genuine economic activity rather than as a facilitator of it or, even less so, as a kind of economic activity in their own right. Commentators have drawn attention to the conspicuous lack of political will to further the movement of workers by referring to "Everything but Labour Globalization".[79]

6.5 Conclusion

GATS Mode 4 commitments involving the temporary entry of natural persons are the rarest to be found in members' schedules of specific commitments, most likely because they touch upon politically sensitive issues such as labour laws and immigration control, which themselves raise questions of cultural cohesion and national security. Yet a substantial share of the world exports in legal services takes place through Mode 4. This is why FTAs that address such modes of service supply directly may have a particularly beneficial impact on trade in legal services.

In virtually all jurisdictions in the world, including the dozen or so that were discussed in this chapter, foreign-qualified lawyers are permitted to practise the law of their home state and international law without additional qualification. These limitations appear to be predicated on the assumption that practice within these areas does not require expertise or qualifications in the local legal system in the case of home state law and, in the case of international law, on the basis that this body of law consists of general principles that are common to the legal systems of the world. The ubiquitous FLC designation often mandates registration, compliance with

[78] Sauve and Ward, "A Trade in Services Waiver for Least Developed Countries" at 572.

[79] L. Pritchett, *Let Their People Come: Breaking the Gridlock on Global Labor Mobility* (Centre for Global Development, 2006) at 30.

ethical standards, and maintaining professional indemnity insurance. Such conditions arguably fit within the recognition provisions of GATS Article VI in as much as it validates the delivery of some kind of legal services within the host state on the basis of educational or professional qualifications achieved elsewhere. This has not prevented commentators from urging that there should be a formal regime for FLCs under the GATS, which should include the removal of all barriers to trade, including the requirement that these foreign lawyers enter into partnership with or hire a domestic lawyer.[80]

Most of the leading legal jurisdictions in the world allow foreign lawyers to become fully licensed in the practice of law of the host jurisdiction through some combination of examination or training that tends to duplicate the procedure available to domestic applicants. This recognition is contemplated by the GATS; however, it achieves little in the way of liberalization other than ensuring that nationality does not act as a bar to the establishment of foreign legal practitioners. Rules that require a foreign lawyer to pass an exam to practise within the jurisdiction could transgress GATS market access rules because they may result in a limitation on the number of foreign lawyers. While such rules are not, strictly speaking, quantitative measures, there is nevertheless a quantitative effect, which arguably falls under the scope of Article VI on Domestic Regulation, not Article XVI on Market Access.

There have been several bilateral agreements that include provisions to facilitate the temporary entry of foreign lawyers who engage in FIFO services supply, which is crucial for the field of international arbitration. The EU-Korea FTA is one such arrangement. Still, with the exception of the EU's internal market and special arrangements between close neighbours such as Australia and New Zealand and Commonwealth of Independent States (CIS) countries, RTAs that offer more under Mode 4 than is offered by the GATS typically do so in the form of best efforts intentions to create MRAs for professional qualifications at some future date. This issue, which is vital to deeper market access for a range of services, including legal ones, will be explored further in Chapter 7.

[80] Muller, *Liberalization of Trade in Legal Services* at 152.

7

Domestic Regulation and Mutual Recognition of Legal Services

7.1 Introduction

Many of the issues that were explored in previous chapters concern the capacity of host jurisdictions to verify the competence of legal services providers as a condition of the providers' entitlement to provide services across various modes. Under international law, this is handled by provisions in trade treaties that require signatory states to observe fair processes with respect to the licensing and verification of competencies, known generally as domestic regulation. This material is enhanced by further obligations on parties to acknowledge that the professional competencies in another jurisdiction are functionally equivalent – a kind of presumptive recognition that eases the regulatory burden on the foreign supplier. Such provisions, which are also common in trade treaties, are known as mutual recognition. While they do not, strictly speaking, constitute liberalization in the sense of creating market access, together these features of public international law nevertheless are instrumental in mitigating the adverse impact of regulatory barriers to trade in services.

This chapter will consider both of these legal strategies for facilitating trade in legal services. It will concentrate on how they are embodied in the GATS, followed by equivalent provisions in free trade agreements (FTAs), examining how these obligations grapple with the fundamental issue of regulatory necessity. This chapter will also explore how multinational initiatives in this regard have been approached, including the important role of professional organizations in standard setting on behalf of governments.

7.2 Domestic Regulation

7.2.1 General Principles

Regulations on any sector of the economy can be a tool of protectionism that shield local interest groups. Inadequate design and weak implementation can lead to harmful market distortions, particularly when there is no compelling analytical or empirical justification for their adoption, as may be the case for legal services. This is even more so in developing countries, where governments often lack the means to implement regulations effectively.[1] In considering the impact of domestic regulation provisions in services agreements, including the GATS, it is important to emphasize the difference between market access and regulation. A Market Access commitment by a country to permit foreign-qualified lawyers to practise does not mean that that state is obliged to accept all foreign lawyers. Acceptance will depend upon whether the lawyer meets the requirements of the relevant domestic laws regarding who is competent to provide legal advice. Following from this, there must be a system in place to allow foreign lawyers to demonstrate their competence with respect to the domestic requirements or else they will be unable to practise in that jurisdiction. Domestic regulation disciplines require that state parties maintain such systems and, more important, that the systems are not arbitrary or excessively trade restrictive. In other words, regulations as an impediment to market access are allowed, provided that the process by which they are administered is fair.

7.2.2 Domestic Regulation and the GATS

Article VI of the GATS on domestic regulation requires WTO members to have adequate procedures in place to verify the competence of foreign professionals. If members do not have such procedures in place, it would be easy to undermine access simply by having no system to verify suitability.[2] More specifically, this section of the GATS deals with licensing requirements, qualification requirements, and technical standards that may operate as barriers to the trade in services. These nonschedulable regulatory measures mean that effective access to a market may not be available even where there is full liberalization under Market Access and National Treatment commitments. These barriers, which are rightly described as qualitative restrictions rather than quantitative ones,[3] are particularly onerous for services professionals such as lawyers who rely upon flexible forms of access, typically through cross-border supply or the presence of natural persons. Such restrictions have the status of de jure less favourable

[1] M. Molinuevo and S. Saez, "Services Trade and Regulatory Reform: A Methodology for Developing Countries" in Sauve and Roy eds. *Research Handbook on Trade in Services.*

[2] J. Neilson, "Trade Agreements and Recognition" in *Quality and Recognition in Higher Education: The Cross-Border Challenge* (OECD, 2004).

[3] Diebold, *Non-Discrimination in International Trade in Services* at 56.

treatment if they have a nationality requirement, such as application of different standards depending on the origin of the supplier. The situation is more complicated for qualification requirements that are origin neutral. For example, in countries where domestic law degrees are required for an individual to be entitled to practise law, even when access to domestic educational institutions is not restricted to national citizens or local residents, this requirement still makes the process more difficult for foreigners because there is a heavier administrative burden than there is for local citizens. This appears to constitute less favourable treatment under the GATS in terms of asymmetrical impact.[4] A more precise definition of "licencing and qualification requirements" would clearly be helpful in improving the transparency of the international delivery of legal services, particularly in Mode 3. Progress on this aspect of domestic regulation seems to be more likely than in other areas, such as the development of a rubric on core values of the legal profession, as many of the bar associations had wished.[5]

GATS Article VI.6 specifies that when a country chooses to make a commitment to allow access for a particular type of foreign professional, such as legal services professionals, that country is required to have adequate procedures in place to verify the competence of those professionals from all other WTO members. The phrase "adequate procedures" is defined, allowing wide discretion to members. This provision of the GATS does not truly embrace recognition substantively; it is more about having procedures in place to evaluate compliance, such as a bar examination or transfer test such as the QLTS in England and Wales. Article VI.6 also says nothing about the standards to be applied, that is, the criteria used to assess competence. It simply mandates that there be adequate procedures. Once again, it is important to note that for the obligation to apply, a member state has to have actually chosen to make a GATS commitment on market access for a particular professional service. If a member allows foreign lawyers to practise the law of their home state but has made no GATS commitment to that effect, the obligation does not apply. Likewise, a member that has allowed foreign lawyers to practise in its territory even without a GATS commitment likely still has an interest in having procedures to verify their competence but is not under a GATS obligation to do so.

It is important to note that the obligation contained in GATS Article VI:5 is subject to the condition of "nullification or impairment" of the rights and obligations of other members. Commentators have suggested

[4] Ibid. at 57.

[5] Muller, *Liberalization of Trade in Legal Services* at 150.

that this reduces it to a variation of the non-violation complaint found in GATT Article XXIII:2, which means that it is of limited practical significance.[6] Non-violation complaints require that the complainant demonstrate that it has been deprived of an expected economic benefit because of the respondent's governmental action. This is an additional evidentiary burden on the complainant that is not required for a conventional violation complaint. Accordingly, the home state of the legal service provider must show that these entities have been denied an actual or potential market because their qualifications have not been recognized; this will be difficult to establish in the absence of actual clients in the respondent state.

The WTO Handbook on GATS states, with regard to domestic regulations, that "governments remain free under the GATS to pursue such policy objectives [e.g. equitable access, consumer protection, job creation etc.] even in sectors where they have undertaken full commitments on market access and national treatment."[7] The examples given here do not correspond to those found in the GATS General Exception clause, suggesting that these policy areas should not be construed as National Treatment violations at all; they are so fundamentally important that they do not constitute discrimination.

To be clear, the GATS specifies that any requirements relating to services sectors in which specific commitments have been made must be based on objective and transparent criteria such as competence and the ability to supply the service and not be more burdensome than necessary to ensure the quality of the service, and licensing procedures must not be, in themselves, a restriction on the supply of the service. These requirements, while aiming to support the liberalization of services, also legitimize restrictions on the provision of services where this ensures quality. Therefore quality, however it may be measured, becomes a normative screen by which the WTO authorizes barriers to international trade. In the words of one commentator, the purpose of Article VI:4 is not deregulation but rather "to promote *better regulation* based on objective and transparent criteria". Reference to "necessary" recalls the balancing tests associated with the chapeau of GATS (and GATT) General Exceptions.

Some comments on the General Exceptions of Article XIV are apposite. In particular, the exception of public order and public morals, which may seem to be highly relevant for restrictions on legal services, is heavily prescribed by an interpretive footnote that explains that the public order

[6] Diebold, *Non-Discrimination in International Trade in Services* at 31.

[7] WTO Secretariat, *Handbook on GATS*, (2005) at 21.

exception may be invoked only when a genuine and sufficiently serious threat is posed to one of the fundamental interests of society. This is unlikely to be applicable to legal services. Still, it is worth noting that the presence of the General Exceptions clause in the GATS is understood to remove any consideration of regulatory purpose from the understanding of "likeness" for the purposes of Most Favoured Nation (MFN) and National Treatment commitments.[8] In other words, members cannot claim that legal services supplied by a foreign lawyer are unlike those supplied by a domestic lawyer simply because there is a policy objective in place to ensure that legal services must be supplied by someone familiar with the local legal culture. This is irrespective of whether the need to have legal services imbued with an understanding of the local legal culture would actually fit within the public morals component of GATS Article XIV, for example.

Under GATS Article XIV, the respondent must demonstrate not only that the regulation fulfils a policy objective that is captured by the list, but also that the measure is necessary to achieve that objective. This test is done by weighing and balancing, through consideration of the relative importance of the interests and values pursued, the contribution of the measure to the realization of that objective, the restrictive impact of the measure on international commerce, and the existence of reasonably available alternative measures.[9] The initial burden on the respondent is addressed by demonstrating the bona fide and reasonable nature of the measure in light of a particular public policy objective. The burden then shifts to the complainant to present a credible case that a reasonably available WTO-consistent alternative exists. It is understood that the necessity test in GATS Article XIV covers nondiscriminatory measures not listed in the Market Access provision and seeks to ensure that such rules are not more burdensome than they need to be for the purpose of achieving policy objectives. In that sense, the test aims to achieve a balance between policy goals and trade liberalization, somewhat in the tradition of the better-known GATT Article XX and, more relevantly, GATS Article XIV.

Furthermore, the chapeau of the General Exception prohibits "arbitrary or unjustifiable discrimination where like conditions prevail". This language may be implicitly relevant for the "necessity test" of GATS Article VI on domestic regulation. In the context of legal services, it is important to ascertain whether like conditions prevail in the relevant countries. The

[8] Diebold, *Non-Discrimination in International Trade in Services* at 86.

[9] Appellate Body Report, Brazil – Retreaded Tires, WT/DS332/AB/R (3 December 2007) at [178].

legal systems and associated educational institutions may be insufficiently "like" such that unequal treatment may be justified. The chapeau also compels a consideration of whether, for example, a requirement that foreign lawyers may practise only in the law of their home state is overly restrictive from the perspective of achieving the pursued objective, such as consumer protection.

To be sure, the necessity test of GATS Article VI appears to be unlike the necessity test of Article XIV, which covers general exceptions to GATS obligations for a range of public policy matters. Necessity under Article VI is an obligation, whereas under Article XIV it is an exception. The types of measures that are engaged by the necessity test of Article VI are unclear. It appears to apply only to regulations that neither are discriminatory nor impose market access limitations; otherwise, the National Treatment and Market Access provisions would be superfluous.[10] The necessity test obligations that are imposed on domestic regulations appear to have the potential to liberalize international trade in legal services well beyond the nondiscrimination obligations but, at the same time, carries with it the risk of significantly interfering with members' regulatory autonomy. The potential threat to sovereignty associated with this obligation is probably why new disciplines have been concluded so far only in relation to accountancy.[11]

The necessity test of GATS Article VI is limited in scope in that it covers only measures relating to qualification or license requirements and procedures and technical standards. Moreover, it applies only to sectors where WTO members have listed specific commitments in their GATS schedules, unlike Article XIV. The scope of Article XIV is further significantly narrowed in that it covers only situations that could not reasonably have been expected by the member at the time the specific commitment was made.[12] For trade in legal services, the relevant nondiscriminatory measures could include requirements of language proficiency, requirements to register with the local bar or courts, and reserved activities such as real estate, caps on fees, or advertising restrictions. An illustrative list of legitimate policy objectives for the purposes of the Article VI necessity test, perhaps along the lines of GATS Article XIV, would be very helpful.

GATS Article VI:4 authorizes the Council for Trade in Services to establish bodies to develop necessary disciplines on measures relating to licensing and qualification procedures and technical standards to ensure

[10] Diebold, *Non-Discrimination in International Trade in Services* at 53.

[11] Ibid. at 31.

[12] Article VI:5 (a) ii.

that they are no more burdensome than necessary to ensure the quality of the service. Negotiations have taken place recently on the development of necessity tests through the Working Party on Domestic Regulation (WPDR), but this has been met with much resistance by WTO members. Consequently, commentators believe that the establishment of a functional necessity test under GATS Article VI is highly unlikely.[13] The WPDR seeks to define technical standards, clarifying that technical standard provisions are only those standards that are "applicable" to the relevant service sector.[14] This appears to be a definitional issue that should not preclude extending the disciplines horizontally.[15]

GATS negotiations on domestic regulation have aimed to resolve transparency problems for measures that affect access to the market as well as the conduct of services suppliers. Doha Round negotiations on domestic regulation have focused on horizontal disciplines covering all services sectors, neglecting the adoption of disciplines on professional services.[16] A possible reason for the failure to achieve progress in domestic regulation disciplines for services in the bilateral or regional context is the MFN obligation. Parties that extend a commitment to abolish all excessive regulation for services, or even one service such as legal services, would be obliged to do so for all WTO members.[17]

Effective market access for professional services suppliers relies on codes of conduct that tend to be adopted by non-state actors, often self-regulated bodies. As in legal services, while these are designed to improve the quality of the service and to protect consumers, they can also restrict competition. The development of pan-European codes of conduct was a key feature of the European Services directive adopted in 2006 and implemented by all EU countries in 2009. Codes of conduct are particularly relevant for regulated professions, in which compulsory registration with the corresponding professional associations exists,[18] as is the case for legal services. The directive does not offer any specific guidance regarding the forms of such codes of conduct, stating only that the objective is to facilitate free movement under the Single Market. This accords a high degree of flexibility,

[13] Muller, *Liberalization of Trade in Legal Services* at 62.

[14] WTO, Working Party on Domestic Regulation, Disciplines on Domestic Regulation Pursuant to GATS Article VI: 4: Chairman's Progress Report (14 April 2011), WTO Doc WT/S/WPDR/W/45 at 1–2; WTO, Article VI: 4: Chairman's Progress Report (2011); WTO, Article VI: 4: Chairman's Progress Report (2011), s 1.

[15] Amos-Stewarta, Broughton, and Schwartz, "All Talk and No Action" at 139.

[16] Muller, *Liberalization of Trade in Legal Services* at 152.

[17] Krajewski, "Domestic Regulation and Services Trade" at 239.

[18] Article 3(1) (a) of Directive 2005/36/EC.

allowing considerable space for professional bodies in the member states to coordinate appropriate rules.

Commentators have viewed this type of use of codes of conduct as emblematic "soft law", in which traditional boundaries between formal governmental regulation and private standard setting collapse. With professional associations becoming the final arbiters in deciding who can participate in the corresponding service at a national (or subnational) level, typically through a governmental act that delegates regulatory powers to the associations, some alignment of the rules governing that profession is key to a healthy global market.[19] In the case of European lawyers, the Code of Professional Conduct adopted by the Council of Bars and Law Societies of Europe (CCBE) included qualities such as independence, impartiality, loyalty, integrity, and confidentiality.[20] Delegating authority to create codes of conduct to the respective professional bodies in this bottom-up way is cost saving because it builds upon existing embedded expertise.

The legal profession does not have a global set of standards or common practices. Without internationally recognized standards to form the basis for multilateral rules on ethics, it would be impossible to subject the legal profession to an even broader horizontal discipline. However, there are common issues in ethical standards between most members that allow for universal international codes of conduct, such as the International Bar Association's International Code of Ethics and the Council of Bars and Law Societies of Europe's Code of Conduct, which governs cross-border legal services in Europe. These international materials could assist regulators in finding common ground on which to establish a global ethical discipline. Given that the legal profession the world over appears to be grounded in universal concepts of loyalty, confidentiality, and the avoidance of conflict of interest, the success of such initiatives is feasible, despite the fact that there are no measurable technical standards that apply across the entirety of the legal profession.

7.2.3 Domestic Regulation and Regional Trade Agreements

A study conducted in 2012 showed that about 80 per cent of FTAs contain a provision similar to that of GATS Article VI:4 on domestic regulation,

[19] P. Delimatsis, "The EU Services Directive and the Mandate for the Creation of Professional Codes of Conduct" in I. Liaons and O. Odudu eds. *Regulating Trade in Services in the EU and the WTO* (Cambridge University Press, 2012) at 323.

[20] Article 2.2.

and about 75 per cent contain a clause similar to that of GATS Article VI:5. The agreements that did not contain this material were viewed as having weaker disciplines than those that did.[21] Other authors have observed that generally speaking, progress in terms of developing rules governing domestic regulation has been weaker at the bilateral level than at the multilateral level through the WTO.[22] Indeed, some recent treaties contain GATS Article VI language but are framed in a best efforts approach.[23] Many bilateral and regional agreements contain sectoral reference papers consisting of regulatory standards for specific sectors beyond telecommunications and finance, which received specific attention under the GATS. This suggests that developing regulatory disciplines for services may be more easily achieved on a sector-specific basis than on a horizontal one.[24]

The Comprehensive Economic and Trade Agreement (CETA) expressly allow parties to enact measures that require that those supplying services obtain a licence, registration, certification, or authorization.[25] It further contains a special chapter on domestic regulation that exceeds the equivalent provision found in the GATS in its level of detail. This chapter applies to licensing requirements and procedures and qualification requirements and procedures but not to technical standards. The definitions for licensing requirements and procedures and qualification requirements and procedures in CETA are very similar to those that were established by the WTO's WPDR. The CETA chapter on domestic regulation does not contain a general necessity test. However, each party is required to ensure that its licensing and qualification requirements and procedures are "based on criteria which preclude the competent authorities from exercising their power of assessment in an arbitrary manner". The relevant criteria must be "clear and transparent, objective, established in advance and made publicly accessible". Procedures should be as simple as possible and not unduly complicated and must not delay the supply of a service. The status of an application and its possible rejection should be promptly provided, with reasons. As commentators have observed, the lack of a necessity test in the domestic regulation chapter of CETA indicates that Canada and the EU were not willing to exceed the GATS status quo in terms of policy justifications.[26]

21 Latrille and Lee, "Services Rules in Regional Trade Agreements" WTO Staff Working Paper, ERSD-2012-19 at 115–122.

22 Krajewski, "Domestic Regulation and Services Trade" at 234.

23 E.g., Korea-Australia FTA Art. 7.7 (2014), US-Colombia FTA Art. 11.7 (2012).

24 Krajewski, "Domestic Regulation and Services Trade" at 217.

25 E.g., CETA Art. 9.3 (a).

26 Krajewski, "Domestic Regulation and Services Trade" at 237.

The US-Korea FTA's provision on domestic regulation for services is similar to that of the GATS; however, it includes a carve-out for a range of sectors and subsectors to which the assessment of qualification and unnecessary barriers to trade obligations do not apply. Thus Korea maintains exemptions for legal services, including restrictions on certification, approval, registration, admission, and supervision of foreign country-licensed lawyers or foreign law firms supplying any type of legal services in Korea; restrictions on foreign country-licensed lawyers or foreign law firms entering into partnerships, commercial associations, affiliations, or any other type of relationship regardless of legal form; restrictions on foreign country-licensed lawyers or foreign law firms hiring *byeon-ho-sa* (Korean-licensed lawyers); and restrictions on senior management and the board of directors of legal entities supplying foreign legal consulting services.[27] The US did not include such provisions in its corresponding Annex. The domestic regulation provision of the US-Korea FTA also expressly reserves parties' "right to regulate" and to "introduce new regulations".[28]

Article 904(4) of NAFTA (as it currently stands) prohibits the preparation, adoption, maintenance, or application of any standard-like measures that intend to create or have the effect of creating any unnecessary obstacle to trade between the parties. However, such measures are permitted when the measure has a demonstrable purpose to achieve a legitimate objective and the measure does not operate to exclude goods of another party that meet the objective. This appears to be another kind of necessity test, shedding light on the way in which domestic regulation is addressed, at least in the context of goods, in that agreement. Chapter Twelve of NAFTA, dealing with cross-border trade in services, contains provisions that are virtually identical to those of GATS Article VI; however, its scope is limited to licensing and certification of natural persons. Moreover, it is phrased in best efforts language only.[29]

As was noted earlier, NAFTA's chapter on trade in services incorporates its own General Exception provisions, which can be used to justify measures that would otherwise violate provisions such as National Treatment and MFN obligations and that can also derogate from its material on domestic regulation. Distinct from the GATS General Exceptions, NAFTA specifies that no obligation in that chapter "shall be construed to prevent the adoption or enforcement by any Party of measures necessary to secure

[27] Korea Annex II.
[28] Article 12.7(2).
[29] Article 1210(1).

compliance with laws or regulations that are not inconsistent with the provisions of [NAFTA] including those relating to ... consumer protection."[30] As yet, there has been no case law under NAFTA to elaborate on this provision. However, it seems to capture the essence of many of the regulations covering trade in legal services.

Perhaps most significantly of all, the Comprehensive and Progressive Agreement for Trans-Pacific Partnership (CPTPP) contains material on domestic regulation in its services chapter that broadly resembles that of the GATS.[31] As was mentioned in Chapter 2, the CPTPP further contains the following text on domestic regulation for legal services, which directly engages with all four modes of supply:

> 9. The Parties recognise that transnational legal services that cover the laws of multiple jurisdictions play an essential role in facilitating trade and investment and in promoting economic growth and business confidence.
>
> 10. If a Party regulates or seeks to regulate foreign lawyers and transnational legal practice, the Party shall encourage its relevant bodies to consider, subject to its laws and regulations, whether or in what manner:
>
> (a) foreign lawyers may practise foreign law on the basis of their right to practise that law in their home jurisdiction;
> (b) foreign lawyers may prepare for and appear in commercial arbitration, conciliation and mediation proceedings;
> (c) local ethical, conduct and disciplinary standards are applied to foreign lawyers in a manner that is no more burdensome for foreign lawyers than the requirements imposed on domestic (host country) lawyers;
> (d) alternatives for minimum residency requirements are provided for foreign lawyers, such as requirements that foreign lawyers disclose to clients their status as a foreign lawyer, maintain professional indemnity insurance;
> (e) the following modes of providing transnational legal services are accommodated:
> (i) on a temporary fly-in, fly-out basis;
> (ii) through the use of web-based or telecommunications technology;
> (vii) by establishing a commercial presence; and
> (iv) through a combination of fly-in, fly-out and one or both of the other modes listed in subparagraphs (ii) and (iii);

[30] Article 2101(2).
[31] Article 10.3.

(f) foreign lawyers and domestic (host country) lawyers may work together in the delivery of fully integrated transnational legal services; and
(g) a foreign law firm may use the firm name of its choice.[32]

The obligations contained here focus on nondiscrimination but make explicit statements covering some of the most controversial issues in trade in legal services, including associations between foreign and domestic lawyers and multidisciplinary firms. This aspect of the CPTPP establishes it as being among the most progressive services instruments in the world.

7.2.4 *Horizontal Sector-Specific Disciplines*

Horizontal and sector-specific disciplines would both assist in opening the legal profession to foreign suppliers. However, a single horizontal discipline covering a single mode of supply across all sectors appears to be ideal. This would allow almost immediate implementation of a new liberalizing regime without the need to develop an individualized system for each service sector.

Regarding specific sectors across all modes, it had been hoped that the WTO – or, more specifically, the Council for Trade in Services – would encourage the development of multilateral disciplines on domestic regulation to help harmonize qualifications with a view to liberalizing trade in services. So far, there have been no such arrangements for legal services. In fact, only the field of accountancy has achieved this goal. The Accountancy Disciplines are not yet binding and will be formally integrated into the GATS only upon the conclusion of the Doha Round, at which point they will become binding on members that have made specific commitments in the accountancy sector. The Accounting Disciplines consist of guidelines on mutual recognition agreements (which will be discussed further later in this chapter) in accounting. Such agreements should include the rules and procedures to be used to monitor and enforce the provisions of the agreement, the means of arbitration for disputes, the contact point for information on all relevant issues, and the procedures of appeal to or review by the relevant authorities.

The key feature of the Accountancy Disciplines is a general necessity test that requires members to ensure that licensing requirements and procedures, technical standards, and qualifications are not more trade

[32] Annex 10-A.

restrictive than necessary to fulfil a legitimate objective. The disciplines also contain provisions regarding transparency and specific requirements for licensing and qualification procedures. The parallels here to the legal profession are obvious. It is worth noting that the preferred modes of supply in both legal and accounting services are Modes 3 and 4.[33] The meaning of "no more trade restrictive than necessary to fulfil a legitimate objective" is uncertain because the terms "necessary" and "legitimate objective" are not defined, much as they are not in the GATS. The inclusion of a precise definition could help to ensure that a necessity test would not undermine a state's capacity to impose regulations that have a genuine purpose. The definition of "legitimate objectives" for legal services providers could include ensuring that ethical requirements, such as privilege and confidentiality, are upheld and that duties to the court and to clients are fulfilled. It may be possible to inform the concept of necessity by establishing that both expert evidence and empirical studies be used to support any restrictions placed on the practice of law. Self-regulating legal professional bodies would have an ongoing role in establishing these requirements and could be called upon to defend them if that they are challenged by independent oversight committees.[34]

As a limiting concept, the restrictive impact on international commerce is particularly interesting in the context of legal services. Adequate access to high-quality legal advice and representation is a cornerstone of the functioning global economy; it is not an end in itself but an instrument by which, arguably, all other kinds of commerce are actualized.[35] As commentators have noted, unravelling necessity is a delicate balancing act that allows determinations to be made on a case-by-case basis according to their merits. No trade agreement could survive in the long term without the "acceptability that can only come from a perceived equilibrium" between trade liberalization and respect for legitimate regulations.[36]

The WTO engaged in several consultations with domestic bar associations regarding the application of the Accountancy Disciplines to the legal profession. The International Bar Association (IBA), the CCBE, and the Canadian Bar Association proposed adaptations to the accountancy

[33] Grosso, Nordås, Gonzales, Lejárraga, and Miroudot, OECD Trade Policy Papers; Paris, Issue 171 (4 November 2014). Services Trade Restrictiveness Index (STRI): Legal and Accounting Services.

[34] Amos-Stewarta, Broughton, and Schwartz, "All Talk and No Action" at 138.

[35] Of course, this argument could be made for other services, such as accounting or telecommunications.

[36] Leroux, "Twenty Years of GATS Caselaw" at 211.

materials by adding the core values of the legal profession and integrating specific characteristics of the legal profession into the necessity test for licensing and qualification requirements.[37] While the Accountancy Disciplines were viewed by many as a model for future general disciplines or specific disciplines in other professional sectors, this has been less the case in recent years. This is because negotiations during the past ten years have resulted in an increasing complexity of the rules and further because consensus regarding the pivotal necessity test was less robust than it had been at the time of the adoption of the Accountancy Disciplines.[38] While the unique features of the legal profession would need to be accommodated, including solicitor-client privilege and, arguably, the pivotal role in ensuring a functioning democracy, some still believe that the Accountancy Disciplines could be generally applicable to legal services.[39] Despite objections, which were based primarily on the uniqueness of the legal profession and its ethical obligations to clients and society, there seems to be room to compromise on the way in which the Accountancy Disciplines would form the basis of a horizontal discipline for legal services.[40]

More recently, the WTO WPDR attempted to examine domestic regulation disciplines with a view towards deriving rules regarding a number of issues, including impacts on regulations covering services in developing countries. The WPDR also looked at the use of international standards, which has traditionally been problematic in the context of services in contrast to goods, given that there is a high degree of variation between sectors. One of the points of contention regarding international standards is the decision-making process in the organization that is applying the requirement. If such standards are to be more than voluntary nonbinding norms, then consensus or near-consensus among WTO members will be required for their adoption. The WPDR also looked closely at the nature of the necessity test in GATS Article VI, considering whether there should be an open-ended list of policy justifications, as in the Accounting Disciplines.

In this regard, it should be repeated that the text of the GATS Article VI does not refer to the degree of trade restrictiveness of a proposed

[37] Muller, *Liberalization of Trade in Legal Services* at 144–146.

[38] Krajewski, "Domestic Regulation and Services Trade" at 221.

[39] Organization for Economic Co-operation and Development, Trade Committee, Managing Request-Offer Negotiations Under the GATS: The Case of Legal Services, OECD Working Paper No. 2, by MG Grosso, TD/TC/WP(2003)40/FINAL (14 June 2004) at 19, online: OECD www.oecd.ord [OECD, Managing Request-Offer Negotiations] (accessed March 2018).

[40] Amos-Stewarta, Broughton, and Schwartz, "All Talk and No Action" at 141.

measure but rather requires that it be no more "burdensome than necessary." Commentators have noted that "less trade-restrictive" is not the same thing as "less burdensome", with "burdensome" potentially capturing measures that were identical in two countries (and therefore did not affect trade) even if the measure was more burdensome for one country than the other. Consequently, less trade-restrictive language should be used in future disciplines, as it was in the accounting disciplines.[41] It has been suggested that future disciplines do take into account costs and local conditions in evaluating the concept of necessity, again as it is in the accountancy regime.[42] Given the absence of concrete negotiations on services in the Doha Round, the WPDR has not continued with text-based negotiations on future disciplines.

7.3 Mutual Recognition

7.3.1 General Features

Mutual recognition is essentially a form of regulatory cooperation in which laws governing services in one jurisdiction are recognized as having authoritative capacity equivalent to that of the laws of another jurisdiction. This is typically granted on a reciprocal basis and tends not to be obligatory but rather is encouraged under most international legal instruments. Mutual recognition agreements (MRAs) acknowledge the differences in two different regulatory regimes over services but permit one party to evaluate the services to certify that they comply with the other party's regulations. MRAs are rarely concluded at the same time as the FTA of which they form a part. This is because the relevant provisions that govern the negotiation and conclusion of the MRAs under a free trade agreement must come into force. Joint bodies supervising the implementation of the MRA must be established to approve the agreements that have been concluded by the relevant professions and subsequently oversee their negotiations and compatibility with the agreement, and this can take time.

Recognition, which can be either unilateral or mutual, is based on the principle of equivalence, a concept that resonates to a degree in the scholarly literature addressing the importance of norm sharing among various branches of international law.[43] In the context of trade in services, equivalence means that when the host state's regulatory purpose is addressed

41 Krajewski, "Domestic Regulation and Services Trade" at 226.

42 Ibid.

43 E.g., T. Broude and Y. Shany eds. *Multi-sourced Equivalent Norms in International Law* (Oxford University Press, 2011).

by the home state's regulation, the host country should accept the home country's regulation as equivalent. The absence of recognition increases the cost of entry for foreign legal services suppliers, which are required to expend additional resources on education and training to prove their suitability as suppliers in that market. In that sense, it may be argued that the purpose of recognition is actually to reduce transaction costs in the form of burden of proof with a view to facilitating market access.[44] In situations in which aspects of the host state's regulatory goals are not met – for example, because local knowledge is required – or there are differences in the scope of the licensed activities between jurisdictions, the host state is permitted to establish additional requirements for recognition. These are called compensatory measures. In practice, recognition is very rarely of the absolute or "pure" variety. Indeed, most MRAs require a considerable degree of ongoing cooperation. This includes interactions between the respective parties' regulatory authorities and, with it, regulatory adaptation, which effectively means compromise.

Generally speaking, MRAs leave considerable residual powers to the host state and consist of mutual monitoring between the regulatory authorities. They are thought to be better than unilateral recognition because unilateral recognition tends to accord a higher degree of discretion to the administrative authority in the host state, impeding predictability in the event of a sudden change of heart.[45] They also involve preconditions before recognition is granted, including the possibility to reverse or remove recognition in view of changes to the other party's regulatory system. In that sense, MRAs are often described as embracing dynamic equivalence, meaning that they can adapt to regulatory changes as conditions change. This is why recognition agreements between states require ongoing resources for monitoring and assessment, typically in conjunction with the relevant professional bodies. Many MRAs include a general safeguard, in addition to the specific rules of recognition, enabling the authorities to reassert regulatory jurisdiction to protect the public good if this becomes necessary in the interests of society.[46]

[44] J. Marchetti and P. Mavroidis, "I Now Recognize You (and Only You) as Equal: An Anatomy of (Mutual) Recognition Agreements in the GATS" in I. Lianos and O. Odudu eds. *Regulating Trade in Services in the EU and WTO* (Cambridge University Press, 2012).

[45] Muller, *Liberalization of Trade in Legal Services* at 116.

[46] K. Nicolaïdis and J. Trachtman, "From Policed Regulation to Managed Recognition in GATS" in P. Sauvé and B. Stern eds. *GATS 2000: New Directions in Services Trade Regulation* (Harvard University/Brookings Institution Press, 2000).

MRAs can provide an effective means of resolving many of the problems associated with reconciling the economic benefits of market access in the field of legal services with the social imperative of preserving the integrity of the legal profession[47] of the WTO member state. In other words, they preserve regulatory capacity for social purposes while minimizing antitrade intrusiveness resulting from excessive provincialism or parochialism. The success of MRAs in terms of trade liberalization has been mixed. Some studies suggest that they are more effective for goods than for services, given the regulatory complexity of the latter.[48]

Negotiation of MRAs is a highly complex and time-consuming task for any sector. Recognition requires that a country have a system in place for regulating a given sphere of service suppliers. Establishing a domestic regulatory framework for any profession (a term that may be loosely applied to any body of service suppliers) is complicated, requiring well-developed and authoritative institutions that are able to set up rules that balance public policy concerns, such as ensuring the quality and competence of members, often including ethical obligations. This can be particularly problematic in developing countries where regulatory frameworks for professions such as legal services are either poorly developed or wholly absent. Recognition additionally necessitates a comparison between regulatory regimes established to meet different sets of cultural, social, and economic circumstances to assess the extent to which rules are genuinely equivalent in terms of outcomes, not simply processes. To say that these are not always easy to compare is an understatement.

The negotiation of mutual recognition encompasses a number of stages: information exchange, analysis of the other party's regulatory regime, evaluation of gaps, and potential compensatory measures. Negotiators must consider whether some aspects of a regime should be excluded from recognition entirely, such as FLCs (which are absent from some systems, including at the regional level), and whether any adaptation of the home state regulatory framework is needed – for example, because the legal profession is united (as in Texas) or split (as in England and Wales). Difficulties with these assessments will also depend upon factors such as the degree of divergence between the parties in terms of their education systems (one-, two-, or three-year law degrees, which may be postgraduate or undergraduate), the substantive nature of their legal systems' standards

[47] International Bar Association, "Standards and Criteria for Recognition of the Professional Qualifications of Lawyers", Adopted at IBA Council Meeting in Istanbul, June 2001 at 7.

[48] A. Correia de Brito, C. Kauffmann, and J. Pelkmans, "The Contribution of Mutual Recognition to International Regulatory Co-operation", OECD Regulatory Policy Working Papers No. 2 (OECD Publishing, 2016).

(common law, civil law, or a combination), approaches to regulation (top-down or bottom-up), and level of development (fully developed, transition, emerging market, or least developing country). The more parties are involved, the harder this process will be, which is one reason why MRAs are commonly pursued under bilateral trade agreements, as will be discussed further later in this chapter. One can only imagine what a multilateral recognition of legal services agreement would look like.[49]

As was noted earlier in the chapter, more dynamic or managed mutual recognition arrangements, in which mutual recognition requires certain conditions to be fulfilled and maintained, may address some of the problems associated with changes in regulations over time. While pragmatic, as will be seen later in the chapter, these systems require institutional arrangements that often involve ongoing supervision by national regulators or joint bodies to establish the parameters of the conditions for recognition as well as for any exceptions to them as they arise.[50] Thus regulatory divergence among jurisdictions is managed systemically rather than being eliminated or suppressed. The creation of joint committees for the purposes of monitoring this process may itself be time consuming and costly.

Given that obtaining qualifications raises the cost of entry into a market (and, in so doing, suppresses competition, increasing prices for consumers), recognition is a way for foreign suppliers to reduce their costs to entry by avoiding at least some of the investment costs in education and training to enter the foreign market. Without recognition, foreign suppliers bear the onus of demonstrating that they meet the domestic licensing requirements. Consumers in turn pay for that burden through higher fees. It is further premised on the notion that consumers trust their own government to regulate the relevant service adequately and to select appropriate recognition partners.[51]

Mutual recognition removes non-tariff barriers to trade, achieving an integrated market for the relevant service. It also facilitates regulatory – that is, institutional – competition and, in so doing, presumptively leads to more socially efficient regulations. Finally and perhaps most importantly, it safeguards regulatory autonomy and avoids centralization, preserving national sovereignty.[52]

[49] Nicolaïdis and Trachtman, "From Policed Regulation to Managed Recognition in GATS."

[50] W. Kerber and R. van den Bergh, "Mutual Recognition in the Global Trade Regime: Lessons from the EU Experience" in Lianos and Odudu eds. *Regulating Trade in Services in the EU and WTO* at 146.

[51] Marchetti and Mavroidis, "I Now Recognize You (and Only You) as Equal" at 419.

[52] J. Pelkmans, "Mutual Recognition in Goods and Services: An Economic Perspective" in F. Schioppa ed. *The Principle of Mutual Recognition in the European Integration Process* (Palgrave Macmillan, 2005).

Critics note that the preservation of sovereignty in the context of an MRA is somewhat illusory because, while states retain the authority to enact regulations on services (and goods), these regulations do not address domestic markets but address only the domestic suppliers of the products. If the preferences of citizen consumers in different countries differ on the need for certain regulations, such as regulations relating to the expertise of the service provider, mutual recognition means that these different objectives cannot be fulfilled. In this sense, the advantages of the removal of trade barriers through mutual recognition must be balanced against the disadvantages of the nonsatisfaction of different preferences of citizens in different countries. An additional problem is what has been described as "reverse discrimination". Services suppliers from a country that enforces weaker standards are allowed to offer their services in a second country that may impose higher standards, which bind the domestic firms in that country. This gives foreign service suppliers from the first country a competitive advantage over local ones in the second country. This could spur pressures from supplier lobby groups and lead to a problematic race to the bottom in regulatory standards.[53]

Mutual recognition is thought to have an advantage over full harmonization because it allows states to retain their own rule-making capacity over the requisite sector, bypassing the political difficulties. Rooted in ideas of tolerance and diversity, it represents economic integration without social or political integration.[54] This is because mutual recognition requires that each service provider be regulated by a single authority only, which in the case of services will be the jurisdiction where the service is consumed. Some have contended that while MRAs appear to be an attractive alternative to fully harmonized rules because of their flexibility in terms of the manner in which regulatory purposes are achieved, they actually have a self-destructive nature. They may be effective in enabling trade, but they also create conditions in which domestic lobby groups agitate for harmonized rules. The harmonization of one aspect of regulation increases the importance of other aspects, which will create a chain reaction. From the supplier's perspective, there will be even greater pressure for harmonization. Because of the nature of harmonization, when cost competition is reduced among states, other costs will increase. If the fact of differences

[53] Kerber and van den Bergh, "Mutual Recognition in the Global Trade Regime" at 134–135.

[54] G. Davies, "Is Mutual Recognition an Alternative to Harmonization? Lessons on Trade and Tolerance of Diversity from the EU" in L. Bartels and F. Ortino eds. *Regional Trade Agreements and the WTO Legal System* (Oxford University Press, 2006) at 277.

in regulation is a major driver of trade, then harmonization will reduce the trade flows that are created by mutual recognition. A system in which regulatory competition is not of great importance is one in which mutual recognition rather than harmonization is most attractive.[55] In sectors where regulatory arbitrage is important, mutual recognition instigates a dynamic process of exploitation of regulatory differences, which is chaotic and unpredictable.[56] Mutual recognition in services is thought to be problematic also because of the fragmented and rapidly evolving nature of services markets. States' capacity to tolerate each other's regulation is not always clear until they try, through mutual recognition, and the act of trying may be precisely what persuades them that full harmonization is a preferable strategy. Moreover, by stimulating trade, MRAs reduce wealth differences between states, which in turn increases the importance of regulatory diversity.[57]

Recognition of educational qualifications could be enhanced by partnerships among law schools, in which students take portions of their degrees in other jurisdictions. Exposure to the legal systems of other countries as part of a degree programme could also address some of the differences across legal jurisdictions. This could be pursued on an optional basis by individuals who are considering practising in other jurisdictions. The law school of the National University of Singapore, for example, encourages students to take classes that consider Asian and Islamic legal traditions along with the core curriculum based on the common law. However, lack of recognition of foreign educational qualifications by their home country may create a disincentive for students to study abroad if their qualifications will not be recognized in their own country. It makes little sense for a Canadian student to obtain a law degree in the UK if the Canadian National Committee on Accreditation (NCA) will not recognize the degree or will recognize only a portion of it. Additionally, rather than obtaining qualifications that are relevant to a particular jurisdiction, law schools could offer more homogenous training, focusing on acquisition of skills such as mediation, mooting, and client interviewing rather than the substantive black-letter content of domestic legal systems. Delocalized legal education has been instigated in Australia, for example.[58]

[55] Ibid. at 276.

[56] Ibid. at 275.

[57] Ibid. at 273.

[58] K. Galloway, "Getting Back to Our Roots: Global Law Schools in Local Context" in Gane and Hui Huang eds. *Legal Education in the Global Context* at 20.

Paradoxically, mutual recognition of professional legal qualifications through MRAs may have an adverse effect on cross-border legal education. Lack of recognition of foreign qualifications can incentivize the seeking of qualifications from other countries as a means of accessing that jurisdiction's market. For example, students seeking admission to the New York bar who have undertaken a two-year law degree in the UK may be motivated to obtain an LLM at a US law school to become eligible to take the New York Bar Exam. Were the New York Board of Bar Examiners to recognize two-year UK law degrees as equivalent to three-year US law degrees, this would obviate the need for the US LLM, depriving a US law school of the considerable tuition fees for that year. The need for a requirement to undertake law school in the jurisdiction in which one seeks recognition is questionable, given that few law school courses in the US, the UK, and Canada are vocational in nature. Moreover, an increasing number of law schools are integrating international elements into their curricula, driven in large part by globalization and the need to serve clients that have an international presence.[59] This is perhaps less true of most US law schools, where international law tends to be viewed as a highly specialized subject area.

Maintaining mutual recognition requires effective oversight and enforcement mechanisms. These ensure that the regulatory regimes do not diverge excessively and that potential conflicts and disputes can be resolved efficiently. The complexity of these matters can be readily seen in the context of the EU, where the recognition regime is enforced at several levels. While regulatory activities in the legal profession are delegated to professional bodies or regulators, the rules themselves are often set out in national legislation. In case of federal countries, such laws are usually enacted at the federal level (as Germany), but the regulation of the legal profession is undertaken at subfederal levels. The Court of Justice of the European Union (CJEU) has been crucial in clarifying the scope and application of relevant treaty provisions and secondary legislation in the field of free movement of persons and services. For example, in *Gebhard* v. *Consiglio dell'Ordine degli Avvocati e Procuratori di Milano*,[60] the CJEU outlined principles of proportionality that are used to justify or to remove barriers to trade in services, and in *Irène Vlassopoulou* v. *Ministerium für Justiz, Bundes- und Europaangelegenheiten Baden-Württemberg.*,[61] the court set out the key elements of mutual recognition of professional qualifications.

[59] Stolker, *Rethinking the Law School* at 142.

[60] (1995) C-55/94.

[61] Preliminary ruling: Bundesgerichtshof–Germany, Case (1991) C-340/89.

7.3.2 *Mutual Recognition and the GATS*

Because MRAs allow members to prefer qualifications from some WTO members and not others, they act as an exception to the MFN obligation in GATS Article II. If the MFN obligation were to apply to any agreements concluded under Article VII, it would effectively preclude their creation. It would force every country to accept lawyers with qualifications from all other countries, even those that were inadequate or poorly aligned with the needs of their consumers. The scope of the MFN obligation under the GATS is limited to less favourable treatment linked to the origin of the service or the service supplier, either expressly or indirectly, and it is not clear that this will be the case when the qualifications held by the service supplier are fundamentally different.

The GATS does not require that members recognize foreign professional qualifications, but it does encourage and facilitate their recognition. In that sense, it is a kind of permission. Article VII:1 states that such recognition may be achieved through harmonization or otherwise and may be based upon an agreement with the country concerned or may even be accorded autonomously, meaning that it may be done either reciprocally or unilaterally. The recognition must be based upon objective criteria and may not discriminate among members for which similar conditions prevail – effectively a reinstatement of the MFN requirement. Put more simply, WTO members can apply whatever standards they want in according recognition, but they must apply the same standards to all WTO members. That is, a member cannot apply different standards in assessing lawyers from country A than in assessing those from country B. This is more permissive than it seems. Lawyers from country A may meet the required standards and those from country B may not, but the same standards must be applied to lawyers from both countries. This capacity on the part of member states is crucial, keeping in mind, for example, different ethical perceptions that may exist with respect to bar associations situated in countries with high or low rankings on the Corruption Perception Index or the Rule of Law Index.

GATS Article VII provides that a member that has recognized the regulatory standards of another member must afford adequate opportunities to countries whose qualifications are not recognized to present their case as to why their regulations deserve recognition. GATS law is silent on the burden of persuasion; it does not specify how much proof is necessary on the part of the party requesting recognition in order for the burden to shift back to the party granting recognition to show that it is not warranted.

There is no case law on this matter yet, leading some to believe that the burden of persuasion in a successful complaint may be high. Panel members would likely view differences in educational requirements, for example, as objective evidence justifying asymmetric treatment.[62] This situation is in contrast to the GATS Annex on Financial Services, which specifies that the member requesting recognition must demonstrate the existence of specific circumstances of equivalent regulation, oversight, and implementation of the regulation as well as procedures regarding information sharing.[63]

Under GATS Article VII, WTO members who are parties to MRAs are required to afford adequate opportunity for other interested WTO members to negotiate to accede to these MRAs. If it is done autonomously, the member extending the recognition must give adequate opportunity for any other member to demonstrate that qualifications acquired within its territory should be recognized. To be clear, other WTO members should be given the opportunity to show that they meet the required standards. Whether they actually do is a matter for the country according recognition to decide. The purpose of this provision is to reassert multilateralism in the face of bilateralism or regionalism, clearly one of the WTO's strategies for securing trade liberalization. This reduces the trade-distorting effects associated with bilateral agreements, such as trade diversion away from a better supplier of a service to one that originates from a state within the bilateral commitment.[64] In one sense, Article VII:2 effectively "corrects" the exception to the MFN principle imposed by an MRA. Members who form an MRA or who grant recognition independently must give other WTO members the opportunity to demonstrate that they meet the same requirement and should benefit from the same treatment.[65]

Recognition is often granted through agreements made by a broad range of parties, including states, subnational governments, agencies acting under delegated authority, and professional bodies such as bar associations that may be independent of government. WTO agreements such as the GATS are an aspect of public international law and as such cover only intergovernmental relations. Therefore it is unclear whether they fall under the rubric of the GATS. Because the relevant provisions of Article VII are very broadly worded, the disciplines of that article should apply to mutual recognition commitments made under RTAs.[66] It has been argued that, even in the context of MRAs that are pursued under an RTA, the relevant professional regulatory

[62] Marchetti and Mavroidis, "I Now Recognize You (and Only You) as Equal" at 423.
[63] Paragraph 3 (b).
[64] See further Bhagwati, *Termites in the Trading System*.
[65] Muller, *Liberalization of Trade in Legal Services* at 62.
[66] Neilson, "Trade Agreements and Recognition."

bodies that typically engage in the negotiations of these agreements are not capable of binding states under international law unless the regulatory bodies have a clear delegation of authority to this effect.[67] Rather, these types of agreements, such as memoranda of understanding between law societies, are more likely to have the legal status of a private contract, although very often they are phrased with such ambiguity (e.g. vague comments about future cooperation) that they would be unenforceable as contracts because they lack sufficient certainty. Even if one of the parties involved in an MRA may be viewed as part of the governmental structure and therefore competent to enter into international agreements, if the other party is merely a professional association, then the MRA would likely be insufficient to constitute a binding international agreement in the sense of public international law. The GATS applies to "measures taken by Members" and defines this to include those measures taken by "(ii) non-governmental bodies in the exercise of powers delegated by central, regional or local governments and authorities."[68] Whether or not an MRA were subject to the discipline of Article VII would depend on the nature of each party to the agreement in terms of its own relationship with the government of the state in which it is located.

So far, mutual recognition has played a limited role in the WTO because its members retain the authority to enact regulations on services and goods, with enlarged capacity to do so for services, given the positive list format for GATS National Treatment and Market Access commitments. There have been a limited number of MRAs regarding legal services, meaning that most recognition is accorded unilaterally. GATS Article VI:6, which requires that members provide for adequate procedures to verify the competence of professionals of other members in sectors in which they have undertaken specific commitments, is important precisely because there are so few MRAs covering legal services. WTO members that have made specific commitments in legal services and have not formed MRAs should still follow through with GATS Article VI:6.[69]

7.3.3 *Mutual Recognition and Regional Trade Agreements*

Few RTAs contain commitments for legal services in excess of those made multilaterally through the WTO. However, there are a significant number of FTAs that include specific provisions on regulatory cooperation in

[67] Beviglia Zampetti, "Market Access through Mutual Recognition: The Promise and Limits of GATS Article VII" in Sauvé and Stern eds. *GATS 2000: New Directions in Services Trade Liberalization*.

[68] Article I.3.

[69] Muller, *Liberalization of Trade in Legal Services* at 122.

professional services, including licensing and certification of professional services. Such arrangements may represent the best way forward for liberalization of the international legal services sector.[70] Mutual recognition of professional titles and qualifications underpins the system set up by the lawyers' directives in the EU. By recognizing each other's qualifications, they allow the practice of law under home country title on a permanent (establishment) or temporary basis without the need to requalify for the host country title. As was discussed in earlier chapters, the directives substantially facilitate free movement of lawyers by setting out common requirements applying to the professional indemnity insurance, professional codes of conduct, salaried practice, representation in courts, use of professional title, cooperation between professional bodies in disciplinary matters, joint practice, and so on.

In practice, WTO members appear to prefer to include MRAs as part of RTAs rather than under GATS Article VII, possibly because the GATS places the additional obligation of opening participation in such agreements to third countries. Bilaterally negotiated MRAs permit countries to limit their commitments to those with countries that have similar standards and also have the necessary implementation capacity.[71] Mutual recognition is not necessary for the establishment of a RTA, under either the wording of GATS Article V or WTO case law that further establishes that the creation of a RTA can allow measures that are necessary for their establishment,[72] such as mutual recognition. It is therefore likely that the creation of a RTA also acts as a shield against claims for extension of recognition in the multilateral context under GATS Article VII on the basis that the very existence of the RTA acts as a justification for granting recognition to that treaty partner and no one else.[73]

Studies have shown that most MRAs that have been concluded through RTAs were done by countries with close cultural congruence based on similar languages and geographic proximity. This may allow a higher degree of trust among parties. Such linkages indicate that WTO members will be in a stronger position to resist requests for recognition from countries that

[70] International Bar Association, "Global Regulation and Trade in Legal Services Report 2014", www.ibanet.org/PPID/Constituent/Bar_Issues_Commission/BIC_ITILS_Map.aspx (accessed March 2018).

[71] B. Hoekman and P. Mavroidis, "A Technical Barrier to Trade Agreement for Services?" in Sauve and Roy eds. *Research Handbook on Trade in Services* at 258.

[72] Appellate Body Report, Turkey – Textiles, WT/DS34/AB/R (21 October 1999) at 58. This is a GATT case, but the logic could be extended to preferential trade agreements in services under the GATS.

[73] Marchetti and Mavroidis, "I Now Recognize You (and Only You) as Equal" at 426–427.

do not share such cultural ties.[74] Legal services are arguably the most jurisdiction specific of all sectors of the economy with the possible exception of the cultural industries.

Best efforts promises to conclude future MRAs in services such as legal in RTAs are quite common. For example, NAFTA's Professional Services Annex[75] contains a General Provision and an FLC section, both of which promote consultation with relevant bodies "to develop mutually acceptable standards and criteria for licensing and certification of professional services providers and to offer recommendations on mutual recognition". This language is now common in US FTAs. Much of the commentary on MRAs in the context of services focuses on the integration that has been achieved under the EU Single Market.[76] Mutual recognition can be found in Article 53 TFEU with regard to "diplomas, certificates and other evidence of formal qualifications" and is regarded as a general principle of EU law.[77] MRAs that are concluded under bilateral treaties are, of course, quite different from what exists in EU law because they are the specific result of bilateral negotiations between two parties often on a sectoral basis and not the consequence of the application of a general principle within a regime of legislative and judicial transnational governance, as in the EU.[78] The EU has adopted a similar approach towards MRAs in its recent FTAs, outlining the general conditions and guidelines for the negotiation of profession-specific agreements, potentially encompassing legal services. These treaties also contain transparency and nondiscrimination rules for licensing and qualifications and promote cooperation between professional bodies. Again, CETA offers a good example of such an arrangement. Australia has included provisions regarding the liberalization of legal services through potential future MRAs in a number of its FTAs.[79] The MERCOSUR services

[74] Ibid.

[75] Annex 1210.5.

[76] E.g., V. Hatzopoulos, "Forms of Mutual Recognition in the Field of Services" in Lianos and Odudu eds. *Regulating Trade in Services in the EU and WTO*; G. Davies, "Trust and Mutual Recognition in the Services Directive" in Lianos and Odudu eds. Regulating Trade in Services in the EU and WTO; and J. H. Weiler, "Mutual Recognition, Functional Equivalence and Harmonization in the Evolution of the European Common Market and the WTO" in Schioppa ed. The Principle of Mutual Recognition in the European Integration Process. Much international law scholarship from outside the US seems to depict the EU as a model or testing ground for developments at the multilateral level.

[77] Case C-225/98, *Commission of the European Communities* v. *French Republic*, Nord Pas de Calais [2000] ECR I-7445, Case C-324/98, Telaustria [2000] ECR I-9315.

[78] Kerber and van den Bergh, "Mutual Recognition in the Global Trade Regime" at 124.

[79] Australia grants lawyers admitted in New Zealand the ability to qualify for mutual recognition under the Trans-Tasman Mutual Recognition Arrangement. Australia's FTA with Japan includes an annex on recognition.

agreement, which was signed in 1997 and entered into force in 2005, contains a provision on domestic regulation that is very similar to GATS Article VI; however, the level of obligations contained in the Mercosur article is not entirely clear and therefore has questionable legal effect in terms of enforceability.[80] The agreement negotiated by the European Free Trade Association with Hong Kong contains best efforts provisions on mutual recognition.[81] The Switzerland-Japan Economic Partnership Agreement urges parties to engage in mutual recognition activities with respect to professional services.[82] The ASEAN Framework Services Agreement has a similar provision but clarifies that parties are under no obligation to enter into MRAs.[83] Another interesting example of an MRA is the one signed in 2009 between the National Bar Council (France) and the Québec Bar (Canada), which was done as a stand-alone agreement outside the context of an RTA. The application process was finalized and the application approved in respect of lawyers (avocats) on 12 August 2010.[84]

MRAs that are concluded as part of RTAs raise questions about coverage by GATS disciplines relating to regional agreements (Article V) or mutual recognition (Article VII). Some MRAs undertaken in the context of RTAs were not notified under GATS Article VII but were included in general notifications of RTAs under Article V. This practice could undermine the efficacy of Article VII notifications because WTO members do not know whether a particular MRA exists and consequently cannot express an interest in joining the agreement or negotiating something similar.

Depending upon how it is worded, an MFN provision could require parties to extend all of the benefits of that chapter to future RTA partners. This could be difficult for states that are unprepared to offer the same level of liberalization to the services sector of a country that is at a different stage of development or one that lacks the same regulatory rigour. A similar MFN problem has been identified in regard to the UK's future trade negotiations with the EU. The EU would in theory be required to offer Canada the same benefits as it does to the UK because of the MFN provision in CETA. Still, CETA's services chapter extends MFN treatment only to services and services suppliers in "like situations",[85] which could be interpreted to mean

[80] Article X:4.

[81] Article 2.7.

[82] Article 49.

[83] Article V:2.

[84] www.immigration-quebec.gouv.qc.ca/publications/fr/arm/ARM-avocats.pdf (accessed March 2018).

[85] Article 9.5.1. To be clear, CETA does not contain any special provisions for lawyers.

those for which there is equivalent regulatory oversight. Thus if an MRA is in place for lawyers from the UK but not for lawyers from Canada, such services providers are arguably not in "like situations", and therefore MFN does not apply, permitting the EU to offer UK lawyers a better deal than it did Canadian lawyers under CETA. In other words, MRAs can be used to constrain the scope of an MFN provision in an RTA, facilitating negotiation of RTAs for services by minimizing risks of overliberalization.

7.3.4 *Joint Committees and Working Groups*

As was mentioned earlier, one of the ways in which parties to RTAs retain flexibility over the fulfilment of recognition commitments in RTAs is by reference to the regular monitoring of verification processes through ad hoc committees. This "managed divergence" or "managed convergence" among professional standards contemplates an active, ongoing role for policy makers, including professional bodies and regulators, rather than binding obligations to which parties must commit from the outset and that presumably may not be departed from over time. These may be variously termed "joint committees" or "working groups". For example, Article 11.5 of CETA creates a Joint Committee for the Mutual Recognition of Professional Qualifications. It states the following:

> The MRA Committee responsible for the implementation of Article 11.3 shall:
>
> (a) be composed of and co-chaired by representatives of Canada and the European Union, which must be different from the relevant authorities or professional bodies referred to in Article 11.3.1. A list of those representatives shall be confirmed through an exchange of letters;
> (b) meet within one year after this Agreement enters into force, and thereafter as necessary or as decided;
> (c) determine its own rules of procedure;
> (d) facilitate the exchange of information regarding laws, regulations, policies and practices concerning standards or criteria for the authorisation, licensing or certification of regulated professions;
> (e) make publicly available information regarding the negotiation and implementation of MRAs;
> (f) report to the CETA Joint Committee on the progress of the negotiation and implementation of MRAs; and
> (g) as appropriate, provide information and complement the guidelines set out in Annex 11-A.

It is clear that facilitating transparency and information exchange is one of the central roles of this committee. The institutional provisions are rather open ended.

Similarly, the CPTPP speaks of establishing a working group for the purposes of mutual recognition of professional services, which expressly includes legal services:

> 11. The Parties hereby establish a Professional Services Working Group (Working Group), composed of representatives of each Party [for mutual recognition]
> 12. The Working Group shall liaise, as appropriate, to support the Parties' relevant professional and regulatory bodies in pursuing [mutual recognition]. This support may include providing points of contact, facilitating meetings and providing information regarding regulation of professional services in the Parties' territories.
> 13. The Working Group shall meet annually, or as agreed by the Parties, to discuss progress towards the objectives [of mutual recognition]. For a meeting to be held, at least two Parties must participate. It is not necessary for representatives of all Parties to participate in order to hold a meeting of the Working Group.
> 14. The Working Group shall report to the Commission on its progress and on the future direction of its work, within two years of the date of entry into force of this Agreement.
> 15. Decisions of the Working Group shall include those Parties that participated in the meeting at which the decision was taken, except if:
>   (a) otherwise agreed by all Parties; or
>   (b) a Party that did not participate in the meeting requests to be covered by the decision and all Parties originally covered by the decision agree.[86]

Considering the broad membership of the CPTPP, this body appears to be particularly flexible, given that it does not require the participation of all parties.

In evaluating the effectiveness of these agencies, which are composed of individuals appointed by both or all parties, it is important to keep in mind that the recognition provisions of the GATS concern the process by which professional qualifications are assessed, not their substantive content. In the context of trade in services, the term "recognition" usually refers to both recognition of the equivalence of the content of the training and recognition of the home country's authority to certify such training through the granting of diplomas or other evidence of qualification.[87]

The emphasis on transparency in these MRA committees is laudable; however, there is lack of clarity regarding their composition. While sector-specific knowledge is unquestionably required to make informed

[86] Chapter 10: Annex A.

[87] Nicolaïdis and Trachtman, "From Policed Regulation to Managed Recognition in GATS."

decisions about recognition, there must also be an effort to guard against self-interest or bias. Representatives of the legal profession may attempt to maintain their lock on the delivery of these services. Some form of consumer representation is therefore essential. Although this could be problematic, since consumers are notoriously poorly organized, lay membership on such bodies could help to achieve such a balance.

7.3.5 The IBA and MRAs

Provisions in trade agreements calling for enhanced cooperation combined with outreach activities related to recognition have a high potential, if properly implemented, at least to increase transparency in domestic regulations. Ultimately, this can lead to the dismantling of practical if not strictly legal obstacles to international trade in legal services, such as those involving the verification of qualifications and experience. As was suggested earlier in the chapter, MRAs can be particularly effective when they require professional bodies or associations to engage in debate and standard setting activities that are then referred back to an associated FTA's ad hoc working groups or joint committees.[88] Indeed, while trade agreements such as the GATS or regional trade agreements (RTAs) play an important role in encouraging recognition, short-term progress may depend more upon the development of incentives to encourage professional bodies to embark on complex and costly negotiations.[89] Of chief importance among these is the IBA, which is among the most important non-state actors governing global trade in legal services. In its report on Standards and Criteria for Recognition of the Professional Qualifications of Lawyers issued in 2001,[90] the IBA provided some insight into the types of issues that should be covered by MRAs for legal qualifications among WTO members concluded under Article VII of the GATS with a view towards encouraging trade in legal services. Here, the IBA highlighted why recognition agreements covering the legal profession should be compatible with the GATS, even though they appear to violate the MFN principle of Article II.

The IBA identified that the legal profession fulfils a special role in democratic societies, facilitating access to justice and upholding the rule of law. As officers of the court, lawyers are guardians of citizens' rights, and this

[88] Moritsch, "Research Paper."
[89] Neilson, "Trade Agreements and Recognition."
[90] International Bar Association, "Standards and Criteria for Recognition of the Professional Qualifications of Lawyers."

responsibility requires the highest standards of integrity so that there is public confidence in the justice system. Therefore, criteria for the recognition of qualifications of the practice of law should include ethical and moral qualifications in addition to intellectual ones based on the competence to supply the service. The IBA further recognized that the exclusion of assessment on the basis of integrity would undermine the practical value of GATS Article VII for the legal profession because no government would be willing to grant mutual recognition without these fundamental criteria as a baseline. Clearly, the principle of mutual recognition requires that the contracting parties maintain a degree of confidence in each other's form of government and regulatory system, which is possible only if the parties have similar political systems, cultures, and values. While this might be the case, for example, among EU member states, it is not necessarily true across the broad membership of the WTO.[91] This may be precisely why MRAs – and indeed many legal services liberalization initiatives – have shifted to the bilateral and regional context among countries that have a closer connection, such as the US and Canada under NAFTA and the APEC member countries.

The IBA also emphasized that the legal profession is distinct because it involves substantive knowledge that is heterogenous. The education and training of legal professionals tend to relate to a particular national or even subnational legal system, a situation that is quite unlike that of the medical profession, for example, in which applicable principles are identical from one country to the next. The IBA pointed further to the regulatory structure of the legal profession, wherein the supervision of the profession is carried out often at the subregional or even local level rather than the national level. In some situations, the regulators are governmental; in others, they are professional bodies acting under delegated authority. As a consequence, the IBA urged that the phrase "competent authorities" found in GATS Article VI on domestic regulation be interpreted broadly.

The IBA went on to recommend a set of reasonable standards and criteria that it considered should feature in MRAs for legal services. First, such agreements should include material on home jurisdiction regulation and discipline. A host country necessarily relies heavily on the integrity and effectiveness of the system of professional regulation that is in place in the home country. The fact that the lawyer has been admitted to practise in the home jurisdiction enables the host jurisdiction to allow that individual to carry out the practice of law within its territory. In that sense, it is based

[91] Diebold, *Non-Discrimination in International Trade in Services* at 43.

on trust; the home state's regulatory rules are an effective means of ensuring that applicants meet the competence and ethical standards of the host state. Second, the MRA should address the character and fitness of the legal practitioner. The host state needs to be satisfied that a lawyer in good standing in the home state has sufficient ethical and moral suitability to act as an agent of the court and as a champion of citizens' rights, even if the lawyer is practising within a restricted scope. Third, education and practical training should be taken into account in evaluating the qualifications of the applicant, depending on the nature of the professional activities the person chooses to undertake. This will include an evaluation of the level and duration of legal education, which some might consider already excessive, as well as the quality of the institution of learning, many of which are authorized by professional associations such as the ABA. The IBA considered, as part of its commentary on education and training in MRAs, that the degree of similarity of legal systems between the home state and the host state is relevant in assessing equivalence. Where the differences are more marked, the host jurisdiction may legitimately require the applicant to complete supplemental education or training for the purpose of curing deficiencies in his or her knowledge of the law of the host jurisdiction. This might suggest that MRAs between two common law countries will be less burdensome than MRAs among common and civil law countries. This reveals potential difficulties in achieving MRAs in the context of regional agreements such as the CPTPP that contains both civil law and common law parties. Establishing legal services markets that are open to foreign suppliers is likely to require law societies and regulating bodies to take a more expansive view of the way in which professional competencies could be verified. This may include accepting nondomestic educational requirements as a complete or partial fulfilment of the necessary standards and eliminating all citizenship and residency requirements.[92]

The IBA urged that states or professional bodies that enter into MRAs for legal services be entitled under the GATS to require that recognition be conditioned upon the completion of a specified period of experience in the practice of law. Seemingly contemplating the chapeau of GATS Article XIV, the period should not be longer than is reasonably necessary to establish the individual's ability to practise law in a competent manner and in accordance with the rules of professional responsibility. The IBA stated that failure to acknowledge the qualifications and training specified in the regulations of some jurisdictions should not be viewed as a violation of

[92] Amos-Stewarta, Broughton, and Schwartz, "All Talk and No Action" at 140.

the MFN obligation under Article II. That this would be an issue at all seems to be a misinterpretation of the MFN concept, which specifies that services suppliers must be "like"; given the vast differences in legal systems among countries, it would be difficult to suggest that a lawyer from one country is like a lawyer from another. Conceptualizations of "likeness" are particularly problematic in the context of services such as legal services for which governments typically adopt regulations for consumer protection reasons.[93] Still, the IBA explained that while Article VII of the GATS does not mention the express criteria of morality and integrity, their application in the context of Article VII is justified by the arguably unique status of the legal profession (which some would challenge) and, seemingly more convincingly, by the objective differences that exist among the many legal systems (and, by extension, legal professions) of the world.

The IBA suggested that MRAs should include material on scope of practice limitations. Such limitations should be set out as clearly as possible, with details regarding whether home state or host state law as well as international law are permitted, along with rights of audience in courts or participation in arbitration. Additionally, the MRA should indicate what forms of association are permitted for foreign lawyers, including whether they can practise with local lawyers or can be hired by them. The agreement should provide details on conditions regarding formation of partnerships and other associations as well as sharing of fees and staff. Disciplinary matters and rules of professional conduct should also be covered. This should be supplemented by a clear definition of the competent authorities in charge of regulating legal services. The decentralized regulatory structure of the legal profession in some countries, such as Russia, can create practical problems in terms of compliance with the obligations contained in the MRA, necessitating a full description of the bodies that are to be bound. The emphasis here appears again to be one of transparency.

The IBA noted that issues regarding the enforceability of the MRA will need to be addressed on a case-by-case basis in a manner that is compatible with the way in which the legal profession is regulated in the relevant WTO member state. Although the IBA did not state so expressly, joint committees created under FTAs for the purposes of mutual recognition could fulfil this function. As was mentioned earlier, MRAs are likely to be particularly effective when they require professional associations to engage in standard-setting activities that are subsequently referred back to

[93] Diebold, *Non-Discrimination in International Trade in Services* at 5.

the working groups.[94] On a multilateral scale, the IBA itself may conceivably have a role in monitoring the implementation of MRAs, possibly in conjunction with the WTO's Council for Trade in Services.[95]

Well-organized and well-resourced professional organizations do not exist in some developing countries, making the conclusion of MRAs by professional bodies problematic. Moreover, many professional associations will not be interested in facilitating access by foreign suppliers to a market over which they hold a monopoly and from which they are able to extract rents such as high membership fees. Establishing mutual recognition is also very resource intensive, so these initiatives will not be feasible in developing states. Taken together, these factors illustrate why the IBA's future role as a global organization in facilitating MRAs must not be understated. Still, it is not clear that the IBA (or other lawyers' associations) should have a direct role in deciding matters relating to recognition because such organizations have foremost in mind the interests of their members (the lawyers and law firms) rather than the general public interest, including the desire to open markets to competition for the benefit of consumers even when this may lower fees. Indeed, non-state actors are often criticized for a lack of independent judgment in such matters, particularly given their growing prominence as norm creators in international law.

7.4 Conclusion

Disciplines on domestic regulation and mutual recognition are the cornerstones of liberalization of legal services because of the sheer volume of regulatory barriers that these sectors face. Without such legal obligations, simple market access guaranteed through specific commitments in the GATS or elsewhere would be largely meaningless. Indeed, commitments contained in schedules under the GATS or under FTAs should not be viewed as a comprehensive indicator of the openness of the legal market in a given state. In legal services, domestic regulations that are not listed into a country's schedule of commitments can create insurmountable barriers for lawyers to access a foreign market; an example might be the conditions for lawyers' requalification.[96] This is precisely why the mere negotiation of trade agreements is not sufficient to liberalize trade in services. Put more

[94] Moritsch, "Research Paper" at 3.

[95] International Bar Association, "Standards and Criteria for Recognition of the Professional Qualifications of Lawyers."

[96] Moritsch, "Research Paper" at 8.

plainly, trade treaties provide only general rules, which require additional effort to implement in order for them to be harnessed by service providers and consumers.[97]

While ensuring fully transparent and nondiscriminatory domestic regulation may be palatable for most countries, there is a concern that MRAs will lead to a loss of regulatory sovereignty. Furthermore, presumptive recognition of legal qualifications from certain jurisdictions may lead to harmonization of standards at the weakest level – in other words, a race to the bottom in the quality of legal services. There is also the plausible concern that essential local knowledge will not be adequately protected under the umbrella of a recognition agreement. This is of clear relevance to law because it is so highly jurisdiction specific. As a creation of humanity rather than a natural science, law is subject to the subjective impressions, cultural beliefs, language, and social conventions of the society from which it originates. Unless partners are culturally similar, recognition initiatives may overreach.

It may yet be possible to engage in an in-depth assessment of educational, training, and licensing criteria in place in foreign jurisdictions, comparing those findings to domestic requirements and then determining, possibly unilaterally, the countries to which recognition should be awarded. Such comparisons will not only be complex and costly but also time-consuming. The participation of law societies or other professional organizations such as the IBA would be helpful but could also raise costs, and conflicts of interest may be unavoidable. It would seem as though the intricate nature of law, as well as its fundamentally local character, severely restricts evaluating equivalency in a functional way. Some of the ways in which the liberalization of legal services may be achieved, including potential responses to these dilemmas, will be explored in Chapter 8.

[97] Molinuevo and Saez, "Services Trade and Regulatory Reform" at 153.

8

Conclusions and Recommendations

Towards a Global Future for Legal Services

8.1 Introduction

This final chapter will consider some of the chief obstacles to the liberalization of trade in legal services coupled with some plausible recommendations for further progress. It will begin with an overview of difficulties encountered in multilateral negotiations under the WTO and then turn to some initiatives undertaken by international organizations. This will be followed by commentary on the potential to achieve the expansion of legal services markets through domestic regulatory reform and deregulation, concluding with a consideration of the possibility of eroding barriers to trade in legal services through the development of global law.

8.2 The Multilateral Regulation of Trade in Legal Services

This section reviews progress in opening legal services markets by WTO members under the GATS and the potential to take this further through a dedicated annex on legal services.

8.2.1 GATS

Negotiations on market access for legal services under the GATS have so far dealt with discriminatory measures with some limited discussion of nondiscriminatory measures. The number of restrictions on legal services under the GATS is comparable to the number of restrictions on other professional services. WTO members that have listed specific commitments have maintained restrictions through the definition of subsectors; for example, commitments are limited to advice on home country or international law. They have also differentiated between modes of supply, tending generally to make commitments for Modes 1 and 2 but not for Modes 3 and 4, with fairly weak commitments in Mode 4 in particular. The most frequently scheduled limitations under the GATS are restrictions on what constitutes a legal entity. These restrictions tend to limit the choice of legal form to natural persons (sole proprietorship) or partnership and tend to exclude limited companies. Nationality and citizenship restrictions are also common, typically involving limits on geographical area or activity. There are other market access restrictions regarding extent of foreign ownership.[1] Current GATS commitments appear to be relatively unattractive for small and medium-sized enterprises such as law firms and sole practitioners that seek to serve foreign markets on a case-by-case basis rather than establishing a commercial presence, although there has been somewhat more progress under free trade agreements (FTAs).[2]

The most common National Treatment barriers for legal services are residency requirements. Some members require full residency; others specify time-limited residency. Other members mandate that legal services suppliers have graduated from a domestic university. On occasion, this requirement applies specifically to the practice of domestic law, which is de facto discrimination against foreign suppliers, which are required to undergo requalification. Language requirements are also included in many GATS National Treatment restrictions, as is recognition of foreign degrees only for home country nationals who studied abroad. Some WTO members specify that foreign lawyers must take an active part in the business and maintain ownership of the local law firm. There are also requirements that suppliers must be members of their home country bar association and use their home country title.[3] It is perhaps no surprise that the WTO members that offer a meaningful right of establishment for foreign lawyers and law firms also tend to make requalification relatively accessible. This is why multilateral negotiations on requalification may not be a useful substitute for negotiations on the right of establishment. In fact, it may transpire that progress in the area of requalification will follow once significant results have been obtained in multilateral negotiations on the right of establishment.[4]

Cross-border supply and presence of natural persons tend to be the modes of service delivery that are most used by legal professionals and therefore are the ones that are most needful of liberalization under the GATS. While it is true that capital is relatively flexible, there are limited options for large foreign investors to purchase established law firms via

[1] Muller, *Liberalization of Trade in Legal Services* at 125.

[2] D. Persin, "Market Access for Small versus Large Service Enterprises: The Preferential and Multilateral Trade Liberalization Tracks Compared", 45:4 Journal of World Trade 785 (2011).

[3] Muller, *Liberalization of Trade in Legal Services* at 125.

[4] Cone, "Legal Services in the Doha Round" at 44.

a commercial presence because law firms, which are not multinational corporations, are not organized in a manner that is conducive to foreign acquisition. A merger or acquisition is therefore not always a feasible option when a greenfield operation meaning setting up an independent law office is not workable. In this regard, international trade in legal services is dominated by Anglo-American law firms, although there are indications that some Asian firms may be gaining traction. Less developed countries tend to start out as importers of legal services and use this to develop expertise, possibly in conjunction with an international hub, with a view towards exporting services via a temporary cross-border presence and then ultimately through full establishment.

The absence of commitments for legal services in the GATS schedules of members such as Brazil, Hong Kong, or Singapore does not mean that foreign legal services providers cannot serve these jurisdictions. WTO members tend not to commit fully, maintaining restrictions to preserve the flexibility to negotiate for liberalization in other services sectors. Indeed, Article XIX of the GATS specifies that WTO members "shall enter into successive rounds of negotiations ... with a view to achieving a progressively higher level of liberalization". This task has become incrementally more difficult as the size of WTO membership has increased, and it is a major reason why future progress on the liberalization of trade in legal services (among other services) may be better pursued at the bilateral or plurilateral level than multilaterally, a theme that has been touched upon in this book. Another possible explanation for the slow progress on services liberalization is the absence of a so-called negotiating currency; it is almost impossible to translate the types of trade measures that exist in various services sectors, including legal services, across all modes into a tariff-like indicator that can then be progressively eliminated through negotiation.[5] Such "currency" may be more feasible if negotiations were to focus on a given sector rather than across sectors. For example, in legal services, the number of years of experience required to be eligible to practise law within a member's territory is a regulatory barrier of a kind that is readily quantifiable and therefore amenable to negotiation with a view towards reduction over time.

Negotiations on market access for services begin with a "request offer" procedure, which takes place bilaterally. After this, WTO members send requests directly to each other showing the improvements they are seeking

[5] W. Martin and P. Messerlin, "Why Is It So Difficult? Trade Liberalization under the Doha Agenda", 23:3 Oxford Review of Economic Policy 347 (2007).

for their services and suppliers. Members respond to such request by specifying in their initial offers the extent to which they are prepared to make binding commitments. This process is generally not publicly disclosed, so it is difficult to determine the content of discussions or even which parties are involved. In contrast, during plurilateral negotiations, a group of WTO members with a common interest make a joint request to individual members to enhance specific commitments in a designated sector or mode of supply. They meet collectively afterwards with the members that have received the request. For legal services, a group of WTO members known as the Friends of Legal Services (including Australia, Canada, Chile, the EU, Japan, New Zealand, Norway, and the US) coordinated a collective request in 2006. They urged liberalization commitments on all four modes of supply, including the removal of restrictions on foreign law firms regarding hiring of domestic lawyers, use of firm names, and the prohibition of foreign capital limitations.[6] Although this collective request was only partially successful in implementing positive steps toward the liberalization of legal services, it was important because in many respects, it reflects the current state of negotiations on market access in the legal services sector, laying out the areas in which improvements are needed and capturing what exporters of legal services seek in foreign markets. Moreover, it has served as a basis for the negotiation of legal services in the context of regional trade agreements (RTAs).[7] It is interesting to observe that many of the Friends of Legal Services group members are also part of the Trade in Services Agreement (TiSA) consortium, so the issues reflected in their collective request are likely to form the basis of legal services negotiations in that forum when it resumes.

The liberalization of legal services under the GATS may face difficulties because it is often unclear whether negotiators have the authority to commit to opening the domestic legal market when national officials do not have direct control over the licensing of legal professionals. Even when national authorities do have this control, negotiators may be unpersuaded by the assurances of their trading partners that commitments to liberalizing legal services market access will be implemented by organizations farther down the chain of authority, such as local law societies.[8] Reciprocity requirements can further frustrate this process. Reciprocity results in what

[6] Joint Statement on Legal Services, TN/S/W/37S/CSC/W/46 (24 February 2005).

[7] Muller, "The EU's Global Europe Strategy and the Liberalization of Trade in Legal Services" at 734.

[8] Chapman and Tauber, "Liberalizing International Trade in Legal Services" at 962.

has been described as "lowest common denominator liberalization", that is, liberalization proceeds only as fast as the rate at which the most restrictive country is willing to relax its rules.[9] This problem is magnified by the Most Favoured Nation (MFN) rule in the GATS, which obliges that improvement in access to any WTO member's legal market must be offered to all members. There is little incentive for one member to offer access if its legal services suppliers will benefit automatically from access gained because of some other member's concession in that regard. Furthermore, improving the access of foreign lawyers to the domestic market under MFN opens the door to lawyers from every WTO member, including those from countries with vastly different – and possibly inferior – training and qualifications. This obligation therefore precludes the ability of domestic authorities to ensure the quality of legal service provided in the domestic market.

Article XIX:1 of the GATS refers to "promoting the interests of all participants on a mutually advantageous basis and securing an overall balance of rights and obligations". This indicates that members should open their own markets as well as pushing for the opening of others rather than expecting unilateral access, although economists would argue that this should be viewed as efficient on its own. More crucially, Article XIX:2 requires that liberalization be regardful of the national policy objectives of each member and the level of development of individual members, in terms of both overall development and individual sectors, meaning that less developed country members of the WTO community may be expected to offer less expansive market access. Whether this applies to legal services is debatable.

Even when specific commitments have been scheduled for legal services, there is the question of whether the National Treatment obligation under GATS Article XVII is relevant, given the questionable "likeness" of legal services or legal services suppliers from two different jurisdictions. The concept of "like services and service suppliers" has been analogized to that of "directly competitive and substitutable", which is understood to apply to the National Treatment provision in the GATT.[10] Thus if foreign-qualified lawyers seek the same clients as domestically qualified ones do, then "likeness" would appear to be confirmed. The same issue could arise in the context of the MFN obligation, with commentators again suggesting that likeness under the GATS is identical to that under the GATT and serves the objective of controlling market distortions.[11]

[9] Ibid.

[10] Article III:2. See also Diebold, *Non-discrimination in International Trade in Services* at 126.

[11] Diebold, ibid., at 139.

8.2.2 A GATS Legal Services Annex

With uncertain progress in scheduling specific commitments under the GATS, some have argued that a dedicated GATS annex on legal services could achieve a significant degree of liberalization of legal services globally. Indeed, the US proposed this some time ago. Annexes are integral parts of the GATS that are binding on all members for the sector that is covered in the annex. An annex-based approach to legal services, containing basic commitments, could help to promote a coordinated reduction in regulatory barriers over time. This could avoid some of the problems associated with reciprocity that have impeded negotiations for specific commitments under the GATS itself. Some of the recommended features of such an annex are as follows.

First, a legal services annex under the GATS should allow for regulatory space for legal services regulators, whether at the national or subnational level, while at the same time removing unnecessary obstacles to trade in legal services across the four modes of supply. This could be achieved through a National Treatment principle covering legal services, allowing any citizen of a WTO member state to become qualified as a lawyer in any other member's territory, provided that the individual satisfies the requirements for membership in the legal profession in the host state.

Second, the annex should establish standardized rules on Foreign Legal Consultants (FLCs). Recall from Chapter 6 that these are individuals who are fully qualified lawyers from one member state who are permitted by many jurisdictions to establish and practise the law of their home state and international law in the territory of another member state. In keeping with most approaches to FLCs, the annex should not guarantee the ability to practise host state law. Registered FLCs should be treated as affiliated members of law societies, not full members. As such, they may be subject to further restrictions on their practice, including no right of audience in all courts. Limitations on practice must be reasonable, be fully disclosed in advance, and be no more burdensome than necessary to ensure the quality of the legal service so that the best interests of clients and society are served. Rules regarding the process of registration for FLCs should be reasonable, ensuring broad consistency across jurisdictions. They should not constitute disguised protectionism and must be based on the principle of full transparency, a cornerstone of the GATS and indeed of the WTO itself. Any restriction that is not expressly listed by the host state should be invalid. The annex should accord FLCs the rights of privilege for conventional lawyers. FLCs should have the right to establish an office to engage in the practice of law in partnership with domestic lawyers. They should also have the right to use official firm names and the right to be included in any official listing of bar members. FLCs must be bound by the host jurisdiction's rules of professional ethics or by those of the home state if the host state considers these as equivalent. FLCs should also bear the affirmative duty to avoid any possibility of being confused with conventional domestic lawyers of the host country. This will require them to use a specified title, such as foreign legal consultant. These professionals must be subject to the same disciplinary procedures and sanctions as conventional members of the profession in the jurisdiction. Authorities in the home and host jurisdictions should inform each other whether there are any disciplinary proceedings involving the individual. The annex should clarify that FLCs have the right to engage in the practice of mediation and arbitration both as advocates and as members of the tribunal.

The annex should also establish institutional framework within the WTO for the purposes of oversight of the annex as well as forum for establishing modifications to rules over time by the WTO members. This could consist of a Committee for Trade in Legal Services to be established by the Council for Trade in Legal Services. This committee should facilitate communication between members regarding qualifications for becoming a full member of the legal profession or an FLC.[12]

A GATS annex on legal services might assist in the harmonization of regulations covering the legal profession through MRAs, as was discussed in Chapter 7. In this regard, it is worth drawing attention to the principles contained in the WTO's Technical Barriers to Trade (TBT) Agreement, which requires WTO members to minimize the trade restrictiveness of regulations and standards covering goods along with a general obligation of nondiscrimination as well as emphasis on mutual recognition when possible.[13] Commentators have drawn attention to the difficulty of adapting TBT disciplines to services. The TBT Agreement covers trade in goods only, constraining the ability of WTO members to use a wide range of product regulations as a protectionist tool. There is far less international standardization in services than there is in goods, and regulation of services generally applies to suppliers as well as to the services themselves, whereas the TBT focuses on the characteristics of products. Additionally, the work of the TBT Committee (along with the SPS Committee) has provided a useful forum for discussion that could be extended to cover

[12] Chapman and Tauber, "Liberalizing International Trade in Legal Services."
[13] Articles 2, 5, and 6, respectively.

services if supported by enough of the WTO's larger members.[14] Thus in laying the foundation for harmonization through MRAs, a GATS annex on legal services could also implement general principles designed to facilitate the process of harmonization. These could include greater time allocations for transposition and implementation; consultation with foreign legal experts, such as professional associations; training of domestic regulators and enhancement of operations in affected institutions, such as ministries of justice; additional executive, legislative, and administrative efforts; and the constitution of ad hoc reform committees.[15]

Although the WTO's Trade Facilitation Agreement includes a number of references to electronic documentation and other digital solutions for facilitating trade at international borders, e-commerce was not included as an explicit component of WTO negotiations on trade facilitation. This could possibly feature in a GATS annex on legal services. Indeed, commentators have noted that developing countries, especially the least developed countries, face the stark reality that there are severe supply-side constraints on active participation in trade in services, including that covering the legal sector. Domestic policy initiatives supported by aid-for-trade efforts and delivered through targeted assistance programmes may be the best way to ensure that developing countries are able to export their expertise in legal services, particularly as the profession appears to be moving towards deprofessionalization or a reduction in the sophistication of many routine legal services, precluding the need for advanced training and qualifications for some kinds of legal work. Aid for trade in services is at an early stage of development, and much of it has focused on assistance for developing countries in trade negotiations, the reform of domestic regulatory frameworks for services trade, and the provision of information on foreign markets to services providers. Further assistance should be geared towards improving the capacity of developing countries to implement the trade agreements they have signed as well as enhancing the capabilities of the private sector.[16]

Finally, an annex on legal services should devote greater attention to transparency regarding policies affecting trade in services to facilitate negotiation and to combat protectionism.[17] While the GATS requires WTO members to publish relevant information affecting market access

[14] Hoekman and Mavroidis, "A Technical Barrier to Trade Agreement for Services?" at 265.

[15] A. Plastas, *The Harmonization of National Legal Systems* (Edward Elgar, 2017) at 105–106.

[16] Sauve and Ward, "A Trade in Services Waiver for Least Developed Countries" at 576.

[17] Roy, "Charting the Evolving Landscape of Services Trade Policies."

in their scheduled service sectors and to establish contacting points, these rules apply only to governmental authorities. Some RTAs, such as the Australia-Korea FTA, have expanded this obligation to cover service supplier associations and have expanded the entitlement to receive this information to service suppliers themselves rather than simply other WTO member states.

Ultimately, including legal services in WTO negotiations may be impractical because these services are fundamentally parochial, being deeply rooted in diverse systems of legal education, legal values, judicial oversight, professional rules, and cultural attitudes. The GATS, while aimed at eliminating protectionist barriers, may be poorly suited to manage the range of issues that arise in dealing with rules on the supply of legal services.[18]

8.3 International Organizations and Soft Law

The International Law Commission's report on fragmentation of international law indicated that the categories from which treaty interpreters can draw are not limited to those specified in Article 31 of the Vienna Convention on the Law of Treaties, which refers to agreements concluded by one or more of the relevant parties and customary international law. Other normative material from international regimes may also be taken into account, including recommendations, guidelines, and statements of best practice made by organizations seeking regulatory coordination, whether public or private.[19] Taken together, these are often described as "soft law". The importance of pragmatic solutions requiring the input of technocratic expertise through informal soft law approaches has been usefully identified under the creative title "minilateralism".[20] Such a strategy may be the best way to address some of the regulatory barriers to trade in legal services. This is in part because these hybrid forms of international law making can help to resolve the paradox that is inherent in the need to preserve accountability or legitimacy (state consent based on internal democratic machinery) and policy effectiveness (socially responsible economically efficient outcomes).[21]

[18] Cone, "Legal Services in the Doha Round" at 46.

[19] International Law Commission, "Fragmentation of International Law: Difficulties Arising from Diversification and Expansion of International Law" Report of the Study Group of International Law Commission, UN Doc.A/CN.4/1682 (13 April 2006).

[20] C. Brummer, *Minilateralism: How Trade Alliances, Soft Law and Financial Engineering Are Redefining Economic Statecraft* (Cambridge University Press, 2014).

[21] Ibid. at 183.

8.3.1 *Model Rules and Guidelines*

A number of statements have been issued by international organizations that underpin the need to achieve balanced liberalization for trade in legal services, some of which were alluded to in Chapter 2. Noteworthy among these is the United Nations 2030 Agenda on Sustainable Development (adopted 25 September 2015), which commits signatory states to the following goals:

> Goal 16: Promote peaceful and inclusive societies for sustainable development, provide access to justice for all and build effective, accountable and inclusive institutions at all levels ...
>
> 16.3 Promote the rule of law at the national and international levels and ensure equal access and justice for all ...
>
> 16.6 Develop effective, accountable and transparent institutions at all levels.

Commentators have suggested that through overregulation of the practice of law, many countries, most notably the US, are breaching their international obligations by not providing for adequate access to legal representation. Because restraints on the supply of legal services at the domestic level may be viewed as a transgression of international law,[22] it follows that international barriers to access to legal representation, particularly in countries where this is already weak, may also be contrary to international law.

Similarly, the Union Internationale des Avocates issued a statement supporting a European Convention on the profession of lawyer.[23] The statement asserts that the specific role of lawyers gives them a central position in the administration of justice as protagonists and intermediaries between the public and the courts. Lawyers play a key role in ensuring that the courts, whose mission is fundamental in a state based on the rule of law, enjoy public confidence. Consequently, harassment, threats, and attacks against lawyers, particularly when these are sanctioned by public officials, are a threat to the independence of the profession. It may be inferred from these statements that unreasonable impediments to access to legal services through trade barriers may compromise a lawyer's capacity to fulfil these important societal goals, which arguably cut across international boundaries, particularly when clients are also mobile. Interestingly, one of the Convention's concerns was "unjustified public criticism" of lawyers. While laudable, this policy could be extended to a range of less

[22] Snyder, *Democratizing Legal Services* at 209–210.

[23] Lahaye-Battheu, "The Case for Drafting a European Convention on the Profession of Lawyer."

glamorous legal services providers, such as real estate purchases or due diligence document review. It is hard to resist the conclusion that some legal services providers are being misguidedly held in unduly high regard to the point at which they are above reproach, which is precisely what empowers their monopolization of the markets in which they operate. This fetishization of the legal profession may, ironically, be precisely what restricts its availability to a broad segment of the public.

Model laws could help to minimize implementation of unnecessary laws that operate as barriers to competition and to international trade.[24] In terms of content, model rules could cover, for example, procedures for allowing and registering FLCs. Countries could be encouraged to adopt these as a basis for their regulations. This approach could be particularly useful for newly liberalizing countries that seek guidance on the optimal regulatory approach to law firms, including foreign law firms.

Perhaps most significantly, in terms of such initiatives pursued by professional organizations, are the IBA's Common Regulatory Principles for Legal Services of the International Bar Association (IBA), which were approved by the IBA Council in 1998. The principles consist of the following declarations:

> Authority to Regulate: The Host Authority has the legitimate right to regulate the establishment of Foreign Lawyers.
>
> Fairness and Uniform Treatment: Regulation and/or admission of Foreign Lawyers should be fair, non-discriminatory, and based upon uniformly applied, objective criteria. Any restrictions on the practice of Foreign Lawyers should be justifiable in the public interest in the Host Jurisdiction.
>
> Transparency: Applicable rules and regulations (including codes of ethics and professional responsibility) governing Foreign Lawyers should be clear and consistently applied.
>
> Public Purpose: Regulation should be designed and administered in a manner which promotes the interests of clients and encourages and facilitates the effective delivery of legal services to the fullest extent practicable, consistent with the protection of the public in the Host Jurisdiction, the maintenance of professional standards and independence of the legal profession of the Host Jurisdiction.
>
> Access: Regulation of Foreign Lawyers should promote access to competent legal advice in the Host Jurisdiction on foreign law, subject to appropriate safeguards consistent with these General Principles.

These guidelines are consistent with the fundamental principle of the IBA: the preservation of an independent legal profession. Again, this is depicted

[24] Hook, "Sectoral Study on the Impact of Domestic Regulation on Trade in Legal Services" at 35.

as essential because of the profession's role in guaranteeing human rights, access to justice, upholding the rule of law, and ensuring the availability of legal services of the highest quality, delivered with appropriate safeguards in a free and democratic society throughout the world.[25] The implication here, which is arguably justifiable, is that liberal trade in legal services via the principles of universal or near universal acceptance is essential for meeting these important goals. Put another way, a state that is not open to foreign legal services providers is one in which its citizens are at greater risk.

One of the problems with adapting model laws across a range of jurisdictions is that there may be conflicting requirements in professional ethical codes, sometimes described as double de-ontology, which was discussed in Chapter 5. These conflicts present difficulties for foreign legal service providers in terms of compliance and its associated costs. There have been a number of discussions among bodies such as the IBA about the promotion of convergence among such codes. Fortunately, most ethical codes of professional conduct for legal professionals contain the same basic provisions. Where conflicts do exist, such as conflicts about regarding referrals, there should be room to accommodate different approaches in accordance with societal distinctiveness, such as allowing for conflicts where there is a shortage of legal practitioners. Clearly, codes of conduct have important social functions. Furthermore, they are usually produced by independent bar associations or law societies, which will not readily relinquish their power to make such rules[26] even at the behest of a global body such as the IBA.

Commentators have noted the importance of codes of conduct to market integration.[27] Such regimes can be used by courts as a supplementary means of interpretation by courts[28] and may be a means of preserving the special status of the profession in the public's eye, potentially justifying the "special status" that accords lawyers different treatment by governmental authorities. Codes of conduct in a sense enshrine obligations to which services suppliers in that sector are required to adhere in order to secure the trust of their clients and of society generally. They further create expectations

[25] IBA Resolution on the Regulation of the Legal Profession 1998. www.ibanet.org (accessed March 2018).

[26] Hook, "Sectoral Study on the Impact of Domestic Regulation on Trade in Legal Services" at 36.

[27] Delimatsis, "The EU Services Directive and the Mandate for the Creation of Professional Codes of Conduct."

[28] Panel Report, EC-Tariff Preferences, WT/DS246 (1 December 2003) at 7.16 (referring to the American Bar Association Model Rules of Professional Conduct).

regarding the quality of a given service. This helps to redress information asymmetries between legal services providers and their customers.

The EC Directive on Services calls upon professional associations to set up Europe-wide codes of conduct in their own discipline, taking into account the nature of their individual professions. Delegating authority to create codes of conduct to the respective professional bodies in this bottom-up way is cost saving because it builds upon existing embedded expertise.[29] In attempting to standardize these concerns through model laws, once again there should be an overriding objective of serving the public interest, which encompasses both competitive markets and consumer interests in confidentiality and trustworthiness.

8.3.2 Memoranda of Understanding

An often underappreciated soft law instrument for the enlargement of legal services trade are the bilateral Memoranda of Understanding between professional bodies such as bar associations or law societies. Such initiatives, while not legally binding, can lay much groundwork for enlarging the scope of legal services trade between willing partners, potentially acting as a basis for MRAs. Such arrangements are often built upon a common legal heritage (e.g., the common law, as between the UK and India) and the recognition of the importance of the movement of lawyers between jurisdictions in strengthening the practice of law in both countries. Participants in such memoranda typically agree to regularly exchange visits with a view towards enabling lawyers from each jurisdiction to gain experience and knowledge in the other's jurisdiction, ideally with the aim of eliminating or reducing barriers to practice rights. While these engagements may initially be framed as short-term visits, such bilateral memoranda will often include language that underpins two-way mobility between the state parties, predicated on the understanding that a rapidly globalizing world has created a situation in which clients require legal services across jurisdictions. The memoranda will both assure the legal professional bodies of the respective states that the legal market is, in principal, open to lawyers from the other jurisdiction and affirm that only authorized persons have the right to practise in accordance with applicable laws and regulations. Such memoranda will typically conclude with a briefing on the nature of

[29] Delimatsis, "The EU Services Directive and the Mandate for the Creation of Professional Codes of Conduct" at 333.

the existing market access with a view towards expansion in the future.[30] The Law Society of England and Wales has concluded many such agreements with foreign professional bodies, often in conjunction with visits of delegations from partner countries.

A good example of such an arrangement is the Internationally Trained Lawyer (ITL) initiative established in 2010 by the Law Society of Upper Canada (Ontario) in conjunction with the University of Toronto. The ITL programme helps foreign-trained lawyers to prepare for requalification exams and for entering the Canadian legal profession. It focuses on addressing language and cultural fluency to assist foreign professionals to better integrate into Canadian society. Currently set up as a one-year course, the ITL programme further includes legal work placements to help foreign lawyers gain employment and make local connections.

On occasion, memoranda of understanding may have a regional dimension. For example, an agreement was signed among thirty-six bar associations in Hong Kong in 2017 containing commitments to explore areas of cooperation in legal services in relation to China's new Belt and Road Initiative. Perhaps the best-known regional concordance of this nature is the APEC Legal Services Initiative, which was sponsored by Australia and cosponsored by Singapore, New Zealand, Canada, Chinese Taipei, and the United States. This project is less than a formal trade agreement, but given that it involves the direct participation of governments, it is somewhat more than a conventional memorandum of understanding. The APEC Legal Services Initiative aims to enhance the transparency of requirements and procedures for professional legal services providers to practise foreign law across APEC economies. It further identifies gaps in information on trade in legal services and promotes the development of best practices for the regulation of foreign lawyers. While respecting the integrity of each economy's regulatory autonomy, the APEC Legal Services Initiative seeks to strengthen the capacity of APEC economies to facilitate the provision of services in foreign and international law.

One of the central purposes of the APEC Legal Services Initiative is to create a database of relevant regulatory frameworks along with other pertinent information such as contact details for regulators in each jurisdiction. This is designed to increase the accessibility of information for regulators, professional bodies, law firms, businesses, and higher education institutions

[30] These documents tend not to be made publicly available. The author has experience reviewing such memoranda as a member of the International Committee of the Law Society of England and Wales.

that train law students. This helps to clarify the licensing procedures of foreign lawyers who provide services in foreign and international law and rights of foreign lawyers to work in association with host economy lawyers.[31] The APEC Legal Services Initiative represents a considerable expansion of the liberalization that has been achieved under the GATS in the sphere of transparency. It has been praised by commentators for its role in clarifying practice rights, especially for lawyers moving on a temporary basis.[32]

8.3.3 Global Professional Indemnity Insurance

Some of the risk associated with allowing the provision of legal services by foreign suppliers may be mitigated through professional indemnity insurance. There may be a role for international organizations to facilitate this process. Professional indemnity insurance is required for the providers of legal services in most jurisdictions. The lack of mandatory professional indemnity insurance in some jurisdictions, such as many Commonwealth of Independent State (CIS) countries, may appear to reflect a more liberal approach to the regulation of the profession generally. Countries where more types of legal work are open to nonqualified individuals tend to be countries where insurance is not necessary. This may be a counterintuitive strategy. Indeed, there may be some room to argue that a stronger regime of indemnity insurance, covering more types of legal services, could be a solution to enlarging the scope of legal advice available to the public. More pertinently, a comprehensive indemnity insurance programme could open up foreign markets to international legal services providers.

Comprehensive professional indemnity insurance could replace the need for tight control over legal qualifications such as those discussed in this book, for either domestically trained or foreign lawyers, precluding heavy restrictions on foreign lawyers. Rather than by limiting the number of market participants in the legal services sector artificially through regulation, the dangers of improper representation posed to clients could be addressed through the availability of monetary compensation by insurance providers. Indemnity insurance can be expensive for lawyers; it is one of the chief financial barriers to the practice of law for sole practitioners in many jurisdictions, where compulsory coverage can be expensive.[33] These

[31] www.legalservices.apec.org/index.html (accessed March 2018).

[32] Muller, *Liberalization of Trade in Legal Services* at 253.

[33] The base premium for standard professional indemnity insurance for lawyers in Ontario, Canada, is $CDN 2950 per year with a deductible of $CDN 5000 per claim. See www.lawpro.ca/insurance/private_practice.asp?section=IT (accessed March 2018).

costs are passed on to consumers, making legal services unaffordable to many and impairing access to justice and, in so doing, undermining the rule of law. There is arguably a need to subsidize the cost of professional indemnity insurance, making the practice of law more affordable and, in so doing, increasing the availability of legal advice.

In the interest of having a free flow of legal advice across international borders, a global professional indemnity insurance regime could act as an alternative to restrictions on practice maintained by national laws, incentivizing the internationalization of legal services in jurisdictions where privately held insurance is too expensive. An analogy to the Multilateral Investment Guarantee Agency (MIGA) of the World Bank is illustrative. MIGA provides political risk insurance coverage to foreign investors seeking to invest in high-risk countries where there is a danger of interference by unstable governments, which makes such projects financially unviable for most investors. By supplying insurance at below market rates, MIGA encourages foreign direct investment in countries where such projects act as an aid to development. Were MIGA – or an agency like it – to support professional indemnity insurance for legal practitioners, it could expand the provision of legal services by foreign-qualified lawyers throughout the world. This could bring down the costs of legal representation in developing countries and for poorly resourced clients in developed countries. Crucially, such a system would preclude the need for a complex regulatory architecture governing trade in legal services. Insurance presents well-known problems, notably adverse selection (insurance is more heavily used by those who pose higher risks) and moral hazard (insurance tends to de-incentivize users to take precautions).[34] Such issues may be mitigated by contributions from the insured in the form of deductibles and some contribution in the form of premiums. MIGA's political risk insurance system operates with these types of controls in place. The cost of professional indemnity insurance tends to be reflected in the price of the service. This is precisely why it is essential to have common rules regarding the extent of professional liability insurance for legal services providers; without them, this cost will act as a market distortion.[35] It is worth noting that the IBA has recently considered supporting a global professional indemnity insurance scheme. Clearly, there are formidable obstacles to such a regime, not the least of which is that the laws governing insurance contracts are far from consistent around the world.

[34] T. Cooter and R. Ulen, *Law and Economics*, 6th edn (Pearson, 2016) at 238 and 240.

[35] Delimatsis, "The EU Services Directive and the Mandate for the Creation of Professional Codes of Conduct" at 326.

8.4 Deregulation and Domestic Reform

Improving the regulatory environment in the host jurisdiction either through a focus on market-based solutions or simply by improving the efficacy of existing regulations may drive the liberalization of trade in legal services.

8.4.1 *Deregulation*

As has been noted several times in this book, there is an argument to be made that many of the regulations that affect the legal profession are unnecessary. If this is true domestically, it may also be true internationally. Corrupt or unethical providers of services are already constrained by general civil and criminal laws, such as those covering fraud and various forms of misrepresentation. Governments can control the extent to which these protections are available to consumers, for example by funding enforcement agencies and facilitating small claims against blameworthy suppliers. This does not mean that the government, via its various regulatory bodies, must dictate through proscriptive rules who is permitted to offer these services, as most do in the case of legal services. Furthermore, risks that consumers face when they are served by unethical or incompetent legal services providers may be mitigated without the intrusion of the government. For larger businesses, the market itself offers a degree of protection because of the importance of reputation to maintaining client base. Insurance is usually available, as was noted earlier. In competitive markets, law firms that ignore complaints about incompetent service performed by their staff will lose clients quickly. Technical advancements in rating systems, such as are common for restaurants, allow businesses to identify issues rapidly and to take remedial action. If asymmetrical information about the quality of the service provider causes a problem for consumers, this does not necessarily need to be resolved by regulators establishing an arbitrary standard of quality to which all providers must conform. The price associated with this level of quality may be too high for some potential consumers who would be prepared either to go without the service, to use cheaper, unlicensed providers, or to perform their own legal work.[36]

A better solution to the problem of overregulation of legal services, including those with an international dimension, could involve encouraging the dissemination of reliable information about the quality of the

[36] Shakleton, "Conspiracy against the Public" at 10–11.

service so that consumers can choose the combination of quality and price that they want or can afford. The government may have a role in helping to provide this information through dedicated platforms, although many privately provided rating systems already do this.[37] As was noted in Chapter 3, there are several legal services comparison websites, including Avvo, Shpoonkle, and MyLawBid, that address the problem of information asymmetry by providing lawyer ratings, pricing information, and even the opportunity for lawyers to compete for business. Of course, these websites cannot compel the participation of all legal services providers either within a jurisdiction or internationally, so the value of the comparisons is somewhat limited, although firms that do not participate may be left out of the market. The revenue of these websites tends to come from the lawyers themselves, which may compromise the sites' legitimacy.[38] Whether such a regime would work for legal services, where many clients are vulnerable, is uncertain. It is important also to consider negative externalities in that poorly performing services providers may cause problems for third parties. For example, incompetent prosecutors could lead to the underprosecution of criminals, resulting in higher levels of crime.

There may be some value in considering a large-scale unilateral reduction in barriers to the regulation of legal services delivered by foreign suppliers. This approach is grounded in the idea that the market for legal services should itself redress any harm that may be suffered by consumers because of information asymmetry between the supplier and the consumer, which is one of the main justifications for the tight regulation of legal services. In the provocative words of one commentator, "Most concerns about the traditional professions are about getting more women, more members of minority ethnic groups or other disadvantaged sections of the community into existing positions of privilege – rather than looking to dismantle that privilege to the benefit of the consumer."[39]

Progress in the liberalization of trade in legal services may begin to unfold when the US begins to move towards the partial deregulation of legal services in the manner of the UK and Australia, which have accepted alternative business structures as well as other legal professionals such as paralegals and legal executives. Some commentators have anticipated this

[37] www.ratemds.com/best-doctors/eng/; www.solicitor.info/ (accessed March 2018).

[38] B. H. Kobayashi and L. E. Ribstein, "Law's Information Revolution", 53 Arizona Law Review 1169 (2011) at 1197.

[39] Shakleton, "Conspiracy against the Public" at 27.

shift in the US (and Canadian) approach to the regulation of legal services as the inevitable consequence of modernity.[40]

Pursuing market-based solutions might be difficult because of the extent of control over the profession by the suppliers themselves. The theory of regulatory capture postulates that self-regulation tends to lead to self-interested outcomes. Members of an occupational group, such as lawyers, have a pecuniary interest in manipulating regulation to serve their own aims, namely, to exclude competition.[41] This theory features prominently in the work of a number of scholars who have resoundingly criticized lawyers for seeking to dampen competition through insistence on self-regulation, often in the guise of independence.[42] It is perhaps not coincidental that most of the negotiators of trade treaties through which liberalization could be achieved are qualified lawyers in their home jurisdictions. It is only natural that these individuals have the self-interested motivation to keep their own sector as closed as possible to outside challengers from overseas. In more tightly regulated jurisdictions, there is normally a statutory framework that establishes the legal profession and gives it some degree of independence from government. This requirement of autonomy is premised on the role that lawyers play in the justice system and typically involves a law society or other bar organization that administers rules of conduct and verifies professional qualification. In contrast, unregulated jurisdictions often have few, if any, rules about the practice of legal advisory services. In these places, the courts are often responsible for ascertaining the basis on which practitioners can appear before them.[43]

The need to ensure access to justice for as many people as possible means that the cost and availability of legal services will decline. This is the case both in developed countries, where legal services are readily available to those who can afford it, and in developing countries, where it may be impossible or impracticable to obtain legal services, regardless of economic status. Legal aid and pro bono work can address some of the deficiencies in this regard. Cross-border legal assistance may be another way of addressing this gap. This may be particularly done in the context

[40] J. Maute, "Global Continental Shifts to a New Governance Paradigm in Lawyer Regulation and Consumer Protection: Riding the Wave" in R. Mortensen, F. Bartlett, and K. Tranter eds. *Alternative Perspectives on Lawyers and Legal Ethics: Re-imagining the Profession* (Routledge, 2010) at 11–12.

[41] M. Pagliero, "What Is the Objective of Professional Licensing? Evidence from the US Market for Lawyers", 29 International Journal of Industrial Organization 473 (2011).

[42] E.g., R. Abel, "Why Does the ABA Promulgate Ethical Rules?" 59 Texas Law Review 639 (1981).

[43] Hook, "Sectoral Study on the Impact of Domestic Regulation on Trade in Legal Services," OECD and World Bank (undated) at 32.

of legal services delivered through alternative business structures, which, because of their size, are better positioned to lower costs for many routine services.[44] Deficiencies relating to access to justice tend to feature more prominently in jurisdictions such as the US that have been slower to adopt regulatory reforms focused on increasing competition with the intent of serving the interests of consumers, as in England and Wales and Australia. Again, the reason for this is, in part, that lawyers in the former jurisdictions, who are largely self-regulated, do not have the same incentives to innovate with a view towards lowering costs,[45] for example, by implementing new technologies such as online delivery of their services.

8.4.2 Domestic Reforms

Trade in legal services may be aided by improvements in domestic regulation, not necessarily through the imposition of market-based reforms but rather by way of innovative approaches to rules aimed at ensuring high quality and integrity. Some believe that there is a need for differential regulation within the legal services profession, with different rules applying to legal services suppliers on the basis of the nature of their organization or the type of law that they practise. Larger law firms have urged a decoupling of the regulations covering the profession for their type of transnational, sophisticated, and commercially focused practice from the type of regulations that are imposed on ordinary consumers, for whom knowledge asymmetry is at its worst. Such an approach would still involve control via the authority of the local bar association or law society, but it could be more appropriate for work with an international commercial dimension. Differential regulation may also have a place with respect to the differences between foreign legal practitioners and local ones, given that foreign firms will tend to serve larger, more sophisticated clients for which consumer protection issues are not as pressing. Such legal services providers are highly segregated from the domestic legal market.

Others have argued that the legal profession should be subject to an international legal "passport", which would essentially lead to a regulatory division between the domestic market, in which there are established policy goals focused on consumers and access to justice, and the international market, in which regulation is justified on public good grounds relating to

[44] G. Hadfield, "The Cost of Law: Promoting Access to Justice through the (Un)Corporate Practice of Law", 38 International Review of Law and Economics 43 (2014).

[45] Semple, *Legal Services Regulation at the Crossroads* at 6.

issues such as corporate governance. In this system, a legal services provider could obtain a worldwide licence to practise certain types of law by holding a commonly accepted FLC qualification in addition to the provider's original legal qualification as authorized domestically. This approach would present many obstacles, including, most notably, restrictions on the unauthorized practice of law in countries such as the US.[46]

Reforms in legal education and training can bring about changes that could enlarge access to legal services. These are important because of the considerable effect they can have on the competitiveness of the domestic legal sector. Globalization continues to place pressure on governments to modernize their legal sectors, either because domestic consumers want more competitive or specialist legal advice or because multinational firms want their legal advisors to be able to accompany them into new markets. Commentators hold that the staging of reforms is important. In this regard, regulation governing cross-border legal practice under Mode 1 or foreign legal establishment under Mode 3 may be possible only after domestic reforms have taken place. Otherwise, the resulting better than national treatment could be problematic for any government. For example, in Japan, regulations permitting foreign lawyers and domestic lawyers to enter into partnership and employment relationships could be achieved only after a series of domestic reforms of the legal profession. Likewise, transparency in the corporate vehicles that could be used by foreign law firms in Russia was possible only after the introduction of regulations covering the local legal profession. The Indian government recognized that market liberalization in legal services had to be preceded by domestic reforms such as the removal of prohibitions on advertising and partnership size. In countries with federal systems, internal mobility regulations may be a prerequisite to the opening up of the regulator regime on an international basis, as in the US, where ABA model rules on transnational practice developed from model rules on multijurisdictional practice within the US.[47]

In pursuing domestic reform with a view towards expanding trade in legal services, local bar associations must maintain open dialogue with their governments in order to optimize regulations. This optimization should be designed to achieve a balance between legitimate regulatory concerns (such as consumer protection) and the maintenance of a competitive environment while ensuring the protection of core values, such as the independence of the profession. There will probably always be de facto

[46] Hook, "Sectoral Study on the Impact of Domestic Regulation on Trade in Legal Services," OECD and World Bank (undated) at 35.

[47] Ibid. at 41.

barriers to the liberalization of legal services, perhaps more so than is the case for many other types of services because the practice of law is so closely tied to language. The interpretation of the meaning of words is such a fundamental part of what lawyers do that deep familiarity with foreign languages will operate as a prerequisite to entering foreign markets successfully. Just as many legal concepts are lost in translation (e.g. there is no word in Japanese for the common law concept of "consideration"), legal services may be notionally open to foreign practitioners, but in reality it will be very difficult for these individuals to penetrate foreign markets in a meaningful way.

As with any plan of regulatory reform, there needs to be further work, especially of an empirical nature, regarding the manner in which the legal profession is regulated around the world. This is especially so with respect to the capacity of foreign lawyers to practise in other jurisdictions as well as, relatedly, the extent to which the legal profession maintains a monopoly over the provision of legal services as well as the impact of that monopoly on access to justice.[48] It is encouraging that many organizations, including the IBA and national law societies, are pursuing these initiatives.

8.5 Global Law and the Transnational Legal Community

Perhaps the most radical path towards the liberalization of trade in legal services is one that is based on reforms to the content of the law itself. As the legal regimes of the many hundreds of jurisdictions around the world begin to move towards convergence in step with globalization, the heterogenous elements of the practice of law will begin to erode and, with it, the justification for placing additional regulatory barriers on legal services providers operating within notionally foreign jurisdictions. If globalization has led to a world in which the lifestyle and consumption habits of middle-class consumers are moving towards parity, then it stands to reason that the laws on which these individuals will rely to safeguard their rights and by which they may suffer liabilities should be tending towards similarity if not unity.[49] Although there will surely never be a genuinely "global law", there may be something not far from it in the coming years, at least in certain practice areas.

[48] L. S. Terry, "Putting the Legal Profession's Monopoly on the Practice of Law in a Global Context", 82 *Fordham L. Rev.* 2903 (2014).

[49] J. B. Auby, *Globalization, Law and the State* (Hart, 2017) at 14.

While this book, let alone its concluding chapter, is not the place to discuss the topic in depth, there is a growing body of academic literature on the internationalization of law, which involves the blurring on the boundaries between domestic and international law and, by extension, the disintegration of the former. This has occurred through processes of construction by legislatures, interpretation by judicial bodies (both domestic and international), and implementation by a wide range of governmental bodies.[50] This is to say nothing of the global *lex mercatoria* that characterizes much of private international dealings, at least in the commercial sphere, and the so-called *lex electronica* or *lex networkia* governing many kinds of interactions on the Internet.[51] There is an unmistakable convergence of laws towards common standards. Governance over international trade through the WTO and over human rights through the European Convention on Human Rights are two obvious examples of this. Some commentators have also observed the development of a global constitutional law through international investment arbitration.[52] The inclusion of international but also comparative law in the curricula of law schools around the world should facilitate the homogenization of the practice of law in the future.

The notion of de-territorialization of legal systems is a persuasive one, drawing upon examples in human rights, the use of force, and conflict resolution. It is linked to the network-oriented creation of law in the modern sphere as distinct from the traditional top-down hierarchy in which the law is imposed by a centralized, authoritative state. The universality of this "global law" is open to criticisms of legitimacy as well as problems of identification and associated issues of predictability in the sense of application to behaviours.[53] Yet the norms associated with globalization itself point towards a commonality of legal approaches and core values. These norms, such as the obligation to perform contractual obligations and to pay compensation for wrongdoing, tend to be characterized by their status as standards of behaviour or guidelines rather than as mandatory rules as in traditionally state-driven law.[54]

It was suggested at the beginning of this book that because situations of extraterritoriality are abundant, there is a demand for legal responses

[50] M. Dias Veralla, *Internationalization of Law* (Springer, 2014); Schiff Berman, *Global Legal Pluralism*; and Auby, *Globalization, Law and the State.*

[51] Auby, *Globalization, Law and the State* at 34.

[52] E.g., D. Schneiderman, *Constitutionalizing Economic Globalization* (Cambridge University Press, 2008).

[53] Dias Veralla, *Internationalization of Law.*

[54] Auby, *Globalization, Law and the State* at 76.

that are also extraterritorial in nature. The environment, the Internet, and the activities of the multinational enterprise are good examples of these phenomena.[55] It has been suggested that the internal regulations of multinational enterprises are themselves a kind of legal order that resists accommodation on either side of the domestic or international law dichotomy. These increasingly powerful entities and the lawyers who serve them pose a further challenge to the centrality and exclusive territoriality of the nation-state.[56] Calls for the harmonization of norms, multilateral and regional treaties, and the establishment of international governing bodies as the embodiment of "world law" are seen by some as a response to the highly fragmented, confusing, and therefore costly nature of the legal processes that govern all varieties of activities. In other words, legal pluralism should be embraced as a way of managing the complexities of a more globalized world.[57] As law becomes more denationalized, the exception seen in most states' legal systems that covers the practice of international law may come to have more significance. Globalization renders the retention of a plurality of legal systems – meaning classic domestic law – costly and impractical.[58] An increasing number of transnational entities are grappling with the high transaction costs that a plurality of legal systems foist on them in the form of distorted markets. These stresses underpin the efforts towards creating model laws or uniform laws that are being made by organizations such as the Organisation for Economic Co-operation and Development (OECD) and the United Nations.[59]

One of the strongest claims supporting the internationalization of law is the notion of a "common legal grammar", which postulates that the process by which laws are created by legislatures has common features across domestic and legal orders. The process of building concepts occurs in a similar pattern, despite distinct normative contexts. An example of this phenomenon is the precautionary principle, which became diffused across a wide range of treaties and statutes around the world in the 1990s from its origin in the UK and Germany decades earlier.[60] The globalization of law has been aided in part by the emergence of many nongovernmental bodies or public international organizations as rule makers that do not have

[55] Ibid. at 17–19.
[56] Lindahl, *Fault Lines of Globalization* at 56.
[57] Schiff Berman, *Global Legal Pluralism* at 9–10.
[58] Auby, *Globalization, Law and the State* at 15.
[59] Ibid. at 92.
[60] Dias Veralla, *Internationalization of Law* at 118–119.

the rigidity associated with the traditional state as law maker.[61] Again, the OECD and the UN are good examples, as is the WTO.

Definitions for concepts produce what has been described as a radiating effect, in which the definitions are repeatedly used in varied forums to avoid contradictions and to facilitate normative integration between national and international levels.[62] This is enhanced by dialogue among judges in different jurisdictions, both domestic and international, through citation of each other's judgments, a process that is often referred to as cross-fertilization.[63] This phenomenon has been described as a "cosmopolitan pluralist jurisprudence" that embraces differences yet charts a functionalist view that seeks harmonization while preserving contextual peculiarities. It is linked to notions of an "international legal consciousness" that is informed by shared sets of assumptions, ideas about justice, and morality.[64]

Legal pluralism, which was described briefly in Chapter 1, suggests that there are other sources of legal authority or ordering beyond the state and its coercive power. These alternative "spaces" provide opportunities for resistance, contestation, and iteration of rights. Multiple sites of normative authority in the global legal system should be viewed, according to some, as interactions to be managed rather than as a problem to be solved.[65] In the spirit of recognizing a more "fluid rubric" for conceptualizing norm development than one that is exclusively state-centric,[66] it is useful to draw attention to the fact that these alternative communities of legal ordering are not necessarily any less complicated or prone to navigation by the non-expert. The key point for legal services providers is that citizens cannot always operate in accordance with the rule systems of alternative environments without specialist assistance. Traditional legal services providers have a role to play in nontraditional spaces. Because these arenas are outside the control of the state, it is odious that legal representation by professionals formally beyond the state's jurisdiction should be excluded.

The fact that many countries allow foreign-qualified legal practitioners to practise international law appears to implicitly recognize the importance of legal services providers to actualize the legal entitlements and obligations associated with extraterritorial spheres of ordering, such as international tribunals. Surely, then, this logic could be extended to

[61] Auby, *Globalization, Law and the State* at 15.
[62] Dias Veralla, *Internationalization of Law* at 119.
[63] Ibid. at 130.
[64] Schiff Berman, *Global Legal Pluralism* at 100.
[65] Ibid. at 54.
[66] Ibid. at 63.

other nontraditional and de-territorialized communities, the Internet being among the most obvious examples. Again, the point to be emphasized here is that the state must not deny individuals the ability to exercise their rights in these arenas on the basis of disallowing legal representation. Postnational law emerges from a plurality of actors and processes of communication. In that sense, it is process based, tied to discourse across and within society at all levels.[67] Self-regulation or, more accurately, co-regulation by non-state authorities exemplifies this process of law making, which defies traditional state-oriented constructs.[68]

The internationalization of law has clear effects on the profession of law itself. Commentators have identified this most obviously in the sphere of business or commercial law. But this process is bidirectional. While the legal services profession has been transformed by globalization with a view to better serving transnational clients, so too have internationally minded lawyers transformed the nature of the laws that they use. For example, the importing by UK law firms of US approaches to loans is seen as a significant factor in the globalization of financial markets.[69]

That most jurisdictions around the world allow foreigners to provide legal services in relation to international law is encouraging and no doubt is a driving force behind what some have referred to as the socialization of international law via a community of engaged practitioners and scholars. This has allowed for the development of a shared language and, with it, an interpretive community that has served to create and reinforce foundational doctrines.[70] Various communities of international lawyers have developed within nongovernmental organizations. There is a vibrant academic community of lawyers interested in international and comparative law who produce scholarship that is occasionally influential in rule making and norm creation. Transnational advocacy networks have been established, bringing international practitioners together in spheres such as human rights and environmental law.[71]

There may be reason to think that lawyers may constitute an especially important "epistemic community" that plays a vital role in the construction of transnational governance regimes. To the extent to which there is a realm of transnational governance, it is composed of a variety of diverse and

[67] Dias Veralla, *Internationalization of Law* at 316.

[68] Auby, *Globalization, Law and the State* at 69–70.

[69] F. Neate, "The Lawyer's Role in International Business Practice" in J. Ross-Harper ed. *Global Law in Practice* (Kluwer Law, 1997).

[70] J. d'Aspremont, *Epistemic Forces of International Law* (Edward Elgar, 2017) at 10–13.

[71] B. Santos, *Law and Globalization from Below* (Cambridge University Press, 2005).

complex fields, each with its own history and dynamics. Yet there may be some features that many of these fields share that can provide the basis for identifying some commonalities among them.[72] For example, legal services providers may be members of at least two epistemic communities. One is a general community that consists of common training and socialization into a particular mode of critical analysis and discourse. The other is a community that is united by shared expertise with respect to particular technical knowledge. Even as they participate in their second communities, legal professionals bring a distinctive perspective to the diagnosis of problems based on their strong preference for the use of law and legal principles as mechanisms to order social life. The use of law as an ordering mechanism may have particular appeal in a transnational realm that lacks a single recognized political authority and conventional institutions, procedures, and modes of normalizing behaviours that serve as a basis for legitimacy on the national level. This set of conditions creates uncertainty about sources of authority, establishing trust between parties, and addressing potentially competing interests. This creates opportunities for a range of actors to acquire de facto authority if they can convince others of their legitimacy in creating conditions that stabilize expectations, which is an essential function of law.[73] Accordingly, lawyers may be in a position to play an especially important role in helping to construct transnational regimes that enhance predictability, furthering globalization.[74] The activities of global lawyers in transnational governance regimes can stimulate the demand for services that their firms supply. They are well situated to invoke the universal norms that drive globalization, such as open markets and human rights. They are further in a position to mediate between those norms in a way that may rebalance the asymmetry in favour of business interests, which are often thought to characterize the transnational legal system.[75]

In light of what has been discussed here, to the extent to which there is or will soon be a global legal system composed of largely homogenous rules, some of which originate from nontraditional sources of authority and which are interpreted and applied by a global network of closely connected legal professionals sharing common approaches, any domestic regulatory barriers that impede these processes appear to be redundant, artificial, or ineffectual.

[72] Regan Jr., "Lawyers, Globalization and Transnational Governance Regimes."

[73] N. Luhmann, *A Sociological Theory of Law*, 2nd edn (Routledge, 2014).

[74] Regan Jr., "Lawyers, Globalization and Transnational Governance Regimes."

[75] Dezalay and Garth eds. *Lawyers and the Rule of Law in an Era of Globalization.*

8.6 Concluding Thoughts

Many challenges face those who rightly seek to liberalize trade in legal services, including achieving global (or regional) consensus in an era when trade protectionism may be reemerging. The main concern in this endeavour would seem to be balancing the important role that lawyers play in properly functioning society, at least in some contexts, against the pressing need to improve competition while adapting to the technological innovations and legal concerns associated with global commerce. While it is vital to safeguard clients and to ensure that lawyers, at a fundamental level, remain free from governmental coercion, it is unquestionable that the profession must reshape itself to serve the modern world in which many types of legal services no longer require high-level technical expertise or even local knowledge as verified by copious, costly qualifications. Governments, professional associations, and international bodies must take these issues into account when crafting solutions, whether these result in more, less, or internationally harmonized regulations. This chapter, as well as the book as a whole, has attempted to illustrate that such solutions must focus on core values such as transparency, nondiscrimination, and consumer choice grounded in presumptive market access. These are principles that are central to international trade and to which legal services and legal service suppliers must conform.

INDEX